Progressive Marketing Plan for a Human Resources Consulting Service

Copyright © 2018 by Progressive Business Consulting, Inc.
Pembroke Pines, FL 33027

Marketing Plan Instructions

1. If you want the digital file for this plan, please send proof-of-purchase to Probusconsult2@yahoo.com

2. Complete the Executive Summary section, as your final step, after you have completed the entire plan.

3. Feel free to edit the plan and make it more relevant to your strategic goals, objectives and business vision.

4. We have provided all of the formulas needed to prepare the financial plan. Just plug in the numbers that are based on your particular situation. Excel spreadsheets for the financials are available on the microsoft.com website and www.simplebizplanning.com/forms.htm http://office.microsoft.com/en-us/templates/

5. Throughout the plan, we have provided prompts or suggestions as to what values to enter into blank spaces, but use your best judgment and then delete the suggested values (?).

6. The plan also includes some separate worksheets for additional assistance in expanding some of the sections, if desired.

7. Additionally, some sections offer multiple choices and the word 'select' appears as a prompt to edit the contents of the plan.

8. Your feedback, referrals and business are always very much appreciated.

Thank you

Nat Chiaffarano, MBA
Progressive Business Consulting, Inc.
Pembroke Pines, FL 33027
ProBusConsult2@yahoo.com

"Progressive Marketing Plan for a
Human Resources Consulting Service"

Copyright Notice
Copyright © 2018   Nat Chiaffarano, MBA
Progressive Business Consulting, Inc
All Rights Reserved.   **ISBN:** 9781980333272

This program is protected under Federal and International copyright laws. No portion of these materials may be reproduced, stored in a retrieval system or transmitted in any manner whatsoever, without the written consent of the publisher.

Limits of Liability / Disclaimer of Warranty
The author and the publisher of "Progressive Marketing Plan for a Human Resources Consulting Service", and all accompanying materials have used their best efforts in preparing this program. The author and publisher make no representations and warranties with respect to the accuracy, applicability, fitness or completeness of the content of this program. The information contained in this program is subject to change without notice and should not be construed as a commitment by the author or publisher.

The authors and publisher shall in no event be held liable for any loss or damages, including but not limited to special, incidental, consequential, or other damages. The program makes no promises as to results or consequences of applying the material herein: your business results may vary in direct relation to your detailed planning, timing, availability of capital and human resources, and implementation skills.

This publication is not intended for use as a source of legal, accounting, or professional advice. As always, the advice of a competent legal, accounting, tax, financial or other professional should be sought. If you have any specific questions about your unique business situation, consider contacting a qualified business consultant. The fact that an organization or website is referred to as a 'resource' or potential source of information, does not mean that the publisher or authors endorse the resource. Websites listed may also have been changed since publication of the book.

Human Resources Consulting Marketing Plan: Table of Contents

Section	Description	Page
1.0	**Executive Summary**	____
1.1.0	Tactical Objectives	____
1.1.1	Strategic Objectives	____
1.2	Mission Statement	____
1.2.1	Core Values Statement	____
1.3	Vision Statement	____
1.4	Keys to Success	____
2.0	**Company Summary**	____
3.0	**Products and Services**	____
3.1	Service Descriptions	____
3.1.1	Product Descriptions	____
3.2	Alternate Revenue Streams	____
3.3	Production of Products and Services	____
3.4	Competitive Comparison	____
3.5	Sale Literature	____
3.6	Fulfillment	____
3.7	Technology	____
3.8	Future Products and Services	____
4.0	**Market Analysis Summary**	____
4.1.0	Secondary Market Research	____
4.1.1	Primary Market Research	____
4.2	Market Segmentation	____
4.3	Target Market Segment Strategy	____
4.3.1	Market Needs	____
4.4	Buying Patterns	____
4.5	Market Growth	____
4.6	Service Business Analysis	____
4.7	Barrier to Entry	____
4.8	Competitive Analysis	____
4.9	Market Revenue Projections	____
5.0	**Industry Analysis**	____
5.1	Industry Leaders	____
5.2	Industry Statistics	____
5.3	Industry Trends	____
5.4	Industry Key Terms	____

6.0	**Strategy and Implementation Summary**	_____
6.1.0	Promotion Strategy	_____
6.1.1	Grand Opening	_____
6.1.2	Value Proposition	_____
6.1.3	Positioning Statement	_____
6.1.4	Distribution Strategy	_____
6.2	Competitive Advantage	_____
6.2.1	Branding Strategy	_____
6.3	Business SWOT Analysis	_____
6.4.0	Marketing Strategy	_____
6.4.1	Strategic Alliances	_____
6.4.2	Monitoring Marketing Results	_____
6.4.3	Word-of-Mouth Marketing	_____
6.5	Sales Strategy	_____
6.5.1	client Retention Strategy	_____
6.5.2	Sales Forecast	_____
6.5.3	Sales Program	_____
6.6	Merchandising Strategy	_____
6.7	Pricing Strategy	_____
6.8	Differentiation Strategies	_____
6.9	Milestone Tracking	_____
7.0	**Website Plan Summary**	_____
7.1	Website Marketing Strategy	_____
7.2	Development Requirements	_____
7.3	Sample Frequently Asked Questions	_____
8.0	**Business Risk Factors**	_____
8.1	Business Risk Reduction Strategies	_____
8.2	Reduce client Perceived Risk Strategies	_____
9.0	**Financial Plan**	_____
9.1	Break-even Analysis	_____
9.2	Projected Profit and Loss	_____
9.3	Projected Cash Flow	_____
9.4	Projected Balance Sheet	_____
9.5	Business Ratios	_____
	Helpful Resources	_____
	Marketing Worksheets	_____

Human Resources Consulting Service Marketing Plan

_____ (date)

Business Name: _____
Plan Time Period: 2018 – 2020

Founding Directors:
Name: _____
Name: _____

Contact Information:
Owner: _____
Address: _____
City/State/Zip: _____
Phone: _____
Cell: _____
Fax: _____
Website: _____
Email: _____

Prepared by: _____
Submitted to: _____
Date: _____
Contact Info: _____

This document contains confidential information. It is disclosed to you for informational purposes only. Its contents shall remain the property of _____ (business name) and shall be returned to _____ when requested. This is a marketing plan and does not imply an offering of securities.

1.0 Executive Summary

Industry Overview
Human Resources Consulting is involved in the practice of helping organizations improve their performance primarily through the analysis of existing personnel problems and development of plans for improvement. Organizations hire the services of Human Resources Consultants for many reasons, including gaining external objective advice and access to the consultants' specialized expertise and awareness of industry "best practices".

Consultancies provide organizational change management assistance, development of coaching skills, technology implementation, strategy development, and/or operational improvement services. Human Resources Consultants generally bring their own, proprietary methodologies or frameworks to guide the identification of problems, and to serve as the basis for recommendations for more efficient ways of performing business tasks related to human resource issues.

Global consulting industry revenues (including HR, IT, strategy, operations management and business advisory services) was about $345 billion in 2010, according to Plunkett Research estimates. This represents a rebound from about $310 billion in 2009 and $330 billion in 2008. As of late 2009 and early 2010, corporate profits in general had grown substantially, meaning that executives may be more willing to authorize new consulting projects as long as they see the potential for a good return on the cost.

Companies in this industry provide advice and assistance to business regarding human resources and personnel policies, employee compensation and benefit planning, and wage and salary administration. Major companies include US-based Aon Hewitt, Mercer, and Towers Watson, as well as divisions of global consulting firms such as Deloitte and Accenture. Major services include compensation and benefits consulting, which accounts for about half of industry revenue. Other services include consulting related to compensation planning systems, personnel management, employee assessment, and wage and salary administration.
Resource:
www.ibisworld.com/industry-trends/market-research-reports/professional-scientific-technical-services/professional-scientific-technical-services/hr-consulting.html

Business Overview
_____ (company name) _____ (was/is in the process of being) formed to provide professional human resources support services to _____ (home office and small office/ small and mid-sized businesses?) Our friendly, knowledgeable and professional staff will help inspire, educate, innovate and problem-solve for our clients in the _____ area. The initial primary service offered will be hourly human resources management support, but we plan to add retainer contracts and project consulting arrangements by the end of the _____ (first?) year.

_____ (company name) will be a human resource consulting company located in

_____ (city), ____ (state). The company has expertise in a wide range of HR areas and is targeting the _____ (start-up?) company market. HCM will offer this market the ability to compensate client's employees with stock options from their company. This will be especially appealing to many start-up companies that find capital scarce.

_____ (company name) will be an HR consultancy committed to developing effective strategic HR Management plans and helping clients implement their HR Department start-up plan. _____ (company name) will be a Human Resources Consulting and technology solutions firm that creates value and enables growth for its clients. _____ (company name) will work with organizations serving the public and private sector, developing and implementing robust HR operational solutions that will generate superior performance. Our core belief is that our success should be measured by our ability to deliver practical, measurable and sustainable financial and operational results for our clients.

Our research indicates that a Human Resources Consulting business is relatively easy to start, requires a modest up-front capital investment of about $ _____ (10000?), has the potential to be a lucrative venture, but does requires a great deal of human resources management expertise, personal branding and networking activities.

Our objective is to help companies to develop successful _____ (strategic HR management?) plans. A 'winner' will be a plan that helps management to gain market share, increase sales and lower employee turnover costs. This is crucial for small businesses that must get the highest return on every dollar spent. _____ (company name) will provide its clients with a broad range of "winning" Human Resources Consulting Services. These services include strategic HR planning as well as tactical implementation. Strategic planning utilizes those processes that lead to an executable HR management plan including identifying areas of improved productivity, market segmentation, benefit administration analysis, personnel planning, training analysis, and culminate in the design of a HR project implementation plan. This will serve as a detailed road map for the planning and supervision of all human resources management activities. Once completed, the tactical process will be initiated leading to the real-world execution of the HR management plan.

Target Market

_____ (company name) is dedicated to providing Human Resources Consulting Services to small and emerging businesses looking for opportunities to increase their potential for success and sustained profitability. The target client of _____ (company name) is the small business that can rarely afford the cost of in-house HR management support and must utilize the outsourced services of a Human Resources Consulting Service to maximize the cost-effectiveness of their operating expenditures. _____ (company name) will be a results-driven Human Resources Consulting Service. We will provide a complete range of management support services. This allows us to evaluate a variety of human resources management tools, choosing those that are best suited to the client's requirements. We will then combine those tools in such a way so as to create meaningful, effective HR management plan that achieves optimal results. Unlike traditional Human Resources Consulting Services that focus on analyzing problems for large clients, we will work exclusively with _____ (small?) business clients to develop concrete, practical, short-term action plans that will start moving their businesses in the right direction. We will take advantage of the business owners' need for HR management skills, the scarcity of those expensive HR skills in the market, and the lack of any major competitor owning the concept of "Small Business Human Resources Consulting Service."

Success Factors:

In order to succeed, _____ (company name) will have to do the following:
1. Make superior client service and the client's business objectives our top priorities.
2. Develop a deep knowledge of the client's business.
3. Stay abreast of trends in the Human Resources Consulting industry.
4. Pursue a niche strategy.
5. Mount a cost-effective marketing and intensive networking campaign.
6. Precisely assess client needs and wants, and then exceed their expectations.
7. Form long-term relationships with clients based on mutual respect, quality and responsive service, and trust to secure profitable repeat business and referrals.
8. Building a reputation for being an innovative firm with bright new HR management ideas.

Client Service

We will take every opportunity to help the client, regardless of what the revenue might be. We will outshine our competition by doing something "extra". We will treat clients with respect and help them like we would help a friend. We will take a long-term perspective and focus on the client's possible lifetime value to our HR consulting business.

Plan Objective

The purpose of this document is to provide a strategic growth plan for our Human Resources Consulting company. The plan has been adjusted to reflect the particular strengths and weaknesses of _____ (company name). Actual financial performance will be closely tracked, and the plan will be adjusted when necessary to ensure that full profit potential is realized.

Business Structure

The business _____ was incorporated on _____ (date) as a _____ (Corporation/LLC/Professional Corporation), and intends to register for Sub-chapter 'S' corporate status for federal tax purposes. This will effectively shield the owner(s) from personal liability and double taxation. The company is/was started by _____ (business owner name), who is the majority owner and a past _____ (indicate relevant business experience or achievements) with ___ years of experience in the _____ industry.

Business Goals

Our business goal is to continue to develop the _____ (company name) brand name. To do so, we plan to execute on the following:

1. Offer quality Human Resources Consulting Services at a competitive price.
2. Focus on quality controls and ongoing operational excellence.
3. Develop long-term client relationships that generate referrals and repeat business.
4. Develop multiple revenue streams that maximize the utilization of our assets and core competencies.
5. Recruit and train the very best ethical and client-focused employees.
6. Create a marketing campaign with a consistent brand look and message.

Location

_____ (company name) will be located in the _____ (complex name) on _____ (street address) in _____ (city), ____ (state). The _____ (purchased/leased) space is easily accessible and provides ample parking for ____ (#) clients and staff. The facilities will include office space for the principals and technical staff, an inventory storage area, and a conference room.

Products and Services

_____ (company name) will work closely with each client's principals and key employees to learn about their respective internal HR systems. Through this process we will be able to develop a customized approach, develop workable HR solutions, make recommendations for improvement and offer assistance with, or take full responsibility for the implementation of each activity. We will offer a wide range of HR services, including executive compensation, corporate governance and recruiting expertise to clients of all sizes, but most are expected to be small businesses. When defining the services, we offer, our HR consultants will be mindful that some clients will ask them to do work beyond their primary areas of expertise. But if that project is outside our HR consultant's area of expertise, it can create headaches and siphon time away from work that is more fulfilling and more lucrative and that can be done more professionally and efficiently. Consequently, we will form referral alliances with other consulting firms that have specialized areas of expertise that we lack.

Competitive Edge

We will coach businesses on how HR can play a lead role in not only ensuring that workers are properly trained and that processes are well-designed, but also that workers are empowered to share their ideas for improving how things are done. We will help our clients to develop the necessary work systems that can assist in tapping workers' knowledge for improving existing processes. We will utilize our entrepreneurial culture and innovative mindset to constantly find new ways to create unique value for our clients. We will continuously engage in the relentless pursuit of greater solutions to improve the lives of our clients' employees.

Differentiation Strategy

To become a high-growth consultancy, we will conduct continuous research, achieve service specialization and focus on the needs of a narrow target market. Specialization will enable our consultancy to offer clearly defined, high-value, high-quality services that will differentiate us from more broadly-based HR consultancies. To document our niche specialization, we will publish case studies of successful engagements and write articles about best practices. This will demonstrate our professionalism and knowledge. The aim will be to build a reputation for excellence, so potential clients perceive our firm as the expert in a specific field.

Marketing Plan

With the help of an aggressive marketing plan, _____ (company name) expects to experience steady growth. _____ (company name) plans to attract its clients through the use of local trade journal advertisements, circulating flyers, a systematic series of direct mailings, news releases in local trade newsletters, a website, online directories, networking with local organizations, and a sales rep to approach commercial accounts. All these marketing methods will be used to communicate our firm's uniqueness and specialized human resources management expertise to separate us from other consulting firms. We will use our website to not only attract business but also to provide a handy resource for prospects and clients. We will use this forum to highlight areas of expertise, showcase case studies and success stories, and provide contact information. To be effective, our website will be professional in appearance, easy to navigate and updated frequently enough to encourage repeat visits.

Target Market

We plan to work with companies of all sizes, but our primary target will be growing companies with roughly 20 to 200 employees, and no formal HR department. Our target market is the 5+ million for-profit and non-profit organizations identified as small to mid-sized businesses (SMBs) in the U.S. with less than 200 employees. Typically, SMBs do not have the financial ability or the HR workload to employ a full-time HR Manager. In these companies, HR functions are usually accomplished in a "band aid" manner by the CEO, CFO/Controller, Bookkeeper, Office Manager, or someone with a designation of HR Coordinator.

Our targeted clients will share the following characteristics:
- Need an immediate, professional solution to a pressing HR problem.
- HR is being handled ineffectively and/or inefficiently by existing resources.
- Too much management time is being spent on one or more HR issues.
- One person is covering too many functional areas.
- Companies wanting to protect and/or grow their businesses.

The Management Team

_____ (company name) will be led by _____ (owner name) and _____ (co-owner name). ____ (owner name) has a _____ degree from ___ (institution name) and a ____ background within the industry, having spent _____ (#) years with ____ (former employer name or type of business). During this tenure, ___ (he/she) helped grow the business from $_____ in yearly revenue to over $___. ____ (co-owner name) has a ___ background, and while employed by __ was able to increase operating profit by __ percent. These acquired skills, work experiences and educational backgrounds will play a big role in the success of our HR Consulting Firm. Additionally, our president, _____ (name), has an extensive knowledge of the _____ area and has identified a niche market retail opportunity to make this venture highly successful, combining his ___ (#) years of work experience in a variety of businesses. _____ (owner name) will manage all aspects of the business and service development to ensure effective client responsiveness while monitoring day-to-day operations. Qualified and trained sales associates personally trained by _____ (owner name) in client service skills will provide additional support services. Support staff will be added as seasonal or extended hours mandate.

Recap of Past Successful Accomplishments
_____ (company name) is uniquely qualified to succeed due to the following past successes:
1. **Entrepreneurial Track Record**: The owners and management team have helped to launch numerous successful ventures, including a _____.

2. **Key Milestones Achieved**: The founders have invested $___ to-date to staff the company, build the core technology, acquire starting inventory, test market the _____ (product/service), realize sales of $_____ and launch the website.

Financial Projections

_____ (company name) is forecasted to gross in excess of $_____ in sales in its first year of operation, ending ____ (month/ year). Profit margins are forecasted to be at about ____ (30?) percent. Second year operations will produce a net profit of $_____. This will be generated from an investment of $___ in initial capital. It is expected that payback of our total invested capital will be realized in less than ___ (#) months of operation. It is further forecasted that cash flow becomes positive from operations in year ___ (one/two?). We project that our net profits will increase from $____ to over $____ over the next three years.

Financial Profile Summary

Key Indicator	2018	2019	2020
Total Revenue			
Gross Margin			
Operating Income			
Net Income			

Exit Strategy

If the business is very successful, ____ (owner name) may seek to sell the business to a third party for a significant earnings multiple. Most likely, the Company will hire a qualified business broker to sell the business on behalf of _____ (company name). Based on historical numbers, the business could generate a sales premium of up to __(#) times earnings.

Summary

Through a combination of a proven business model and a strong management team to guide the organization, _____ (company name) will be a long lasting, profitable business. We believe our ability to create future product and service opportunities and growth will only be limited by our imagination and our ability to attract talented people who understand the concept of branding.

1.1 Key Strategic Objectives   (select)

The following strategic objectives of this business plan will specify quantifiable results and involve activities that can be easily tracked. They will also be realistic, tied to specific marketing strategies and serve as a good benchmark to evaluate our tactical marketing plan success.

1. To create a Human Resources Consulting company whose primary goal is to exceed client expectations.
2. To develop a cash flow that is capable of paying all salaries, as well as grow the business, by the end of the _____ (first?) year.
3. To be an active networking participant of the community by _____ (date).
4. Create over ____ (50?) % of revenues from repeat clients by _____ (date).
5. Develop a follow-up strategy to evaluate performance with all clients and achieve an overall client satisfaction rate of ____ (100?) % by _____ (date).
6. Get a business website designed, built and operational by _____ (date), which will include an online shopping cart.
7. Achieve total sales revenues of $_____ in _____ (year).
8. Achieve net profit of at least ____ (45?) % by the ____ (first?) year.
9. Increase overall sales by _____ (20?) percent from prior year through superior service and word-of-mouth referrals.
10. Reduce the cost of new client acquisition by ___ % to $ ___ by ____ (date).
11. Turn in profits from the _____ (#) month of operations.
12. Expand operations to include all of the _____ (city) area, including _____,
13. Provide employees with continuing training, benefits and incentives to reduce the employee turnover rate to _____ %.
14. To pursue a growth rate of ____ (20?) % per year for the first ____ (#) years.
15. Achieve a client mix of ___% small business, ___% entrepreneurial, ___% individual per year.
16. Move into a small office space by the end of the first year.
17. Achieve total sales revenues of $_____ in _____ (year).
18. Achieve net income more than ___ percent of net sales by the ____ (#) year.
19. Increase overall sales by _____ (20?) percent from prior year through superior service and word-of-mouth referrals.

20. Reduce the cost of new client acquisition by ___ % to $ ___ by _____ (date).
21. Provide employees with continuing training, benefits and incentives to reduce the employee turnover rate to _____ %.
22. To pursue a growth rate of ____ (20?) % per year for the first ____ (#) years.
23. Enable the owner to draw a salary of $ _____ by the end of year ____ (one?).
24. To reach cash break-even by the end of year ____ (one?).
25. Increase market share to ___ percent over the next ___ (#) months.
26. Become one of the top ___ (#) players in the emerging _____ category in __ (#) months.
27. Increase Operating Profit by ___ percent versus the previous year.
28. Achieve market share leadership in the ____ category by ____ (date).

1.1.1 Strategic Objectives

We will seek to work toward the accomplishment of the following strategic objectives, which relate back to our Mission and Vision Statements:
1. Improve the overall quality of our Human Resources Consulting Services.
2. Make the buyer experience better, faster and more client friendly.
3. Strengthen personal relationships with clients.
4. Enhance affordability and accessibility.
5. Foster a spirit of innovation.
6. Develop a sustainable start-up consultancy firm that can survive off its own cash flow by _____ (year) and has significant equity holdings in ___ (#) emerging companies.

1.2.0 Mission Statement   (select)

Our Mission Statement is a written statement that spells out our organization's overall goal, provides a sense of direction and acts as a guide to decision making for all levels of management. In the mission statement, our goal will be to identify the client pain we intend to satisfy, and what our company will do to satisfy it. In developing the following mission statement, we will encourage input from employees, volunteers, and other stakeholders, and publicize it broadly in our website and other marketing materials.

Our primary focus is to work closely with clients and help them succeed in setting and meeting their marketing goals. We offer total support and a commitment to communicate their ideas in a strategic, creative, and cost-effective manner.

It is the Mission of _____ (company name) to provide fast, reliable, high quality human resources management support and solutions to small and mid-sized businesses. Our mission is to provide customized Human Resources Consulting Services and products that will enable our clients to optimize their employee productivity, sales revenues and assist in the realization of their business goals and objectives.

Our mission is to help clients develop the HR strategy, motivation and accountability required to succeed in their business. The company sees each contract as an agreement between partners who wish to create a close and mutually beneficial long-term relationship. This will help to provide greater long-term profits through referrals and repeat business. We will strive to provide our clients with the best customized solution to meet their Human Resources needs. Our mission is to help our clients to integrate their core values into their Human Resources practices.

Our mission is to provide human resource consulting for _____ (start-up?) companies. Our mission is to realize 100% client satisfaction, and generate long-term profits through referrals and repeat business. Our mission is to serve our clients as trusted advisors, providing them with the loyalty of a business partner, and the economic savings of an outsourced vendor. Our goal is to set ourselves apart from the competition by making client satisfaction our number one priority and to provide client support that is responsive, informed and respectful.

1.2.1 Mantra

We will create a mantra for our organization that is three or four words long. Its purpose will be to help employees truly understand why the organization exists. Our mantra will serve as a framework through which to make decisions about product and business direction. It will boil the key drivers of our company down to a sentence that defines our most important areas of focus and resemble a statement of purpose or significance.
Our Mantra is _____

1.2.2 Core Values Statement

The following Core Values will help to define our organization, guide our behavior, underpin operational activity and shape the strategies we will pursue in the face of various challenges and opportunities:
- Being respectful and ethical to our clients and employees.
- Building enduring relationships with clients.
- Seeking innovation in our industry.
- Practicing accountability to our colleagues and stakeholders.
- Pursuing continuous improvement as individuals and as a business entity.
- Performing tasks on time to satisfy the needs of our internal and external clients.
- Taking active part in the organization to meet the objectives and the establishment of continuous and lasting relationships.
- Offering professional treatment to our clients, employees, shareholders, and the community.
- Continuing pursuit of new technologies for the development of the projects that add value for our clients, employees, shareholders, and the community.

Personal and professional improvement through education.
Teamwork to achieve our goals.
Honesty and integrity in all areas of our professional relationships.
Loyalty to the team and dedication to achieving our mission.

1.3 Vision Statement

The Vision Statement will set the long-term direction for our business and describe what goals we want to achieve in the long term. The following Vision Statement will communicate both the purpose and values of our organization. For employees, it will give direction about how they are expected to behave and inspires them to give their best. Shared with clients, it will shape clients' understanding of why they should work with our HR Consultancy.

_____ (company name) will strive to become one of the most respected and innovative Human Resources Consulting Service firms in the _____ area. It is our desire to become a landmark business in _____ (city), ____ (state), and become known not only for the quality of our Human Resources Consulting products and services, but also for our community citizenship and charity involvement. To generate a sufficient number of satisfied repeat clients to build a stable retainer base.

_____ (company name) is dedicated to operating with a constant enthusiasm for learning about the Human Resources Consulting business, being receptive to implementing new ideas, and maintaining a willingness to adapt to changing market needs and wants. To be an active and vocal member of the community, and to provide continual reinvestment through participation in community activities and financial contributions.

In five years, _____ (company name) will be an area leader in the Human Resources Consulting industry, and plans will be developed and implemented to pursue national business through the franchising of our business model concept.

1.4 Keys to Success   (select)

In broad terms, the success factors relate to providing what our clients want, and doing what is necessary to be better than our competitors. The most significant success factor will be effective market segmentation through the identification of the needs and wants of several specific niche markets and detailed implementation strategies. The following critical success factors are areas in which our organization must excel in order to operate successfully and achieve our objectives:

1. Deliver a Human Resources Consulting experience that is completely confidential, and reliable, with trustworthy expertise and information.
2. Develop the visibility to generate new business leads.
3. Leverage from a single pool of expertise into multiple revenue generation opportunities, such as retainer coaching, project consulting, workshop facilitation and individual coaching.

4. Consistently develop productive and thought-provoking learning experiences to maintain growth and success with each client.
5. Incorporate the usage of state-of-the-art technology.
6. Provide easy access to our Human Resources Consulting Services.
7. Assemble a seasoned advisory team.
8. Possess the technical management expertise to minimize the learning curve for our clients and minimize their expenses.
9. Be a part of our client's business team.
10. Generate new innovative strategies for our clients that result in high-quality and cost-effective product and/or service introductions.
11. Service our client needs with personalized attention, confidential trustworthiness, superior reliability, two-way collaboration, open and honest communication and expert knowledge.
12. Develop a wide range of Human Resources Consulting skills due to the small budget size of the projects that typically come from small to mid-size firms.
13. Act as an on-call problem-solver with prompt response times.
14. Launch a website to showcase our products, services and client testimonials, provide helpful information and benefit from an online e-commerce catalog.
15. The people skills to establish long-term business relationships and secure repeat business.
16. Conduct a highly targeted and cost-effective advertising campaign.
17. Institute a program of profit sharing among all employees to reduce employee turnover and improve productivity.
18. Control costs at all times without exception.
19. Institute management processes and controls to insure the consistent replication of services and operations.
20. Recruit employees with a passion for delivering exceptional client service.
21. Institute an employee training to insure the best consultative sales techniques are consistently practiced.
22. Network aggressively within the business community, as word of mouth will be our most powerful advertising asset.
23. Develop the ability to operate across a range of markets to reduce the impact of local demand conditions.
24. The flexibility to respond to changing client buying habits and needs.
25. Leverage our capabilities with the help of an outside alliance pool of experts.
26. Build brand awareness, which will drive clients to increase their usage of our Human Resources Consulting Services and make referrals.
27. Business planning with the flexibility to make changes based on gaining new insightful perspectives as we proceed.
28. Build trust by circulating and adhering to our Code of Ethics and Service Guarantees.
29. The development of a niche or focused marketing strategy.
30. Continuous training of our staff to update their technical skills and create a depth of human resources and business knowledge.
31. An understanding of the needs that potential clients believe to be the most critical and how they see them.

32. A set of criteria for selecting profitable clients.
33. Remotely coordinating a wide range of skills and experiences from a diverse network of consultants and alliance partners.
34. Develop a local presence in a strong small business market.
35. Define a clear value proposition that can be communicated into the target market
36. Show leadership in professional associations, and if possible speak before groups, and write articles about accomplishments and ideas.
37. Seize every opportunity to interface with clients, develop new HR Consulting services, and improve core competencies.
38. Thoroughly research the client's company to suggest improvements in HR Procedures.
39. Offer a flexible means of obtaining compensation from clients.
40. Do the upfront research to determine which types of human resources services are in high-demand in our area.
41. Develop some top Key Performance Indicators (KPIs) for measuring employee success.
    Resource: www.entrepreneurshipinabox.com/12605/human-resources-kpis-employee-success/
42. Document, in writing, the agreement and expectations of the consulting relationship to help manage expectations and avoid misunderstanding.
    Note: At a minimum include: a description of the services that will be performed, the deadline by which services will be completed, and the fees that will be charged.
43. Consistently listening to employee feedback, and measuring their preferences will promote employee satisfaction, and help manage rising benefit costs, creating the classical win-win relationship for both employees and employers.
    Source: www.aon.com/human-capital-consulting/thought-leadership/communication/article_employees_consumers.jsp

2.0   Company Summary

_____ (company name) is a start-up _____ (Corporation/Limited Liability Company) consisting of __ (#) principle officers with combined industry experience of __ (#) years. _____ (company Name) will be a HR consultancy firm serving the _____ area market. It will be set up as an _____ (state) Corporation owned by _____ and will focus on _____ (type of companies?) companies.

We will provide human resources consulting to all size businesses throughout the state, and will offer a variety of services including HR program development, creating and revising employee handbooks, recruiting, employee satisfaction surveys, employee training programs, and more. The firm will employ ___(#) people initially, and ___ (#) people by the end of the _____ (first?) year in business.

The company was formed to offer a wide range of quality, affordable and expert Human Resources Consulting support services and for sale products, such as packaged software, a company newsletter, special reports, books, seminars and paid public addresses.

The owner of the company will be investing a significant amount of ____ (his/her) own capital into the company and will also be seeking a loan of $ _____ to cover start-up costs and future growth. _____ (company name) will be initially located in a ____ (purchased/ rented/ home office?) ____ (suite/ complex) in the _____ on _____ (address) in _____ (city), _____ (state).

The facilities will include office cubicles for the owner and staff, locker/snack room, reception area and conference room/classroom area. The company plans to use its existing contacts and client base to generate short-term sales. Its long-term profitability will rely on focusing on referrals, networking within community and business organizations, and a comprehensive marketing program that includes public relations activities and a structured referral program. Sales are expected to reach $_____ within the first year and to grow at a conservative rate of ____ (20?) percent during the next two to five years.

Facilities Renovations

The necessary renovations are itemized as follows:	Estimate
Partition of space into functional areas and admin offices.	_____
Painting and other general cosmetic repairs	_____
Build storage area for product and supplies inventories.	_____
Installation communications lines.	_____
Build reception area and conference rooms	_____
Other _____	_____
Total:	_____

Operations

_____ (company name) will open for business on _____ (date) and

will maintain the following business hours:
Monday through Thursday: _____ (9 to 6?)
Friday: _____ (9 to 5?)
Saturday: _____ (Closed?)
Sunday: _____ (Closed?)

The company will invest in client relationship management software (CRM) to track sales and collect client information, including names, email addresses, key reminder dates and preferences. This information will be used with email, e-newsletter and direct mail campaigns to build personalized fulfillment programs, establish client loyalty and drive revenue growth.

2.0.1   Traction (optional)

We will include this section because investors expect to see some traction, both before and after a funding event and investors tend to judge past results as a good indicator of future projections. It will also show that we can manage our operations and develop a business model capable of funding inventory purchases. Traction will be the best form of market research and present evidence of client acceptance.

Period _____
Product/Service Focus _____
Our Sales to Date: _____
Our Number of Users to Date: _____
Number of Repeat Users _____
Number of Pending Orders: _____
Value of Pending Orders: _____
Reorder Cycle: _____
Key Reference Sites _____
Mailing List Subscriptions _____
Competitions/Awards Won _____
Notable Product Reviews _____
Actual Percent Gross Profit Margin _____
Industry Average: GPM _____
Actual B/(W) Industry Average _____

Note: Percent Gross Profit Margin equals the sales receipts less the cost of goods sold divided by sales receipts multiplied by 100.

3.0 Products and Services

In this section, we will not only list all our planned products and services, but also describe how our proposed products and services will be differentiated from those of our competitors and solve a real problem or fill an unmet need in the marketplace.

_____ (company name) will be a team of experienced Human Resources Consultants with a successful track record of developing HR management systems. We will offer the customized solutions that firms require for mission-critical strategic initiatives in HR strategy formulation, HR process design, HR program management, and HR organizational development. We will work collaboratively with client talent in an integrative, inclusive style that is both more effective and more cost efficient than the typical consulting firm. If additional outside resources are needed to round out a team's talent base, we will bring in additional experts from our extensive consulting network to fulfill the specific need. We will offer exceptional value by focusing on results, and always ensuring the value created for our clients greatly exceeds our fees. Our clients will benefit from our unique combination of real world HR management experience, formal business education, knowledge of best practices, collaborative style, and client driven focus.

We will put our client's company in the strategic position necessary to manage talent acquisition, leadership development, workforce planning, HR compliance, and re-engage their employees. _____ (company name) will provide human resource consulting to _____ (start-up?) companies in the _____ (city) market. We will charge a below market rate and offer to take stock options in the client company.

Services: (select)

_____ (company Name) will offer the following Human Resources Consulting Services:
1. Human resource management.
2. Organizational management.
3. Professional development.
4. Employee relations.
5. Labor relations.
6. HR Audit.
7. HR policy and procedure.
8. Executive search.
9. Sexual harassment.
10. Position classification.
11. Personnel management systems.
12. Performance evaluations.
13. Diversity.
14. Executive Compensation
15. Corporate Governance
16. Talent Acquisition Services
17. Leadership Development

18. Leadership Assessment
19. Retirement Planning
20. Benefits Administration
21. M & A Transaction Services
22. Public Training Programs
23. Custom Employee Handbooks
24. Set up Human Resources Department
25. Career Management
26. Competency Development
27. Downsizing/Outplacement
28. Employee Referral Programs
29. Employee Incentive Programs
30. Interviewing/Recruiting
31. Writing Job Descriptions
32. New-hire Orientations
33. Policy Guides/Employee Handbooks
34. Resume Writing
35. Customized Employee Training
36. Diversity Training
37. Harassment training
38. Motivational Speaking
39. Motivational Workshops
40. Sales Training
41. Skill-based Training
42. Employee Surveys
43. Exit Interview Programs
44. HR Coaching
45. Employee On-boarding Programs
46. Form I-9 Audits

Resource:
https://www.the-arnold-group.com/employerservices/hrconsulting/

The pricing structure will either be an hourly rate or a per project fee. These options will be settled on in an upfront negotiation with the client. In general, _____ (company name) will be receptive to a flexible payment arrangement.

As a diversified human resources management consultancy firm, we will also help companies with going public, mergers and acquisitions, shell corporations, venture capital, stock exchanges, corporate finance, private placement etc.

Our business Human Resources Consulting Service's goals will be to help new and existing companies or businesses with performance improvement, plus offer objective advice that can be real valuable to a client company. _____ (company name) will practice organizational change management assistance, company HR strategy development, technology implementation and any other HR skills coaching, if needed.

Products:
We will use the sale of the following products to even out dips in the uncertainty of consulting, provide additional revenue streams, brand our image and as marketing tools to keep our name out in the marketplace.

1. Human Resources Software
2. HR Topic Papers
3. Special Report Fees
4. Affiliate Book Sales (via Amazon)
5. Consultant Authored Book Sales
6. Newsletter Subscription Fees
7. Seminar DVD Sales
8. Survey Results
9. HR Planning Guides
10. Workbooks
11. Speech CDs and DVDs
12. Compensation Management Software
13. Recruitment Software
14. Benefits Administration Software

3.1 Service Arrangement Descriptions   (select)

We will offer our clients the following service arrangement options:

1. **Hourly Technical Support**
   A short term or temporary assignment, designed to help a company solve a particular marketing challenge or issue. We will seek to establish an hourly or daily rate that will ensure profitability for our company and a firm time frame for rates to remain in effect, before scheduled increases. The hourly rate will be tied to each consultant's level of expertise and the scope of the project.

2. **Retainerships**
   A traditional form of consulting that involves a fee-for-services relationship, usually for a specific skill and deliverable on short notice. Our retainerships will be based on a specific activity and at a stated cost and very clearly stated objectives. The retainer relationship will assure our clients that they will have access to our HR advisory services for a fixed monthly fee. They will provide our company with a known flow of income for a specific period. The owner's particular area of expertise is in _____ (consulting). In accordance with Retainer Consulting, we will represent a client company as an extension of its business development and market development functions. This begins with complete understanding of the client company's situation, objectives, and constraints. We will then represent the client company quietly and confidentially, sifting through new market developments and new opportunities as is appropriate to the client, representing the client in initial talks with possible allies, vendors, and channels.

3. **Project Consulting**
   Project consulting is proposed and billed on a per-project and per- milestone basis. Project consulting offers a client company a way to harness our specific

qualities and use our expertise to solve specific problems, develop and/or implement plans, develop specific information. This will include such things as consulting on major media purchases, networking activities, market testing, and project management. Requires a clear assessment of the salaries, benefits and overhead expenses to be incurred to meet the client's needs and our project profitability goal.

4. **Contingency Arrangements**
Our fee will be based on the achieving of agreed-on project results. According to this arrangement, we will receive a one-time specified percentage of the gains (revenue enhancements) or savings (cost reductions) resulting from the project. In this case, it will be very important that the measurement standards are clearly specified and defined and the client can be trusted to honor their commitment.

5. **Value-Based Fee Arrangement**
According to this arrangement, our fees will be tied to the value the project generates and the fees are not limited to a one-time percentage of the results or benefits realized. To eliminate some of the financial risk, we will ask for a good-faith payment at the beginning of the project, set checkpoints to measure progress against goals and request interim payments.

6. **Composite Pricing Arrangements**
Involves creating an innovative combination of the aforementioned arrangements.

3.2 Service Descriptions

In creating our service descriptions, we will provide answers to the following types of questions:
1. What does the service do or help the client to accomplish?
2. Why will people decide to buy it?
3. What makes it unique or a superior value?
4. How expensive or difficult is it to make or copy by a competitor?
5. How much will the service be sold for?

Human Resources Consulting
_____ (company name) will help clients to optimize performance, control costs and risks, modify systems and processes, and use change as a catalyst for profitable growth. We will do this by identifying strategies for success, managing change across the enterprise and developing the workforce to achieve their potential.

HR Process Management
We will help our clients to evolve their HR operations to accommodate an increasingly complex, volatile and interconnected global marketplace. Our unique combination of six sigma skills, approaches, assets and tools will help clients to develop and operate

scalable, efficient, defect free and agile business processes to deliver immediate and long-lasting value and improved levels of client satisfaction.

Coaching Services
We will meet once a month at a prescheduled day and time for about an hour with the client. We will talk about whatever the client wants, or we can take the client through a process that walks through their entire HR management approach. The session will generally end with tasks outlined and assigned. In between our phone or actual meetings the client can email their questions. This service will cost $____ (700.00) per month.

Benchmarking & Best Practices
Our Benchmarking and Best Practices service line will provide sales executives with data and insight into the processes and practices that drive world class sales productivity. Participating executives will be able to identify and scale areas of strength as well as diagnose and correct areas of under-performance. We are committed to providing sales executives with the benchmarks they need to make fact based decisions on how to cover their target markets and provide specialized comparisons and benchmarks in select industries.

Leadership Exchange
The objective of this service is to foster the kind of innovative thinking that leaders need to create high performance organizations, as innovation is a prominent hallmark of today's high-performance organization. The Leadership Exchange will be a source of ideas and insights that promote such innovation. This specialized family of events and research topics designed for business leaders will offer access to content and to a network of peers from which clients can learn and profit.

HR Executive Workshops
These workshops are designed to help senior executives deal with specific, high impact topics. These keynote practitioners and small-group facilitated HR workshops will help executives develop both a blueprint for action and a network of peers they can call upon for HR advice and input.

Executive Roundtables
These tele-roundtables will consist of ___ (#) executives and one facilitator. Participants in the topic groups will vote for the topics they want to discuss. A summary document, called the Chief Sales Executive Digest, will be produced after each roundtable and distributed free to participants. The report will summarize the issues, root causes, action alternatives and outcomes.

Change Management
_____ (company name) will help organizations and their people to benefit from and adjust to change, whether it is a HR technology system that requires training, processes that need integrating into existing work patterns, or a new HR strategic direction that depends on the understanding and support of stakeholders.

Seminar & Special Event Management

We will work closely with clients to identify opportunities for firm sponsored and outside sponsored HR seminars and other special events. In addition to identifying the event, and determining whether it makes sense for the firm, we will work closely with clients to coordinate and implement the actual event. Many items need to be considered and decided upon well in advance: What are the overall goals? Is the purpose to go after prospective clients or to solidify relationships with existing clients? Who is the target market and how easy will it be to identify and reach them? What's the pre- and post-event follow up plan? Planning for a seminar or other special event is as important as its effective implementation. We will assist firms throughout the entire event consideration and planning process, from the decision to commit to the post follow-up activities.

Public Training Programs

Our public training programs will focus on combining fundamental concepts, practical experiences, consulting frameworks and real-world examples that will help participants apply the learning at work.

On Demand Coaching

This service, for time restricted clients, will include, but is not limited to, private and objective professional HR coaching, affordable and "on-demand," access to coaching via phone/email.

Special Projects Management

Special Projects Management will include strategic HR planning and implementation, leadership development, people management and systematizing HR processes.

Corporate Governance

We will help clients develop executive compensation philosophy, director compensation, and Compensation Committee charters. In addition to this development we will also provide:

- Director education
- External market and legislative updates
- CD&A and Proxy development
- CEO evaluations
- Committee evaluations
- Tally sheet preparation
- Pay/performance analysis
- Disclosure review and analysis
- Testing vs. Risk Metrics models for acceptable practices

Executive Compensation

Communication of Executive Compensation
We will help clients develop the right messaging to communicate their plans to across internal and external constituents, through:
- Communication strategy development
- Individual participant statements
- Shareholder education materials
- Plan documents

Program Design
Our design capabilities will be comprehensive; from full total rewards strategy and design down to individual contract analysis. Other areas include:
- Equity and cash based long-term incentive design
- Performance metrics analysis and selection
- Employment contract analysis
- Change in control & severance plan design and costing
- Non-qualified SERP and restoration plan design and costing
- Deferred compensation plan design/costing
- Total Rewards architecture and monitoring
- Peer group selection and analysis
- Pay/performance analysis

Corporate Change and Transition
We will help companies conduct plan design and integration work for spin-offs, divestitures and public offerings. This work will include:
- Equity design and transition from parent company's plans
- Bankruptcy planning, testimony, and emergence planning and design
- Global or domestic restructuring

Executive Compensation and Analysis
We will use our technical resources to regularly perform:
- Custom peer group selection and performance/pay analysis
- External market studies and job pricings
- Competitive market valuations for salary, bonus, long-term incentives, benefits and perquisites
- Pay and performance alignment
- Best practice and emerging trends research
- Outside Director compensation design/analysis
- Equity grant run rate and dilution analysis
- Tally sheet preparation
- Interactive modeling of proposed compensation programs and business strategy

Technical Support Services
Other technical support we will provide clients include:
- Special program design, implementation and communications
- Long-term incentive plan design and shareholder approval
- Share pool analysis and usage

Internal revenue code section 162m assistance
409a compliance and analysis
Plan documentation and award agreements
Tax, accounting and securities law analysis and excise tax calculations
Ongoing research and tracking of all legislative and regulatory changes

Pay and Performance Alignment
We will perform pay and performance alignment evaluations, and we will identify "performance" definitions for use at all levels. Alignment work will include:
Annual and long-term metrics selection, hurdle selection, and modeling
Pay element mix selection to ensure consistency with total rewards strategy
Company differentiator identification and the success factors for inclusion in reward plans
Review of checks and balances to reward structure, goal setting and pay-out curves
Annual risk assessment of compensation programs, metrics, governance practices and outcomes

Recruiting/Talent Acquisition Services

From workforce planning to new hire engagement, our Talent Acquisition Services will ensure a pipeline of performance-ready employees to drive client success. We will offer the following programs:

1. Developing job descriptions
2. Determining the best strategies for locating qualified candidates
3. Creating an innovative approach to advertising
4. Receiving and reviewing resumes
5. Conducting phone screens and in-person interviews
6. Providing detailed feedback on each candidate presented
7. Verifying previous employment and credentials
8. Conducting reference checks, background checks, and employment testing

Leadership Development

Our consultancy will attract, identify, develop, and coach high-potential talent, from entry-level supervisors to boardroom executives. Our award-winning, web-based leadership assessment will provide in-depth skill measurement and detailed developmental results. Our leadership development workshops will provide proven results in improving leaders' knowledge, competence and confidence.

Our leadership development solutions will include:
Help organizations improve their global leadership bench-strength and quickly build a strong leadership pipeline. Through our leadership development programs, target employees will have improved scores on leadership competencies, increasing leadership performance ratings by nearly _____ (20?) percent.

Increase leadership retention by approximately _____ (85?) percent.

Help leaders perform better on the metrics that matter, such as _____ (three?) times higher client service scores, ____ (15?) percent more sales, _____ (65?) percent fewer team terminations, and ____ (5?) % lower costs.

Reduce the organization's administration costs by ____ (50?) percent through the use of virtual and remote solutions.

Leadership Assessment
Our suite of assessment tools will provide a robust, cost-effective, easily-tailored approach to assessing leadership capability and potential including:
    Identifying individual contributors for selection into front-line leadership
    Assessing high potential leaders to support accelerated development
    Evaluating the adequacy of leadership capability for talent and succession planning
    Selecting internal and external candidates at all leadership levels

Sales Force Performance
Sales Force Effectiveness
Our Sales Force Effectiveness Practice will understand that sales people are expensive resources that often operate remotely from headquarters, interact directly with clients and have significant impact on business results. Given these factors, we will operate under the belief that proper client targeting, organization deployment, sales talent management and motivation of sales people will be critical to our clients' success.

Targeting specific markets and clients is one of the primary growth, retention and profit levers for sales. We will help our clients with the key elements in strategically targeting clients:
Sales Potential Estimation–Using statistical algorithms, we will help clients predict the total sales opportunity from a client. This is important when deciding whether to target that client for new sales, further penetration or retention-focused programs

Client Segmentation–By grouping clients with common traits we will more effectively align the sales force to meet clients' needs and improve a company's value proposition.

Sales Organization Deployment is a critical factor in improving revenue and decreasing cost of sales. We will provide the basis for a structured, intelligent sales territory plan that puts the right skills in the right place to achieve strategic objectives.

Sales Force Sizing–Sales force sizing based on historical data analysis, market potential, future growth projections and a sales team's productivity are all considerations in deploying the optimal sales force. We will analyze these factors to support effective client coverage.

Coverage Modeling–Best in class sales forces recognize that selling has evolved to a profession of specialists, requiring sales talent that aligns to specific skills, clients, channels, products and productivity levels. We will help clients understand and improve sales results prior to deployment so that risk is minimized.

Talent Selection and Management are common hurdles that prevent a sales force from being successful. Attracting and retaining top talent provides an important advantage over competitors.

Selection Criteria–Our team will help clients to develop job profiles and test candidates based on proven success factors to guide recruitment efforts. We will adapt the sales competencies in these profiles as our client needs and target markets evolve.

Engagement–Improved engagement of the sales force can motivate productivity and reduce turnover. We will provide leading indicators that identify engagement issues and drivers to scientifically improve sales performance.

Sales Force Rewards are the primary means of motivating salespeople. Incentive plans influence the activities and behaviors of salespeople and push them to higher levels of performance. We will help our clients to develop plans that direct sales behavior to drive strategy and revenue goals.

Goals & Quotas–To execute a sales strategy successfully, goals and/or quotas must be set to effectively evaluate sales activities and achieve results. We will help clients to develop targeted, achievable performance objectives to align sales performance with strategy and territory potential.

Sales Compensation–The success of a sales organization is often driven by the compensation plan. A well-designed sales compensation program focuses salespeople on activities that support the company's strategy and revenue objectives, and in turn, rewards salespeople for their contributions. We will design sales compensation plans based on our proprietary survey data and our clients' needs for sales and profit growth.

Retirement Planning
We will create sustainable retirement programs for our clients that engage the workforce and protect the business financial health.

Benefits Administration
We will offer best-in-class benefits delivery to ease the client's administrative burden and increase the effectiveness of their health and retirement programs so their employees can live, work, and retire well.

M & A Transaction Services
As the deal close draws near, we will help with the preparations to develop and implement the HR strategy for the acquired operations in compliance with legal and regulatory requirements and in accordance with sound business practice. To avoid last minute fire drills and lead to a smooth transition, we will help clients to focus on the critical priorities during the do-by-close and integration planning and execution phases.

HR Audits

Our HR Audit will identify the state of the client organization's compliance programs while clearly identifying areas of opportunity that will make the greatest impact to the success of their organization. Business leaders will gain a clear picture of:

1. Gaps in regulatory compliance
2. Areas where risk can be further mitigated
3. Opportunities for improving employee retention and productivity
4. Ideas to better position your organization as an "employer of choice"

The human resources audit will evaluate human resources health in the following areas:

1. Talent acquisition and orientation
2. Policy administration
3. Benefits administration
4. Health and safety
5. Communication and employee relations
6. Training
7. Leave of Absence

We will focus on how these activities are performed by the client, and will thoroughly analyze their human resources policies, procedures, practices, documentation, and systems to gain a clear understanding of the changes that need to be made to streamline their existing operations. Our audit process will reveal the client's system's strengths and identify new, innovative processes that can dramatically improve their daily operations. We will provide the client with a comprehensive audit report of our findings that suggests practical, customized solutions guaranteed to improve their human resources operation.

Custom Employee Handbooks

We will prepare custom employee handbooks with company policies and guidelines that are compliant with state and federal employment laws. These custom employee handbooks will be a foundational component of the client's business, and provide significant value to both the employer and employee, including:

1. An introduction for new employees to the policies, procedures and culture of the company.
2. A helpful tool for employees and supervisors to understand and consistently adhere to organizational practices.
3. A reliable basis for employee performance management and disciplinary actions.
4. Legal evidence that your company's policies are consistent with and encourage adherence to employment laws.

Set up Human Resources Department

A human resources department is a critical component of employee welfare and general business administration regardless of size. We will work with small and growing companies to efficiently set up their human resources functions. We will then help with the client with their human resources needs on an ongoing basis, or we can turn it over to the client when they are ready to hire a full-time, human resources professional. Our primary goal will be to put into place all of the systems and processes necessary to get the client's human resources department setup and running smoothly. Set up will include:

1. New employee packets
2. Employee file setup
3. Workers compensation and safety
4. Job description design
5. Reviewing current costs, structure, and compensation
6. Working with their current broker or helping to select one that will assist with health benefit administration
7. Analyzing current benefit plans and evaluating cost and coverage
8. Standardization of all files and forms
9. Creating policy and procedure manual
10. New hire orientation programs
11. Succession planning
12. Recruiting procedures

We also provide a detailed assessment of the client's existing human resources functions and recommend areas that should be added or improved. We will work to ensure that the client is in compliance with all regulations and that they are providing employees with the best possible benefits.

3.3 Alternative Revenue Streams

We plan to pursue the following alternative revenue streams:

1. Classified Ads in our Newsletter
2. Referral Commissions
3. HR Audits
4. HR Department Documentation Preparation
5. HR Software Installing, Training and Customization
6. HR Classes in Federal Contracting Personnel Requirements.
7. Sales of Instructional DVDs
8. Affiliate Program Sales (Ex; Commissioned Book Sales for Amazon.com)

3.4 Production of Products and Services

We will use the following methods to locate the best suppliers for our business:

- Attend trade shows to spot upcoming trends, realize networking opportunities and compare prices.

- Subscribe to appropriate trade magazines, journals, newsletters and blogs.
    Top HR Blogs
    Thecynicalgirl.com

Tlnt.com
Hrbartender.com
Hrexaminer.com
Askamanager.org
Hrcapitalist.com
Theemployeehandbook.com
Womenofhr.com
Human Resource Executive Magazine
Octane Magazine
Personnel Today				www.personneltoday.com

- Join our trade association to make valuable contacts, get listed in any online directories, and secure training and marketing materials.

Society for Human Resource Management.   www.shrm.org/pages/default.aspx
The world's largest HR membership organization devoted to human resource management. Representing more than 275,000 members in over 160 countries, the Society is the leading provider of resources to serve the needs of HR professionals and advance the professional practice of human resource management. SHRM has more than 575 affiliated chapters within the United States and subsidiary offices in China, India and United Arab Emirates.

National Association of Human Resource Consultants   www.nahrc.com/
NAHRC is geared towards training individuals hoping to operate as HR Consultants, as well as advance the professionalism of current members and employees of HR Consulting firms or the HR Department of an organization.

The Human Resources Independent Consultants Network
The HRIC Network was established in January of 2013, is now comprised of human resources independent consultants from various specialties within that group, such as recruiters, generalists, attorneys, safety and health specialists, talent management, benefits specialists, loss prevention, HR technology, training, etc.

Certified Management Consultant (CMC)
International Human Resources Information Systems (IHRIM)
Professional Exchange of HR Solutions (PEHRS)
The HRIS World.
Department of Labor – Compliance – www.dol.gov/compliance
US Department of Labor/State Labor Laws – www.dol.gov/whd/state/state.htm
Free Management Library –www.managementhelp.org/humanresources
Department of Labor – Benefits –www.dol.gov/elaws/ebsa/health/2.asp
Employee Benefits Security Administration –www.dol.gov/ebsa
Bureau of Labor Statistics – www.bls.gov/nce/ebs
Occupational Outlook Handbook –www.bls.gov/ooh

3.5 Competitive Comparison

The Human Resources Consulting business is competitive, as the barriers to entry and exit in this market are relatively low. Buyers have a significant amount of power since they have a number of companies to choose from, including several national companies. Human Resources Consulting companies must compete on quality and timeliness of the service, as the pursuit of these goals will produce client loyalty and repeat business.

Competition in the Human Resources Consulting industry arises from the following sources:

1. Companies choosing to do HR department development, channel development and market research in-house. Our key advantage in competition with in-house development is that managers are already overloaded with daily responsibilities. Also, we can approach alliances, vendors, and channels on a confidential basis.
2. The high-level prestige Human Resources Consulting Services, such as McKinsey, Accenture, Bain, and the Boston Consulting Group are essentially generalists who take their name-brand Human Resources Consulting into specialty areas. We will compete against these brand name firms as niche experts in our specific fields, and with the guarantee that our clients will have the top-level people doing the actual work.
3. The third general kind of competitor is the international market research company: International Data Corporation (IDC), Dataquest, Stanford Research Institute, etc. These companies are formidable competitors for published market research and market forums, but cannot provide the kind of high-level Human Resources Consulting that we will provide.
4. The fourth kind of competition is the market-specific smaller house.
5. Sales representation and brokering are ad-hoc business forms that will be defined in detail by the specific nature of each individual case.

_____ (company name) believes that it can improve on the quality and diversity of programs in this industry by instituting management control procedures, developing a preferred retainer program, expanding on the range of basic HR service offerings and initiating pay-for-performance compensation practices for associates that will assure a consistently superior service offering.

The company will be competitive in price and will maintain close relationships with accounts to secure valuable feedback and realize their lifetime value to the business. Through these steps, _____ (company name) will be able to build up a brand reputation for offering better quality Human Resources Consulting products and services at competitive prices than its competitors.

We plan to reinvest major dollars every year in technical and consultative sales training programs for our staff. We will also attend trade association seminars to bring industry trend information to our clients. Additionally, we will offer our clients an Unconditional Satisfaction Guarantee.

3.6 Sales Literature

____ (company name) has developed sales literature that illustrates a professional organization with vision. ____ (company name) plans to constantly refine its marketing mix through a number of different literature packets. These include the following:
- direct mail with introduction letter and product price sheet.
- product information brochures
- press releases
- new product/service information literature
- email marketing campaigns
- website content
- corporate brochures

A copy of our corporate informational brochure is attached in the appendix of this document. This brochure will be available to provide referral sources, leave at seminars, and use for direct mail purposes.

3.7 Fulfillment

Our Order Fulfillment will be a _____ (manual/automated/outsourced?) process.
1. Order Shipment will be determined by the location of the product stock, which will be _____ (local/remote/a drop shipper arrangement?)
2. Client Notification will be given via email whenever the order status changes.
3. Client Service will be facilitated by posting our telephone number on our website. This will serve to make potential clients more comfortable with the contact options available.

The fulfillment process will be managed by our director/owner, and implemented by our certified associates. We will develop a training and mentoring program for all new staff members. The real core value is the industry expertise of the founder, staff experience and company training programs.

Our real core value is our professional marketing expertise, provided by a combination of experience, hard work and education. We will turn to qualified professionals for free-lance back-up in _____, presentation and report development, which are areas that we can afford to contract out without risking the core values provided to the clients.

3.8 Technology

___(company name) will employ and maintain the latest technology to enhance its office management, project scheduling and HR management, inventory management, payment processing, client profiling, HR auditing and record keeping systems.

_____ (company name) will maintain the latest Windows and Macintosh capabilities including:
1. Complete presentation facilities for preparation and delivery of multimedia presentations on Macintosh or Windows, in formats including on-disk presentation, live presentation, or video presentation.
2. Complete desktop publishing facilities for delivery of regular retainer reports, project output reports, marketing materials and market research reports.
3. Expertise in constructing an Internet presence through Web development and Web hosting.

Resources:

SimpleHR   www.simplehr.ca/
Affordable human resource software for small businesses. Integrates with **QuickBooks**. Supports all common HR tasks such as tracking vacation, attendance and performance reviews. View salary and job history online. Record incidents and accidents and have access to a Document Library of over 110 reports, HR letters and forms.

EffortlessHR   www.effortlesshr.com/pricing.php
Web based human resources software for small business. Provides labor laws, compliance posters, employee benefits management and time tracking.

HR Software Solutions   http://hrssolutions.com/

HR Software Directory   www.hr-guide.com/HRIS/HRIS_Vendors_Consultants.htm

Competency Toolkit (CTK)   www.competencytoolkit.com.
The world's only competency marketplace and community, provides expert-created resources and support that talent management professionals worldwide need for successful hiring, employee assessment and development, career development, succession planning, and performance planning and reviews. CTK offers 450+ competencies spanning cross-functional (e.g., communication and planning skills) and technical areas (e.g., IT and marketing) and 900+ competency models. Interview guides, competency assessments, performance reviews and other competency-based products are also available in the marketplace.

Business Decisions, Inc.   www.businessdecisions.com.
BDI is a talent management software and services company with a 30+ year track record of providing effective talent management solutions to organizations around the world. They work collaboratively and flexibly with clients to design and deliver tailored, practical solutions in competency modeling, employee and candidate competency assessments, performance management, career development, succession planning, and behavioral interviewing.

Ascentis   https://www.ascentis.com/

Offers a comprehensive suite of on-demand HRIS/HRMS HR software, employee self-service, online payroll, applicant tracking system, and time and attendance software solutions. Their HRIS software/HR management software, online payroll services, recruiting software, and online timesheet products are easy to set up, use, and are fully backed by friendly customer support professionals.

Mobile Phone Credit Card Reader https://squareup.com/

Square, Inc. is a financial services, merchant services aggregator and mobile payments company based in San Francisco, California. The company markets several software and hardware products and services, including Square Register and Square Order. Square Register allows individuals and merchants in the United States, Canada, and Japan to accept offline debit and credit cards on their iOS or Android smartphone or tablet computer. The app supports manually entering the card details or swiping the card through the Square Reader, a small plastic device which plugs into the audio jack of a supported smartphone or tablet and reads the magnetic stripe. On the iPad version of the Square Register app, the interface resembles a traditional cash register.

Google Wallet https://www.google.com/wallet/

A mobile payment system developed by Google that allows its users to store debit cards, credit cards, loyalty cards, and gift cards among other things, as well as redeeming sales promotions on their mobile phone. Google Wallet can be used NFC to make secure payments fast and convenient by simply tapping the phone on any PayPass-enabled terminal at checkout.

Apple Pay http://www.apple.com/apple-pay/

A mobile payment and digital wallet service by Apple Inc. that lets users make payments using the iPhone 6, iPhone 6 Plus, Apple Watch-compatible devices (iPhone 5 and later models), iPad Air 2, and iPad Mini 3. Apple Pay does not require Apple-specific contactless payment terminals and will work with Visa's PayWave, MasterCard's PayPass, and American Express's ExpressPay terminals. The service has begun initially only for use in the US, with international roll-out planned for the future.
Resource:
www.wired.com/2015/01/shadow-apple-pay-google-wallet-expands-online-reach/

WePay https://www.wepay.com/

An online payment service provider in the United States. WePay's payment API focuses exclusively on platform businesses such as crowdfunding sites, marketplaces and small business software. Through this API, WePay allows these platforms to access its payments capabilities and process credit cards for the platform's users.

Chirpify

Connects a user's PayPal account with their Twitter account in order to enable payments through tweeting.

3.9 Future Products and Services

We will initially use small assignments to polish our craft and progressively go for high-end HR projects, where there is a larger funding budget.

_____ (company name) will continually expand our offering of HR products and consulting services based on industry trends and changing client needs. We will not only solicit feedback via surveys and comments cards from clients on what they need in the future, but will also work to develop strong relationships with all of our clients and vendors, as it is our understanding of the needs of our target market segments that will be one of our competitive advantages. It will also be important to stay up-to-date on knowledge to remain competitive in the future.

In the future _____ (company name) will broaden the coverage by expanding into additional geographic markets and additional HR product areas, such as database technology installation and integration. We are also studying the possibility of newsletter or electronic newsletter services, or perhaps special monthly on-topic HR reports. And, as the existing team gains experience working together, we plan add new consultants who will bring various skill sets to the company, and open up additional offices in other cities and states to provide more "points of local contact" for our clients.

Virtual HR Consulting Services
We also plan to offer Virtual Human Resources Consulting Services. As the Virtual HR Director, we will remotely create the ideas and manage the implementation process. The client will be able to activate the Virtual Marketing Manager only when they need it, and not have to pay for the gaps in between like a full-time employee. Plus, the client will get all the experience of a seasoned HR management veteran, unlike hiring a low cost entry-level person. We will own the client's strategic management efforts for $_____ (2,500) per month. We will offer an online service that gives clients access to our network of independent, certified management support experts capable of handling virtually any management issue. We will do it all, from writing employee handbooks to handling personnel forms to setting up and administering 401(k) programs. The advantages to this business are that we can work at home and the field is recession-proof. Our clients will be small and midsized businesses that either have no human resources departments or might prefer to downsize and outsource to our consultancy. We will direct-mail our brochure and sales letters to these firms, then follow up with phone calls. We will network among professional and civic organizations in our area. We will write articles for the business section of local publications, and give talks to business groups. We will introduce our consultancy to bankers, accountants, attorneys specializing in small business, and insurance agents, and any business that deals with small and start-up businesses.
Example:
http://jumpstart-hr.com/hr-advisor-hr-consulting-for-small-businesses-and-start-ups/

Online Courses

Plan to develop the following types of online courses:

Essential Skills of Leadership

This online course will focus on three critical management skills, the program establishes a methodology for productive interactions between team members and team leaders. This course will help experienced managers, new managers, and aspiring managers refocus on the basics - the skills required to manage the individual while also leading the team.

Resolving Conflict

This online course will help managers develop skills to identify the source of team member conflicts. Using effective communication and management techniques, managers can help individuals understand another point of view and move beyond the conflict.

Source:
http://www.hrconsults.com/shop-online/online-courses

HR Specialization

To charge higher fees, our goal is to specialize in one aspect of HR, such as:
- Compensation and benefits
- Compliance
- Community relations
- Crises communications
- Diversity
- Employee recruitment, development and training
- Health and wellness
- Labor relations
- Legal issues, including immigration
- State and Federal regulations, such as overtime and new laws.
- Workplace safety
- Sexual harassment, including training and responding to complaints.
- Strategic planning, such as lowering turnover, retaining top talent, improving the recruitment process, or reviewing programs from a cost perspective.

Improve Client's Recruitment Process

We will develop the procedures and software systems to make the client's recruitment process more efficient and lower turnover. We will develop self-service, front-end, web-based assessment tools that will help clients to weed out unqualified people, reduce their turnover rate and improve productivity.

Provider of HR Outsourcing Services

We will become a provider of certain HR services, because it will allow Companies to focus on their core competencies. Additionally, a more defined focus on the outsourcing of different aspects of HR will assure that the client's employees are being taken care of to the maximization of every dollar spent.

Develop Customized Staff Assessment Systems
Although staff assessment is a standard procedure in many companies today, there is often a lack of systematic, professional implementation. Jointly with our clients, we will prepare or optimize customized staff assessment systems. We will help to develop the guidelines for conducting comprehensive assessment interviews in specific industries. We will also coach the executives in conducting actual staff interviews and in preparing for them.

HR Starter Kit Package
We will develop HR Starter Packs, for startup businesses, that include basic employee contracts, forms, tutorial videos, white papers and generic documents, which we will sell at a fixed rate. We will develop different starter packs for each of the industries that we specialize in. The package will also include a satisfaction survey and a client referral form.
Examples:
http://www.silvershr.com/services/start-up-kit/

Job Description Software
We will develop a copyrighted electronic job analysis/description tool to provide client organizations with current, data driven, legally compliant job descriptions for each position, as well as a plan to maintain them as the organization evolves. The program will dramatically improve job description writing productivity and completeness, and contain industry salary data for comparison purposes.

Top Talent Retention Strategies
As the economy proceeds towards full-employment, companies are becoming increasingly concerned with keeping or retaining their top people. As HR consultants, we will help the client to design and execute proven retention strategies. Retention strategies will include how to assess the talent and determine the right retention approach to use. Our HR consultants will help the organization to structure the retention plan and apply the right approach to individual staff members.

4.0 Market Analysis Summary

Our Market Analysis will serve to accomplish the following goals:
1. Define the characteristics, and needs and wants of the target market.
2. Serve as a basis for developing sales, marketing and promotional strategies.
3. Influence the e-commerce website design.

We will target start-up companies for the following reasons:
1. They are in need of HR services as they are growing rapidly.
2. They often do not have a large enough in-house solution as they are increasing in size.
3. Capital is a scarce resource for emerging companies so the ability to accept stock options in replace of cash is attractive.

The market will also be composed of the following segments:
1. Home Office Businesses
2. Small Businesses
3. Medium Businesses
4. Large Businesses
5. Federal, State, County and City Agencies
6. Educational Institutions

We will focus our marketing efforts on the _____ (start-up/ medium) businesses, because they have a need for HR management support, and are usually billed at an hourly rate.

_____ (company name) will have a unique and broad offering of Human Resources Consulting Services that will appeal to a large client base. The company will concentrate on mid-sized corporations because they are the easiest and quickest to penetrate and provide good profit potential. The following sections outline key information regarding the target markets.

There are a significant number of competitors in the _____ area, but they are widely specialized and sized. This gives our company the opportunity to create and exploit the start-up niche in the chosen market segments. It is also important to note the growth trend for this market, which is estimated to be about ___ (9?) percent annually for the next ____ years.

4.1 Secondary Market Research

We will research demographic information for the following reasons:
1. To determine which segments of the population, such as Hispanics and the elderly, have been growing and may now be underserved.
2. To determine if there is a sufficient population base in the designated service area to realize the company's business objectives.
3. To consider what products and services to add in the future, given the changing demographic profile and needs of our service area.

We will pay special attention to the following general demographic trends:
1. Population growth has reached a plateau and market share will most likely be increased through innovation and excellent client service.
2. Because incomes are not growing, and unemployment is high, process efficiencies and sourcing advantages must be developed to keep prices competitive.
3. The rise of non-traditional households, such as single working mothers, means developing more innovative and personalized programs.
4. As the population shifts toward more young to middle aged adults, ages 30 to 44, and the elderly, aged 65 and older, there will be a greater need for child-rearing and geriatric mobile support services.
5. Because of the aging population, increasing pollution levels and high unemployment, new 'green' ways of dealing with the resulting challenges will need to be developed.

We will collect the demographic statistics for the following zip code(s):
_____

We will use the following sources: www.census.gov, www.zipskinny.com, www.city-data.com, www.demographicsnow.com, www.freedemographics.com, www.ffiec.gov/geocode, www.esri.com/data/esri_data/tapestry, www.brainyzip.com, and www.brainyzip.com, www.claritas.com/claritas/demographics.jsp. (www.claritas.com/MyBestSegments/Default.jsp). This information will be used to decide upon which targeted programs to offer and to make business growth projections.

Resources: www.sbdcnet.org/index.php/demographics.html
Sperling's Best Places   www.bestplaces.net

Snapshots of consumer data by zip code are also available online:
http://factfinder.census.gov/home/saff/main.html?_lang=en
http://www.esri.com/data/esri_data/tapestry.html
http://www.claritas.com/MyBestSegments/Default.jsp?ID=20

1. **Total Population** _____
2. **Number of Households** _____
3. **Population by Race:** White ____% Black ____%
   Asian Pacific Islander ____% Other ____%
4. **Population by Gender** Male ____% Female ____%
5. **Income Figures:** Median Household Income $_____
   Household Income Under $50K ____%
   Household Income $50K-$100K ____%
   Household Income Over $100K ____%
6. **Housing Figures** Average Home Value - $_____
   Average Rent $_____
7. **Homeownership:** Homeowners ____% _____
   Renters ____% _____
8. **Education Achievement** High School Diploma ____% _____
   College Degree ____% _____
   Graduate Degree ____% _____

9.	**Stability/Newcomers**	Longer than 5 years % _____
10.	**Marital Status**	___% Married ___% Divorced ___% Single ___% Never Married ___% Widowed ___% Separated
11.	**Occupations**	___%Service ___% Sales ___% Management ___% Construction ___% Production ___% Unemployed ___% Below Poverty Level
12.	**Age Distribution**	___% 20-29 ___% 30-39 ___% 40-49 ___% 50-59 ___% 60-69 ___% 70-79 ___% 80+ years
13.	**Prior Growth Rate**	_____% from _____ (year)
14.	**Projected Population Growth Rate**	_____ %
15.	**No. of Computers/Household**	_____
16.	**No. of Small Businesses**	_____
17.	**No. of Mid-sized Businesses**	_____
18.	**Unemployment Rate**	_____
19.	**Overall Business Growth Rate**	_____

Secondary Market Research Conclusions:
This area will be demographically favorable for our business for the following reasons:
_____
_____

Resources:
www.allbusiness.com/marketing/segmentation-targeting/848-1.html
http://www.sbdcnet.org/industry-links/demographics-links
http://factfinder2.census.gov/faces/nav/jsf/pages/index.xhtml

4.1.1   Primary Market Research

We plan to develop a survey for primary research purposes and mail it to a list of local home and business magazine subscribers, purchased from the publishers by zip code. We will also post a copy of the survey on our website and encourage visitors to take the survey. We will use the following survey questions to develop an Ideal Client Profile of our potential client base, so that we can better target our marketing communications. To improve the response rate, we will include an attention-grabbing _____ (discount coupon/ dollar?) as a thank you for taking the time to return the questionnaire.

1. What is the primary benefit you would like to receive from using management consulting services?
2. What publications does your organization subscribe to?
3. How many employees do you have?
4. What are the annual sales revenues of your company?
5. What is your target market?
6. What organizations are you a member of? _____

7. Please describe your current management configuration?
8. What is your annual management staffing budget?
9. How important is marketing to the success of your company?
10. Why do you lose clients?
11. What is the next market your company wants to enter?
12. What company offering is slowing down? Why?
13. What management related problems are you interested in solving?
14. How do you evaluate your return on invested dollars?
15. How frequently do you use the services of a HR management consultant?____
16. For what types of projects would you consider using the services of a HR management consultant?
17. What is your preferred fee arrangement with a HR management consultant firm?
18. Describe your experience with other HR management consultant firms.
19. What can be done to improve HR management consultant products and services?
20. Please rank (1 to 16) the importance of the following factors when choosing a management consultant:

    ___ Quality of Services   ___ Product Selection
    ___ client Service   ___ Salesperson Knowledge
    ___ Salesperson Friendliness   ___ Program Selection.
    ___ Scheduling Convenience   ___ Value Proposition
    ___ Price   ___ Referrals from colleagues
    ___ Past Experience   ___ Staff Recommendations
    ___ Industry Analyst Advice   ___ Web-based Research
    ___ Business Trade Press Reports ___ Trade Shows/Conferences
    ___ Other _____

21. Who currently provides your Human Resources Consulting Services?
22. What are their business strengths?
23. What are their businesses weaknesses or shortcomings?
24. What would it take for us to earn your management consultant service business?
25. What is the best way for us to market our management consultant services?
26. If you switch to another service provider, please indicate your reasons for doing so. (Select all that apply).

    ___ Better Quality Products   ___ Better Value
    ___ Service easier to use.   ___ Friendlier Service
    ___ Better Support Availability ___ Faster Service
    ___ Cheaper Price   ___ Better Progress Reports

27. Have you purchased Human Resources Consulting Services within the past year? What?
28. Describe why you are not interested in purchasing Human Resources Consulting Services?
29. What information would you like to see in our company newsletter?
30. Which online social groups have you joined? Choose the ones you access.

    ___ Facebook   ___ MySpace
    ___ Twitter   ___ LinkedIn
    ___ Ryze   ___ Ning

31. What are greatest HR management challenges facing your company?
32. What prevents your company from achieving its goals?
33. What do you see as the greatest need for improvement?
34. What types of new HR management service programs would most interest you?
35. Please describe the qualities of your ideal Human Resources Consulting Service.
36. On average how much does your firm spend each year on management consulting services?
37. What are your suggestions for realizing a better Human Resources Consulting experience?
38. Are you on our mailing list? Yes/No   If No, can we add you?   Yes / No
39. Would you be interested in attending one of our HT seminars on innovative employee cost reduction techniques?

We very much appreciate your participation in this survey. If you provide your name, address and email address, we will sign you up for our e-newsletter, and enter you into our monthly drawing for a free _____.

Name   Address   Email   Phone
Resource: http://www.questionpro.com/survey-questionnaire.html
                www.surveymonkey.com

4.2   Market Segmentation

The purpose for segmenting the market is to allow our marketing/sales program to focus on the subset of prospects that are "most likely" to purchase our Human Resources Consulting services. If done properly this will help to insure the highest return for our marketing/ sales expenditures. A market segment is a classification of potential private or corporate clients by one or more characteristics, in order to identify groups of clients, which have similar needs and demand similar HR products and/or consulting services concerning the recognized qualities of these products, e.g. functionality, price, design, etc.

_____ (company name) will concentrate on initially building clients in the ____ (city) area before expanding into other areas. We will be concentrating on all businesses that employ less than ____ (100?) individuals. We will not initially segment our market to any greater degree since the company wants to build clients as quickly as possible.

Initially, small businesses will be our most important market segment because they will give the opportunity to build our reputation and standardize our human resources consulting approaches. Small firms are more likely to handle HR activities in-house. With penetration of between 3-5%, this supports the notion that today most small firms have the "do-it-yourself" mentality.

Mid-size and larger firms will be more open to outsourcing selected functions, such as

payroll and benefits. Small firms are also less likely to have a full-time HR person while mid-size firms will typically have an HR generalist and large firms will have several specialists reporting to powerful HR executives who manage a complex and comprehensive HR infrastructure. For medium sized growth companies _____ (company name) will be able to offer an attractive HR management development alternative to the company that is management constrained and unable to address opportunities in new markets and new market segments. Large manufacturer corporations will be our least important market segment. These companies will be calling on _____ (company name) for HR development functions that are better outsourced than managed in-house, and for market research, and for market forums.
Source: http://www.hrmarketer.com/selling_to_HR.pdf

Our market will also be segmented into two different groups, emerging high-tech companies and emerging non-high-tech companies. The emerging high-tech companies are going to be the larger of the two segments, as there are many different emerging high-tech companies proliferating. This is evidenced by the Business Journal of _____ (city) which in their annual list of fastest growing companies for this year, ___ of the top ___ (#) were technology companies. There are also non-technology companies that are emerging in the _____ area and _____ (company name) will be able to serve them as well.

We will define the niches that we serve in the following ways:
1. The role that we will play: Ex: trainer, coach, HR management consultant, etc.
2. Level of the organization approached: Ex: Managers vs. Executives
3. Topic of expertise: Ex: HR Department Set-up
4. Structure of groups approached: Ex: Teams vs. Individuals
5. Industry _____
6. Special Situations: Ex: Start-ups vs. High Growth Businesses
7. Organization Size: Ex: Mid-sized businesses vs. Fortune 500 Companies
8. For-profit or Non-profit: _____
9. Work Location. Ex: Local, County, State, Regional, National, International

We will precisely define market segments to better understand the specific needs of our market. The following represents the market segmentation for our human resources consulting business:
1. **Home Office Businesses**
    This is a large and growing segment. It is defined by small businesses that are based primarily out of the owner's home. The modern concept of Small Office and Home Office or SoHo, or Small or Home Office or Single Office/Home Office deals with the category of business which can be from 1 to 10 workers. This segment can further be divided into 'high-end' and low-end home offices. These home-based clients typically request jobs that are easier, faster and less resource intensive than larger business clients. In addition, this market tends to offer more flexibility for service scheduling, allowing for a more productive workday.

2. **Small Businesses**

   According to the U.S. Department of Commerce, a business employing less than 100 people. Small businesses play a disproportionately important role in innovation as well as in the economic and employment growth in the United States. This is the second largest and fastest growing segment in the _____ area. This segment can further be divided into high technology and low-technology small businesses.

3. **Mid-Sized Businesses**

   These businesses are normally privately owned corporations, partnerships, or sole proprietorships and have 100 to 499 employees. Mid-sized businesses generally have smaller workforces, lower budgets, and less complex environments than large enterprises. But, they must meet the same types of demands as enterprise organizations to optimize service levels to support business objectives, control costs, and align marketing programs with what matters to the business.

4. **Large Businesses**

   These businesses have 500 or more employees, and most often have their own internal marketing management staff. We can help the managers in these large businesses to access company data and information, which is needed for their decision making processes. We can also help these businesses to realize opportunities in new market segments and achieve incremental productivity gains in back office operations by introducing them to new marketing technologies. Large businesses continue to create consulting requirements that increasingly become segmented and specialized. We expect to see the highest hourly rates billed in this market segment.

5. **Education**

   Encompasses institutions focused on teaching and learning.

6. **Government**

   Includes government agencies at federal state, county & city management levels.

Composite Client Profile:

By assembling this composite client profile, we will know what needs and wants to focus on and how best to reach our target market. We will use the information gathered from our client research survey to assemble the following composite client profile:

Ideal Client Profile

Who are they?

Location of business headquarters (city) _____
Type of Business _____
Number of employees _____
Approximate annual revenues _____
Years in business _____
Company growth stage _____
Publications subscribed to _____
Trade associations the company belongs to? _____
What is the total sq/ft. of the facility? _____
Where are they located (zip codes)? _____
Trend Preferences? Trendsetter/Trend follower/Other _____
How often do they buy? _____
What are most important purchase factors? Price/Brand Name/Quality/Terms/Service/ Convenience/Green/Other_____

What is their key buying motivator? _____
How do they buy it? Cash/Credit/Terms/Other_____
Where do they buy it from (locations)? _____
What problem do they want to solve? _____
What are the key frustrations/pains that these clients have when buying? _____
What info search methods do they use? _____
Wh
at is preferred problem solution? _____

Table: Market Analysis

Potential clients	Growth	Annual Sales Dollars		
		2018	2019	2020
Home Office Businesses	10%			
Small Businesses	10%			
Medium Businesses	10%			
Large Businesses	9%			
Education	10%			
Government	10%			
Other	10%			
Totals:	10%			

4.3 Target Market Segment Strategy

Our target marketing strategy will involve identifying a group of clients to which to direct our Human Resources Consulting Services. Our strategy will be the result of intently listening to and understanding client needs, representing clients' needs to those responsible for product production and service delivery, and giving them what they want. In developing our targeted client messages, we will strive to understand things like: where they work, worship, party and play, where they shop and go to school, how they spend their leisure time, what magazines they read and organizations they belong to, and where they volunteer their time. We will use research, surveys and observation to uncover this wealth of information to get our product details and brand name in front of our clients when they are most receptive to receiving our messaging.

Target Market Worksheet (optional)

Product Benefits: Actual factor (cost effectiveness, design, performance, etc.) or perceived factor (image, popularity, reputation, etc.) that satisfies what a client needs or wants. An advantage or value that the product will offer its buyer.

Products Features: One of the distinguishing characteristics of a product or service that helps boost its appeal to potential buyers. A characteristic of a product that describes its appearance, its components, and its capabilities. Typical features include size and color.

Product or Service	Product/ Service Benefits	Product/ Service Features	Potential Target Markets

Our marketing strategy will basically involve matching the right products and services to the specific needs of the right targeted client. _____ (company name) will target the following market segments:

1. Small businesses not presently using a developed HR plan, and therefore lack the skills and manpower to handle the implementation of such a program.
2. Large companies seeking problem-solving assistance on a specific HR management project.
3. Government agencies, companies and organizations seeking sales training programs.
4. Mid-sized companies seeking a custom designed personnel plan and implementation guidance.
5. Small businesses seeking HR project management skills.
6. Small businesses wanting to more fully exploit the database organizing and candidate recruiting potential of the internet.

Target Venture Capitalists and Angel Investors
We will target these types of organizations because they frequently make Human Resources Consulting recommendations to business ventures that they get involved with. We will offer to give speeches at their trade association meetings and trade exhibitions. We will also offer to perform our 'Business HR Evaluation Analysis' at a reduced rate for trade association members.
Resources:
https://www.mycapital.com/index.php
https://www.vcgate.com/res_venture_capital_directory.asp
http://www.vcaonline.com/directory/invdir.asp#.WohIpudOmUk

https://www.angelcapitalassociation.org/directory/
http://www.boogar.com/resources/venturecapital/angels.htm

Target Organizations Supporting Entrepreneurs
We will target entrepreneurs because they often have good business start-up ideas, but a lack of human resources management experience. We will offer to give seminars through the 'National Association of Entrepreneurs' and other local entrepreneur groups and clubs. We will also participate in their networking events and advertise in their newsletters and magazines.

Resources:
www.entrepreneur.com/article/253283
www.entrepreneur.com/article/241192
www.forbes.com/sites/johnhall/2012/10/09/the-best-organizations-for-entrepreneurs/#3e764840628b

Examples:
Young Entrepreneurs Council	https://yec.co/
Entrepreneur's Organization	www.eonetwork.org/
Founder's Card	https://founderscard.com/
Startup Grind	www.startupgrind.com/

Target Commercial Real Estate Agents
We will target commercial real estate agents, because new businesses to this area often ask for business support service recommendations.

Target Office Supply Companies
We will seek permission to offer HR seminars to their clients, on their premises, to establish our expertise and support community businesses.

Target Lawyers and Accountants
We will seek to establish mutual referral relationships with lawyers and accountants because these professionals often make HR consultancy recommendations to their clients.

Target Software Development Companies
We will target these companies because they have been known to achieve remarkable early growth rates, and have a known knowledge gap with regard to best human resources practices.
Resources:
http://asp-software.org/www/
https://www.monster.com/career-advice/article/top-it-organizations
www.techrepublic.com/blog/career-management/top-networking-organizations-for-it-professionals/

Helpful Resources:
U.S. census Bureau Statistics	www.census.gov
U.S. Dept. of Labor/Bureau of Labor Statistics	www.bls.gov/data/home.htm

4.3.1 Market Needs

Regardless of the services and expertise offered, our HR consultants will always remember that private-sector clients need to make money. Our HR consultants will focus on their clients' profitability and productivity. Sometimes we will have to focus on rules and regulations, but that will be done in the context of a business that needs to be profitable.

Companies around the world are increasing their investment in HR infrastructure. They are not only becoming more attuned to the benefits of recruiting, hiring and retaining top talent, but they are also buying more products and services to help them realize the best return from their people and investing in automation to streamline the delivery of these services. As the market for HR products and services expands, so does the competition.

The most important market needs are for timely and cost-effective HR management support, and sales training by small companies that cannot cost justify a dedicated HR staff. The following opportunities exist for Human Resources Consultants:

1. Temporary HR management support to find solutions for personnel challenges and achieve growth objectives.

2. Delivering the following in-demand skill sets:
    - Strategic Personnel Growth Plan
    - HR Process Improvement
    - Data Mining
    - HR Software Installation
    - Sales Training Programs
    - Website HR Database Access
    - HR Project Management
    - Personnel Plan Development

3. The number of new businesses starting each year in the U.S. and specifically in the _____ area of _____ (state) create a sizeable market. Many of these businesses are started by an entrepreneur with a solid idea, but little experience in creating the formal HR business strategies necessary to turn their idea into a successful business.

4. To maintain strong business valuations, founders need to effectively define and communicate their value propositions, and since this is not a core competency for many entrepreneurs, there is an opportunity to provide this skill set through outsourcing Human Resources Consulting arrangements.

5. Business owners need experience and coaching in HR management to exploit market opportunities and create early revenue wins.

6. No business currently exists with dominant mind-share as a "small business HR consulting" firm.

4.3.2 Market Forces

The following market forces will determine _____ (company name) ability to succeed:

1. **Buyer Power:**
   With almost 1 million new businesses starting each year, there is ample demand for human resources consulting services. Buyers have power in this market, but the size of the market makes it unlikely that buyer power will have any significant negative impact on our human resources consulting firm.

2. **Threat of Conventional Competitors:**
   No other competitor owns the idea of "small human resources management consultant" in the minds of today's business owners. A number of high-profile management and human resources consulting firms exist, yet most of these firms have a reputation for being expensive and much too theoretical for small business owners who have practical, short-term concerns. By beginning our efforts in the ____ area of ___ (state), we will exploit an area that has a very strong market of small businesses, but does not have many high-profile competitor offices.

3. **Supplier Power:**
   Suppliers have minimal power over a consulting firm, and by crafting supplier contracts in a careful manner, we hope to limit our exposure to risk due to suppliers' power.

4. **Threat of Substitutes:**
   Potential substitutes are a very real threat. Venture Capitalists could add more HR consulting services to their portfolio in order to have more points of contact with the new business. Additionally, non-profit groups such as SCORE offer basic HR planning services. We intend to form relationships with potential substitutes. By working with Venture Capitalists, we will be able to provide a set of core competencies in HR management strategy that complements the VCs funding and business model assessment competencies. Also, by becoming more involved with non-profit organizations, we will gain access to a number of firms who will be potential prospects for Human Resources Consulting once they receive their initial funding.

5. **Threat of New Entrants:**

This threat is significant as there are very few barriers to entry in a HR management consulting market. HR Consulting firms do not normally have significant intellectual property that can be patented, and the requirements for creating these firms are minimal. Fortunately, the size of the new business market should sustain a number of firms in this area.

4.4 Buying Patterns

A Buying Pattern is the typical manner in which /buyers consumers purchase goods or services or firms place their purchase orders in terms of amount, frequency, timing, etc. In determining buying patterns, we will need to understand the following:
- Why consumers make the purchases that they make?
- What factors influence consumer purchases?
- The changing factors in our society.

The key element in purchase decisions made at the client level is trust in the professional reputation and reliability of the Human Resources Consulting Service.

Research indicates that larger businesses tend to hire larger Human Resources Consulting Services. The home business and small business owners tend to feel intimidated by larger consulting firms and actually prefer the personal relationships that can develop with the smaller consulting firm.

Additionally, clients who have established a relationship with a management consultant tend to remain loyal as long as the service and results remain acceptable.

Overall, buying patterns are driven by the need for value pricing, expert management support, good client service and prompt response times.

Demand is driven by the needs of businesses, nonprofit institutions, and government agencies for outside HR advice. The profitability of individual companies depends on the efficiency of their operations and their ability to maintain a steady flow of business. Large firms have advantages in being able to offer broad ranges of services and to take on more complex projects. Small firms can compete effectively by specializing. The US HR consulting services industry is concentrated: the top 50 companies account for about 75 percent of industry revenue.

Service availability is of utmost importance to buyers. The buyer tends to want customized and prompt solutions to their growth and cost control challenges, and is willing to pay a slight premium for such support.

_____ (company name) will gear its offerings, marketing, and pricing policies to establish a loyal client base. Our affordable pricing, educational clinics, basic quality Human Resources Consulting Services and broad product selection will be welcomed in _____ (city) and contribute to our success.

4.5.0 Market Growth

We will assess the following general factors that affect market growth:

Current Assessment

1. Interest Rates _____
2. Government Regulations _____
3. Perceived Environment Impact _____
4. Consumer Confidence Level _____
5. Population Growth Rate _____
6. Unemployment Rate _____
7. Political Stability _____
8. Currency Exchange Rate _____
9. Innovation Rate _____
10. Home Sales _____
11. Gasoline Prices _____
12. Trend Linkage _____
13. Overall Economic Health _____

According to recent research from the U.S. Small Business Administration office, a record number of new small businesses opened their doors in _____ (year). The growth of the market is not nearly as important as its size. We will need to focus on how to capture the most out of the existing market, even if it declines in size, before thinking about expanding. Potentially, the low growth may dissuade some competitors from entering the market, providing _____ (company name) with an opportunity to capture market- and mind-share before more competitors enter.

The _____ area is expected to grow _____ % annually. The _____ zip code area is expected to grow _____% annually. These estimates are based on the most recent census data and projected growth rate for the _____ area.

The _____ Chamber of Commerce predicts continued growth particularly in the small office/home office (SOHO) market segment.

In summary, the general industry analysis shows that _____ (city) is expected to experience substantial population, housing and commercial business growth, which makes it a prime location for a Human Resources Consulting business. The Human Resources Consulting industry is expected to continue to grow at an annual rate of _____ (8?) percent.

4.5.1 Growth Strategy

We will adopt the following growth strategies to achieve a sustainable growth pattern:

1. Schedule marketing programs to generate a consistent string of inquiries and leads.
2. Develop annuity products from the sales of articles, books, audiotapes, workbooks, software, speeches, etc.
3. Develop a Virtual Practice Arrangement through flexible subcontractor or partner relationships.
4. Form a corporation to hire employees.
5. Raise fees to control growth and improve profitability and re-investment.
6. Enable employee telecommuting to reduce overhead expenses.
7. Utilize sales reps to open new territories.
8. Use penetration pricing tactics to enter new markets.
9. Develop new types of customized management coaching programs directed at niche market segments.
10. Develop an annual rebate program to encourage client consolidation of vendors.
11. Improve Product Quality by improving reliability and client Service.
12. Decease Product Costs increasing base program standardization.
13. Introduce New Branded Image to foster awareness and remembrance.
14. Use incentives, sampling and comparisons to Attract Competitor Clients
15. Increase Referrals with a structured referral program.
16. Form alliances to Reposition the Brand
17. Use online marketing as a New Distribution Channel.
18. Increase Pricing to convey a Better image
19. Accelerate R & D to develop new products and services.

4.6 Service Business Analysis

Human resources consulting companies provide a variety of services to assist businesses with different human resources functions. The Bureau of Labor Statistics expects this type of industry to grow between 2008 and 2019, due to increasing changes in employment laws and regulations, as well as many organization's needs to reduce personnel-related costs.

An HR consultant will perform advanced, specialized and administrative duties in a designated human resource program or section area" and is responsible for providing high-level support in the administration of a human resources program. Human resource consultants undertake a lot of administrative responsibility in their day-to-day tasks. In essence, they interpret human resources policy and offer advice on its implementation in an organization or business. From answering questions on policy to presenting training sessions on complex HR procedures, HR consultants are largely responsible for a company's continued compliance with human resources policy.

Although there already exists a large number of Human Resources Consultants in the _____ area, there is an opportunity to locate and develop a particular niche market for our company. We have chosen to pursue the following niche market needs:

1. _____
2. _____

clients in this industry tend to be loyal, and rely on the same consultant for future needs once a relationship has been established. In fact, it is often worth making concessions in any single service to maintain a client relationship that brings the client back for future lifetime services.

An analysis of our main competitors reveals no overwhelming strengths that would act as significant barriers to our success. Additionally, we have identified the following competitor weaknesses that we can exploit and target in our marketing strategy.
1. _____
2. _____

_____ (company name) seeks to provide it clients with affordable Human Resources Consulting products and quality service in a convenient and supportive environment.

In order to develop our branded reputation for industry specific Human Resources Consulting Services, we have chosen to work solely within a specific industry, such as _____ (manufacturers/retailer/wholesalers), to market our services to. And, by combining the marketing and management experience, small business focus, and local presence in key markets, _____ (company name) will help the growing number of small businesses increase their chances for financial success.

_____ (company name) is incorporated in the state of _____ where it will initially focus its HR consulting operations. The rapidly growing _____ area of ____ (state) which includes the cities of _____, _____ and _____ was recently ranked #___ on the list of large metropolitan areas in Dun and Bradstreet's *Entrepreneur* magazine's annual listing of the "Best Cities for Small Businesses." However, with networked consultants distributed across the nation, we can easily expand our target client base to encompass other regions through the use of existing and tested technology.

In summation, this business area is far from saturated and does present an opportunity for an aggressive company with a comprehensive marketing strategy and a diversified range of Human Resources Consulting products and services, offered at value price points.

4.7 Barriers to Entry

_____ (company name) will benefit from the following combination of barriers to entry, which cumulatively present a moderate degree of entry difficulty or obstacles in the path of other Human Resources Consulting businesses wanting to enter our market.

1. Industry and Technical Expertise.   2. Business Software Evaluation
3. Vendor Research   4. Community Networking Connection

5. Referral Program Set-up
6. Marketing Skills
9. Website Design
11. Process Improvement Skills
13. Analytical Skills
5. People Skills
7. Operations/Cash Flow Management
10. Financial Analysis Skills
12. Cost Reduction Skills
14. Problem-solving Creativity Skills

4.7.1 Porter's Five Forces Analysis

We will use Porter's five forces analysis as a framework for the industry analysis and business strategy development. It will be used to derive the five forces which determine the competitive intensity and therefore attractiveness of our market. Attractiveness in this context refers to the overall industry profitability.

Competitors   The degree of rivalry is high in this segment, but less when compared to the overall category. There are _____ (#) major competitors in the _____ area and they include: _____

Threat of Substitutes
Substitutes are high for this industry. These include other management and HR consulting firms, lawyers, accountants, DIY business owners, etc.

Bargaining Power of Buyers
Buyer power is moderate in the business. Buyers are sensitive to quality and pricing as the segment attempts to capitalize on the pricing and quality advantage.

Bargaining Power of Suppliers
Supplier power is low in the industry. Inventory can be obtained from a number of distributors. A high level of operational efficiency for managing supplies can be achieved.

Threat of New Entrants
Relatively high in this segment. The business model can be easily copied.

Conclusions: _____ (company name) is in a competitive field and has to move fast to retain its competitive advantage. The key success factors are to develop operational efficiencies, innovative programs, cost-effective marketing and client service excellence.

4.8 Competitive Analysis

Competitor analysis in marketing and strategic management is an assessment of the strengths and weaknesses of current and potential competitors. This analysis will provide both an offensive and defensive strategic context through which to identify our business opportunities and threats. We will carry out continual competitive analysis to ensure our market is not being eroded by developments in other firms. This analysis needs to be matched with the target segment needs to ensure that our products and services continue to provide better value than the competitors. The competitive analysis needs to be able to show very clearly why our products and services are preferred in some market segments to other offerings and to be able to offer reasonable proof of that assertion.

Competitor	What We Can Do and They Can't	What They Can Do and We Can't

We will conduct good market intelligence for the following reasons:
1. To forecast competitors' strategies.
2. To predict competitor likely reactions to our own strategies.
3. To consider how competitors' behavior can be influenced in our own favor.

Overall competition in the area is _____ (weak/moderate/strong).

Competitive analysis conducted by the company owners has shown that there are ____ (# or no other?) companies currently offering same combination of Human Resources Consulting products and services in the _____ (city) area. However, the existing competitors offer widely specialized Human Resources Consulting Services. In fact, of these _____ (#) competitors only _____ (#) offered a range of Human Resources Consulting Services comparable with what _____ (company name) plans to offer to its clients.

Type of competitors include:

Large consultancy firms and franchises: these firms offer a wide range of consultancy services. These firms generally have top-quality services and bill out at the correspondingly top-of-the-market rates. Larger companies will typically go with the larger firms because of name recognition.

Small independent firms: these firms typically have one office that serves a general area, and bill out at market rate. Some will specialize in one or a few different areas within HR, while others offer a wide range of areas of expertise. Smaller companies will go with whom they know, or can afford.

Independent contractors/consultants: these people are individuals who do HR work as an independent consultant. They usually offer a wide variety of services.

Generally, the larger competitors appear to be grouped into the following categories:
1. Those who provide branding expertise to large businesses.
2. Those who provide consulting service for business software products they sell, install and modify.

A number of other firms will compete with ____ (company name). But, due to the size of the available market, it will be exceptionally difficult for any of the following competitors to gain significant market share. However, it will also be difficult for _____ (company name) to control the market.

Self-assessment

Competitive Rating Assessment: 1 = Weak .... 5 = Strong

	Our Company	Prime Competitor	Compare
Our Location	_____	_____	_____
Our Facilities	_____	_____	_____
Our Products	_____	_____	_____
Our Services and Amenities	_____	_____	_____
Our Management Skills	_____	_____	_____
Our Training Programs	_____	_____	_____
Our Research & Development	_____	_____	_____
Our Company Culture	_____	_____	_____
Our Business Model	_____	_____	_____
Our Distribution System	_____	_____	_____
Overall Rating	_____	_____	_____

Rationale: _____

The following establishments are considered direct competitors in _____ (city):

Competitor	Address	Market Share	Primary Focus	Secondary Prod/Svcs	Strengths	Weaknesses

Indirect Competitors include the following:

_____
_____

Alternative Competitive Matrix

Competitor Name:　　　　　Us　　_____　_____　_____
Location　　　　　　　　　_____

Comparison Items:

Sales Revenue	_____
Profitability	_____
Market Share	_____
Brand Names	_____
Services	_____
Specialties	_____
Products	_____
Target Markets	_____
Operating Hours	_____
Pricing Strategy	_____
# Yrs in Business	_____
# Yrs Experience	_____

Reputation _____
Marketing Strategy _____
Sales Brochure/Catalog _____
Guarantees _____
Website _____
No. of Staff _____
Competitive Advantage _____
Skill Sets _____
Comments _____

Competitor Profile Matrix

Critical Success Factors	Our Score	Competitor 1 Rating	Score	Competitor 2 Rating	Score	Competitor 3 Rating	Score
Advertising							
Product Quality							
Service Quality							
Price Competition							
Management							
Financial Position							
Client Loyalty							
Brand Identity							
Market Share							
Total							

We will use the following sources of information to conduct our competition analysis:

1. Competitor company websites.
2. Mystery shopper visits.
3. Annual Reports (www.annual reports.com)
4. Thomas Net (www.thomasnet.com)
5. Trade Journals and Associations
6. Local Chamber of Commerce
7. Sales representative interviews
8. Research & Development may come across new patents.
9. Market research surveys can give feedback on the client's perspective
10. Monitoring services will track a company or industry you select for news.
    Resources: www.portfolionews.com   www.Office.com
11. Hoover's   www.hoovers.com
12. www.zapdata.com   (Dun and Bradstreet) You can buy one-off lists here.
13. www.infousa.com   (The largest, and they resell to many other vendors)
14. www.onesource.com (By subscription, they pull information from many sources)
15. www.capitaliq.com   (Standard and Poors).
16. Obtain industry specific information from First Research (www.firstresearch.com) or IBISWorld, although both are by subscription only, although you may be able to buy just one report.

17. Get industry financial ratios and industry norms from RMA (www.rmahq.com) or by using ProfitCents.com software.
18. Company newsletters
19. Industry and Market Research Consultants
20. Local Suppliers and Distributors
21. Client interviews regarding competitors.
22. Analyze competitors' ads for their target audience, market position, product features, benefits, prices, etc.
23. Attend speeches or presentations made by representatives of your competitors.
24. View competitor's trade show display from a potential client's point of view. 25. Search computer databases (available at many public libraries).
26. Review competitor Yellow Book Ads.
27. www.bls.gov/cex/ (site provides information on consumer expenditures nationally, regionally, and by selected metropolitan areas).
28. www.sizeup.com
29. Business Statistics and Financial Ratios   www.bizstats.com

4.9 Market Projection

For each of our chosen target markets, we will estimate our market share in number of clients, and based on consumer behavior, how often do they buy per year? What is the average dollar amount of each purchase? We will then multiply these three numbers to project sales volume for each target market.

Target Market	Number of Clients		No. of Purchases per Year		Average Dollar Amount per Purchase		Total Sales Volume
	A	x	B	x	C	=	D

Using the target market number identified in this section, and the local demographics, we have made the following assessments regarding market opportunity and revenue potential in our area:

Potential Revenue Opportunity =

	_____	Number of Local Businesses
(x)	_____	Expected Market Share
(=)	_____	Number of likely local business clients
(x)	$ _____	Average transaction dollar amount
(x)	_____	Average number of orders per year
(=)	$ _____	Annual Corporate Revenue Opportunity.
(=)	$ _____	Total Annual Revenue Opportunity

Or…

                No. of Clients   (x)   Avg. Sale   (=)   Monthly Income

	Per Month			
Services	_____	_____		_____
Product Sales	_____	_____		_____
Other	_____	_____		_____
Total:				_____
Annualized:		(x)	12	
Annual Revenue Potential:				_____

Recap

Month   Jan Feb Mar Apr May Jun Jul Aug Sep Oct Nov Dec   Total

Products

_____

_____

Services

_____

_____

Gross Sales: _____

(-) Returns   _____

Net Sales   _____

Revenue Assumptions:

1. The sources of information for our revenue projection are:

   _____

2. If the total market demand for our product/service = 100%, our projected sales volume represents ____% of this total market.

3. The following factors might lower our revenue projections:

   _____

5.0 Industry Analysis

Human Resources Consulting Services (SIC 7361)
A May 2013 report by market research firm IbisWorld on HR consulting in the U.S. concluded that the profession has low barriers to entry, low startup costs and little regulation. The industry is also highly fragmented.

The largest HR consulting companies—including global giants such as Aon Hewitt, Mercer and Towers Watson—are responsible for less than 20 percent of the industry's revenue, which IbisWorld projected would be roughly $26 billion in 2013. The remaining 80 percent of U.S. HR consulting revenue is divided among tens of thousands of small regional and local firms. Joint research from IbisWorld and the U.S. Census Bureau indicates that nearly 74 percent of HR consulting firms have 0 to 4 employees, in addition to their owners. There are roughly 205,000 HR consultants in the U.S.

The variety of HR consulting services matches the range of work HR professionals do within organizations. Some consultancies offer generalist services to small companies that don't possess the expertise to manage recruiting and hiring, benefits, performance management, training, and other HR basics, many of which have regulatory compliance requirements. Other consultants specialize in more-strategic services that they typically sell to large companies. Some small HR consultancies do both.

Consulting engagements are now relatively short-term or less profitable than assignments of the recent past. Corporate clients now focused on a provable return on investment for their consulting dollars spent. Specific goals will be set early in the process, and consultants will be under intense pressure to meet those goals. Large, multifaceted consulting companies will face fierce competition from smaller, niche companies. U.S. governments at local, state and federal levels have been providing lucrative consulting contracts. Government at all levels has large needs for consulting in IT, security, human resources and other areas.

Demand comes largely from corporations that sell consumer products, and telecommunications, entertainment, and financial services. The profitability of individual HR consulting companies depends on creative skills and good marketing. Large companies are advantaged in being able to serve the varied needs of large clients, but small companies can be competitive through special talent or lower pricing or through specialized services. The industry is labor-intensive, but the high value of the product produces annual revenue per employee of about $150,000.

5.1 Industry Leaders

We plan to study the best practices of industry leaders and adapt certain selected practices to our business model concept. Best practices are those methods or techniques resulting in increased client satisfaction when incorporated into the operation.

As of 2015, Mercer, Towers Watson, Aon Hewitt, Hay Group, and Buck Consultants were referred to as the largest HR consulting firms. While the MBB and Big Fours may not have the largest HR Consulting practice, some of them are known to be among the best in this field.
Source:
https://en.wikipedia.org/wiki/Human_resource_consulting
www.firstresearch.com/Industry-Research/Human-Resources-Consulting-Services.html

Some of the major players of the global workforce management market are IBM Corporation, Oracle, SAP SE, Kronos Incorporated, ADP, LLC, Ultimate Software, Workday, Inc., Verint Systems Inc., Workforce Software, LLC, Reflexis Systems, Inc., NICE, ActiveOps Limited, Infor, and others.
Source:
https://thefinancialconsulting.com/what-are-the-major-factors-for-global-workforce-management-market-and-why-it-is-rising-in-ict-industry/72564/

Aon Hewitt www.aon.com/human-capital-consulting/consulting/default.jsp
The leading global provider of risk management, insurance and reinsurance brokerage, and human resources solutions and outsourcing services. Their key advantage is our broad view of two of the most important issues in our economy today: risk and people. With an employee base of 66,000 people working in more than 120 countries, they can anticipate how changes in one sector impact another. Aon Hewitt is among the world's top global human capital and management consulting firms, providing a complete array of consulting, outsourcing and insurance brokerage services. Their professionals possess extensive knowledge and experience in a variety of fields and help companies of all sizes attract and retain top talent. They can help their clients achieve better business results by finding, developing, motivating and rewarding employees in ways that fit with their broad financial and business goals.

Mercer www.mercer.com
A global consulting leader in talent, health, retirement, and investments. Mercer helps clients around the world advance the health, wealth, and performance of their most vital asset – their people. Mercer's more than 20,500 employees are based in more than 40 countries, and they operate in more than 130 countries. Mercer is a wholly owned subsidiary of Marsh & McLennan Companies (NYSE: MMC), a global team of professional services companies offering clients advice and solutions in the areas of risk, strategy, and human capital.

Towers Watson www.towerswatson.com
A leading global professional services company that helps organizations improve performance through effective people, risk and financial management. With 15,000 associates around the world, they offer consulting, technology and solutions in the areas of benefits, talent management, rewards, and risk and capital management.

Alexander Mann Solutions www.alexandermannsolutions.com

They are passionate about helping companies and individuals fulfil their potential through talent acquisition and management. Today, over 3,500 of their talent acquisition and management experts are partnering with blue-chip clients across multiple sectors and in more than 80 countries. Delivering a distinctive blend of outsourcing and consulting services, their experience, capability and thought leadership helps their clients attract, engage and retain the talent they need for business success.

Resources Connection, Inc
A multinational consulting firm. The Company's operating entities primarily provide services under the name Resources Global Professionals (RGP). The Company provides consulting and business initiative support services to its global client base in the areas of accounting; finance; corporate governance, risk and compliance (GRC) management; corporate advisory, strategic communications and restructuring; information management; human capital; supply chain management, and legal and regulatory.

Randstad North America   www.randstadusa.com
A wholly owned subsidiary of Randstad Holding nv, a €23.3 billion global provider of flexible work and human resources services. Through its unique approach of delivering HR innovation with human interaction at the center, Randstad secures and manages a workforce of more than 100,000 people for thousands of clients each week. As a trusted partner in the post-digital world of talent, Randstad advances the careers and business success of our candidates and clients through a combination of the best of high-tech and high-touch processes. Employing over 6,500 recruiting experts through approximately 1,100 offices and client-dedicated locations, Randstad North America provides outsourcing, staffing, consulting and workforce solutions within the areas of engineering, finance and accounting, healthcare, human resources, IT, legal, life sciences, manufacturing and logistics, office and administration and sales and marketing.

AugmentHR.com
A collective of HR specialists who provide flexible talent acquisition and customized HR services on the client's terms to fit their needs. AugmentHR is a flexible offering that partners with clients to provide access to HR consulting on an as-needed basis. Solutions are customized to the short, mid, or long-term needs of the client. AugmentHR can work as either a standalone HR consultant or in conjunction with their existing HR team, remotely or onsite.

5.1.1 Corporate HR Leaders

The 30 Most Innovative Corporate Human Resources Departments

Google (#1) is consistently ranked as the best company to work for in the world. What truly makes Google a great place to work is the people. The company is more than just an Internet juggernaut, its Mountain View, California headquarters offer a seven-acre sports complex, three wellness centers, indoor roller hockey rinks, horseshoe pits, and over 100,000 hours of subsidized massages doled out each year. Google's philosophy is that with the right tools, you can attract the best talent, and develop happier and more productive employees.

Source: www.humanresourcesmba.net/worlds-30-innovative-corporate-human-resources-departments/

5.2   Key Industry Statistics

1. A survey of consultants shows that at any given time 38% are using daily or hourly rate, 27% are using fixed price contract, 19% are using fixed fee plus expenses and the other 16% are using more complicated variations.
2. In 2007, management, marketing and technical consulting services generated $160.3 billion in income in the U.S. alone. This figure increased by 3% from 2006. Although the 2008 economy is reeling, the demand for expert consultants may rise even further
3. Only one in ten solo consultants lasts for ten years, because of the difficulty of maintaining credibility and marketing oneself.
4. Research indicates that 60 percent to 70 percent of a consulting company's revenue (regardless of the company's size) comes from repeat business with existing clients.
5. According to Global Industry Analysts, Inc. (GIA), HR outsourcing remains strong with an expected combined global market of almost $54 billion by 2020
6. According to Bloomberg BNA, 65 percent of employers outsourced at least one HR activity in 2015.
7. There are roughly 86,000 discrimination and retaliation cases filed with the U.S. Equal Employment Opportunity Commission each year.
8. According to a 2017 survey by Bloomberg BNA, there are now 1.4 HR professionals for every 100 workers, vs. 1.0 a decade ago.
9. The US human resources consulting services industry includes about 7,200 establishments (single-location companies and units of multi-location companies) with combined annual revenue of about $17.5 billion.
Source: www.firstresearch.com/Industry-Research/Human-Resources-Consulting-Services.html

5.3   Industry Trends

We will determine the trends that are impacting our consumers and indicate ways in which our clients' needs are changing and any relevant social, technical or other changes that will impact our target market. Keeping up with trends and reports will help management to carve a niche for our business, stay ahead of the competition and deliver products that our clients need and want.

1. To provide a complete range of services to clients, the large consulting

companies have been built by acquisition during the past decade. Rather than absorbing acquired agencies into a larger organization, the companies operate them mainly as separate entities. Consolidation has been encouraged by the growth of clients and of large media companies, like Viacom and Disney.

2. "Relationship Consulting" is on the rise and involves working with a company over many years to ensure continued monitoring, discussion and implementation of new ideas.

3. Firms are looking for consultants with very specific knowledge in areas like logistics management, knowledge management, data warehousing, multimedia, client-server development, sales force automation, electronic commerce, brand management and value management.

4. With the Hispanic population quickly gaining importance in the US market, agencies are searching for HR management expertise to appeal to this audience.

6. The continued growth in the outsourcing of Human Resources Consulting to avoid the fixed costs of salaries and staying updated with new regulations.

7. The continued growth of SOHO businesses as compared to traditional mid-sized and large businesses.

8. The combination of big bucks and less-than-optimum advice may have more and more company owners turning away from "experts" and to laypeople they trust, such as college whiz kids, business managers and local retailers.

9. Consultants are becoming more accountable, more involved, and more a part of their clients' teams.

10. An improvement in documentation of results from consultants has resulted in measurable impacts and ROI.

11. Companies are proactively seeking the services of consultants to assess, improve and implement change at many levels within their organizations.

12. Consultants, rather than being seen as an expense, are more and more often viewed as an investment in the growth potential of a company.

13. New research shows that the ability to deliver results quickly and save client's money, are where the real opportunities for differentiation lie today.

14. Clients are cutting projects down into small pieces that they can give to specialist firms.

15. It has become easier for small Human Resources Consulting Services to navigate the marketplace due to better electronic tools, availability of relevant datasets and the general escape of qualified professional consultants from the larger firms.

16. Human Resources Consulting Services are more focused on delivering good product - development businesses; analyzing profitability; executive growth potential; competitive dynamics and segmenting clients.

17. In 2015, attracting and retaining younger employees aged 18 to 25 will be challenging, because they tend to demand flexibility, transparency, benefits, and training.

18. Many large consulting firms have practices targeted at particular industries--for example, pharmaceuticals, chemicals, and electric power--which require specific technical qualifications.

19. Video has become a more valued tool for recruiting, employee training, recording questionnaire responses and testimonials, etc.

20. Human Resources Consulting is becoming more prevalent in non-business related fields, such as in government, quasi-government and not-for-profit agencies.
21. A mobile-capable HR website for recruiting purposes has become vital.
    Source: http://jumpstart-hr.com/whats-trending-in-small-business-hr-for-2015/
22. Large, diversified organizations, Medium-sized management consultancies and Boutique firms have focused areas of consulting expertise in specific industries, functional areas, technologies, or regions of the world.
23. Consolidation is increasing competition as large national HR suppliers are offering end-to-end solutions and penetrating markets that were once the domain of smaller, regional suppliers. Thus, any marketing strategy must also consider differentiating the value of the message from other vendors clamoring to gain the attention of influencers and buyers.
    Source: http://www.hrmarketer.com/selling_to_HR.pdf
24. The continued rise of Artificial Intelligence (AI) and digital transformation will have an increasing impact on the HR industry, and enhance the importance of agile organizations and agile leadership, thus placing more importance on how quickly new technologies are being adopted.
    Source:
    http://markets.businessinsider.com/news/stocks/Alexander-Mann-Solutions-Uncovers-2019-HR-Trends-at-their-Annual-Catalyst-Summit-1011329668
    https://victorhrconsultant.com/category/h-r-technology/
25. Many HR Consultants find that having a specialty area of niche focus is an important way to develop name awareness and a steady stream of clients.
26. Compensation and benefits consulting continue to be in high demand as companies seek new ways to attract and retain top employees.
27. New and emerging companies continue to outsource key components of their business, especially human resources, allowing them to remain lean, maintain flexibility, and scale their HR needs as their company evolves.
    Source: www.augmenthr.com/blog/5-hr-consulting-trends-for-2017/
28. There has been a renewed focus on productivity, and the better use of existing employees.
29. Analytics are being used to help determine what the characteristics are of the best performing people and teams, and the findings are being used in recruitment and team development.
    Source: https://hrtrendinstitute.com/2017/11/27/8-major-hr-trends-for-2018/
30. New solutions like Workday Learning, Fuse Universal, SAP Jam and other tools focus on scaling video learning to the enterprise.
    Source: www.shrm.org/hr-today/news/hr-magazine/0217/pages/9-hr-tech-trends-for-2017.aspx
31. Expect to see employers work both externally and internally to shore up their talent pipelines.
    Source: www.hrdive.com/news/10-trends-that-will-shape-hr-in-2018/513665/

Resources:
https://www.fastcompany.com/3066976/the-top-five-hr-trends-for-2017

www2.deloitte.com/us/en/pages/human-capital/articles/introduction-human-capital-trends.html

5.4 Industry Demand Trends

1. Government policies are driving consulting demand in the following areas:
   - Health care reform, with a new focus on digital health records.
   - Renewable energy projects
2. Consultancies that focus on projects that reduce business costs and improve operating ratios, such as cash flow enhancement, supply chain efficiency and manufacturing efficiency will thrive.
3. Consultancies that have deep experience in debt restructuring, financial workouts and assisting firms that are emerging from bankruptcy will be in high demand.
4. There are opportunities for consultants who can show companies how to navigate rapidly changing relationships between government and certain industries, or deal with government oversight, particularly in financial services.
5. Consultants who assist firms in managing layoffs or lowering benefits costs are in high demand.

Source: Plunkett Research, Ltd.

5.5 Key Industry Terms

We will use the following term definitions to help our company to understand and speak the language of our industry.

Best Practice
A method or technique that has consistently shown results superior to those achieved with other means, and that is used as a benchmark. In addition, a "best" practice can evolve to become better as improvements are discovered. Used to describe the process of developing and following a standard way of doing things that multiple organizations can use.

Certified Management Consultant (CMC)
An international professional certification for Human Resources Consulting professionals, awarded by institutes in 46 countries (as of December 2009). The CMC enjoys global reciprocity; consultants certified in one country are recognized in most other countries. The standards for CMC in technical competencies and professional conduct were developed by various of the international associations.

Consultant Brokers
Charge clients a billing rate multiple of 1.3 to 1.5 times the wage paid to the consultant.

Independent Contractor (IC)
A consultant who enters into a consultant contract directly with the client. The client must furnish the IC and IRS a Form 1099 at the end of year listing the amounts paid to

the IC.

Human Resources Consulting

Indicates both the industry and practice of helping organizations improve their performance primarily through the analysis of existing organizational, leadership, recruiting and training problems, and development of plans for improvement.

Human Resources Planning

The process of anticipating future staffing needs and ensuring that a sufficient pool of talent possessing the skills and experience needed will be available to meet those needs.

Sexual Harassment

Unwelcome sexual advances, requests for sexual favors and other verbal or physical conduct of a sexual nature constitute sexual harassment when this conduct explicitly or implicitly affects an individual's employment, unreasonably interferes with an individual's work performance or creates an intimidating, hostile or offensive work environment.

Virtual Service Provider

Provides limited service from a remote location. Support can range from monitoring, reporting, remote management, back-ups, security and updates. Organizations can outsource some of their smaller functions of their office to a Virtual Service Provider.

Resources:

www.shrm.org/templatestools/glossaries/documents/glossary%20of%20human%20resources%20terms.pdf

http://awards.hrinz.org.nz/Site/Resources/Knowledge_Base/Glossary_of_HR_terms.aspx

6.0 Strategy and Implementation Summary

We intend to offer our clients a wide range of Human Resources Consulting products and services, and develop a training program for commissioned sales reps to pursue _____ (start-up?) business accounts.

Our first step in formulating our consulting marketing plan will be to research which companies could use our HR specialty services, afford to pay for them, and who we would like to work for.

Sales associates will be highly skilled and trained to meet our high-performance standards. They will participate in continuous consultative sales training and receive regular sales coaching. Sales closes will be based on demonstration of satisfying the client buying criteria.

Our sales strategy is based on serving our niche markets better than the competition and leveraging our competitive advantages. These advantages include superior attention to understanding and satisfying client HR management needs and wants, creating a one-stop solution, a 100% guarantee and value pricing.

We will use our competitive edge of compensation flexibility to attract start-up and mid-sized companies. This competitive advantage is especially valuable to emerging companies who are typically struggling to find enough capital to grow their business. Accepting stock options as compensation will be useful because equity is one thing these companies have lots of, unless they have given it all away to the Venture Capitalists.

Our strategy will revolve around the following factors:
1. Emphasize results
    We will differentiate ourselves with measurable results and will seek to establish our business by offering a clear and viable alternative for our target market.
2. Build a relationship-oriented business
    We will strive to build long-term relationships with clients, not single-visit deals, and become their HR advisor and trusted partner of choice.
3. Focus on target markets
    We will need to focus our offerings on _____ (start-up/mid-sized?) business owners and entrepreneurs who have a real passion for growing their businesses.

The objectives of our marketing strategy will be to recruit new clients, retain existing clients, get good clients to spend more and request our services more frequently. Establishing a loyal client base is very important because such core clients will not only generate the most lifetime sales, but also provide valuable referrals.

We will generate word-of-mouth buzz through direct-mail campaigns, exceeding client expectations, developing a Web site and getting involved in community events with local businesses, and donating our services at charity functions, in exchange for press release coverage. Our sales strategy will seek to convert potential and first-time clients into long-term relationships and referral agents.

The combination of our competitive advantages, targeted marketing campaign, referral program, web-based promotion and networking activities, will enable _____ (company name) to continue increasing our market share.

6.1.0 Promotion Strategy

The primary promotion strategy will be to focus on cultivating existing relationships, using known networking techniques to develop referrals and new client leads. The ultimate promotion strategy will be in guaranteeing client satisfaction.

Our promotional strategies make use of the following tools:
- **Advertising**
    - Grand Opening Event celebration with invitations to local businesses.
    - Yearly anniversary parties to celebrate the success of each year.
    - Multiple Yellow Pages ads in the book and online.
    - Flyers promoting new HR Audit services to local businesses.
    - Doorknob hangers for businesses.
- **Local Marketing / Public Relations**
    - Participation in local civic groups.
    - Press release coverage of complimentary HR Audit offerings to nonprofit organizations and school contests.
    - Article submissions to magazines describing the importance of creating a strategic human resources plan.
- **Local Media**
    - Direct Mail - Containing our prices and an explanation of our HR service support programs.
    - Radio Campaign - We will make "live on the air" presentations of our discount coupons to the disk jockeys, hoping to get the promotions broadcasted to the listening audience.
    - Newspaper Campaign - Placing several ads for special seasonal promotions. We will include a discount coupon in the ad to track the return on investment.
    - Website – This will give the internet users access to our online affiliate book catalog and provide some selection, implementation and comparison tips. We will also collect email addresses for a monthly newsletter.

6.1.1　Grand Opening

Our Grand Opening celebration will be a very important promotion opportunity to create word-of-mouth advertising results.

We will do the following things to make the open house a successful event:
1. Enlist local business support to contribute a large number of door prizes.
2. Use a sign-in sheet to create an email/mailing list.
3. Schedule appearance by local celebrities.
4. Create a festive atmosphere with balloons, beverages and music.
5. Get the local radio station to broadcast live from the event and handout fun gifts.
6. Giveaway our logo imprinted T-shirts as a contest prize.
7. Print promotional flyers and pay a few kids to distribute them local businesses.
8. Arrange for snacks for everyone.
9. Arrange for local politician to do the official opening ceremony so all the local newspapers came to take pictures and do a feature story.
10. Arrange that people can tour our facility on the open day in order to see our facilities, collect sales brochures and find out more about our services.
11. Allocate staff members to perform specific duties, handout business cards and sales brochures and instruct them to deal with any questions or queries.
12. Organize a drawing with everyone writing their name and phone numbers on the back of business cards and give a voucher as a prize to start a marketing list.
13. Hand out free article reprints.
14. Distribute introductory discount coupons for HR Audits.

Human Resources Audit
A method to review current human resources policies, procedures, documentation and systems to identify needs for improvement and enhancement of the HR function as well as to ensure compliance with ever-changing rules and regulations.
Resources:
http://smallbusiness.chron.com/conduct-effective-hr-audit-11213.html
www.slideshare.net/mekbib-mulat/human-resource-auditing-questionnaries

6.1.2　Value Proposition

_____ (company name) offers a set of services designed to improve overall business execution for small and emerging businesses. Unlike traditional Human Resources Consulting Services that concentrate on helping large clients identify problems, we will focus exclusively on working with small businesses to implement practical, short-term actions designed to start implementing a custom designed business improvement plan.

_____ (company name) will create a value proposition based on the following differential advantage ideas:
　　Focus on helping small businesses to start moving in the right direction;
　　Practical, actionable, short-term HR services strategy help;

Local presence for availability and minimization of costs;
Broad HR skill base combining major corporation training with small business experience.

Our value proposition will summarize why a client should use our Human Resources Consulting Services. It will convince prospects that our HR consulting services will add more value or better solve their need for a responsive, value priced and one-stop service.

We will use this value proposition statement to target clients who will benefit most from using our one-stop Human Resources Consulting Services, and, this will help to maintain an economic benefit separation from our competitors. Our value proposition will be concise and appeal to the client's strongest decision-making drivers, which are timely and practical profitability solutions, delivered at a reasonable rate, and a 100% satisfaction guarantee to reduce client perceived risk.
Resource: www.marketingexperiments.com/improving-website-conversion/powerful-value-propositions.html

In developing our 'Value Proposition', we will seek answers to the following questions:
1. What are we passionate about?
2. What experiences or specialized HR skills will our clients most benefit from?
3. What type of clients or law motivates us the most?
4. What niche aspect of the HR laws are we interested in learning more about?
5. Who is our target audience?

Recap of Our Value Proposition:

Trust – We are known as a trusted business partner with strong client and vendor endorsements. We have earned a reputation for quality, integrity, and delivery of successful HR solutions.

Quality – We offer _____ experience and extensive professional backgrounds in _____ at competitive rates.

Experience – Our ability to bring people with ___ (#) years of _____ experience with deep technical knowledge of _____ is at the core of our success.

True Vendor Partnerships – Our true vendor partnerships with _____ and _____ enable us to offer the resources of much larger organizations with greater flexibility.

Client Satisfaction and Commitment to Success – Through partnering with our clients and delivering quality HR solutions, we have been able to achieve an impressive degree of repeat and referral business. Since ____ (year), more than ____% of our business activity is generated by existing clients. Our philosophy is that "our client's satisfaction is our success." Our success will be measured in terms of our client's satisfaction survey scores and testimonials.

6.1.3 Positioning Statement

Our ideal client is the _____ (start-up business/small business?) owner who needs a custom HR plan so that the business can continue to grow and make money.
It is the objective of _____ (company name) to become the local leader in delivering quality of HR solutions, convenience, speed of service, value proposition, innovativeness and service experience of all the Human Resources Consulting Services within the _____ area.

We also plan to develop specialized HR services and program plans that will enable us to pursue a niche focus on the _____ (leadership development?) aspect of the Human Resources Consulting industry. We want to be known as the Human Resources Consulting Service that delivers profitable growth to small businesses by providing expert HT management support, virtual remote HR services, customized software solutions, and regular follow-up and benchmarking services.

These objectives will position us at the _____ (mid-market level/high-end) of the market. This will allow the company to realize a healthy profit margin in relation to its low-end, discount rivals and achieve long-term growth. We will also stand apart from the competition by offering a 100% satisfaction guarantee.

Market Positioning Recap

Price: The strategy is to offer competitive prices that are lower that the market leader, yet set to indicate the value and worth of our HR consulting services.
Service: On-time and customized service, based on client delivery specifications, will be the key to success in this type of business. Personal attention to the clients will result in higher sales and word of mouth advertising. We will do absolutely everything in our power to exceed client expectations.
Product Quality: Sourcing top-of-the-line HR training materials.
Design: Offering superior aesthetic or functional design.
Innovation: Introducing new and unexpected variations on existing HR products and consulting services.
Niche Focus: Comprehensively serving a subset of a HR product or service category.
Authenticity: Establishing unique credibility in a particular HR specialty area.

6.1.4 Unique Selling Proposition (USP)

Our unique selling proposition will answer the question why a client should choose to do business with our company versus any and every other option available to them in the marketplace. Our USP will be a description of a unique important benefit that our Human Resources Consulting Service offers to clients, so that price is no longer the key to our sales.

Our USP will include the following:
Who our target audience is: _____
What we will do for them: _____
What qualities, skills, talents, traits do we possess that others do not: _____

What are the benefits we provide that no one else offers: _____
Why that is different from what others are offering: _____
Why that solution matters to our target audience: _____

Resources:
https://www.haleymarketing.com/how-to-tips/whats-your-usp/
https://www.businessnewsdaily.com/5521-unique-selling-proposition.html
http://fizzle.co/sparkline/unique-selling-proposition

Some USP Options:
1. Lowest Prices Everyday
2. The Best Client Service Quality
3. The Only Place to Get It
4. Client Friendliness
5. Broadest Selection of HR services
6. State-of-the-Art HR software
7. Deliverables always on-time

6.1.5 Distribution Strategy

Consulting is sold and purchased mainly on a word-of-mouth basis, with relationships and previous experience being by far the most important factor. The major name-brand houses have locations in major cities and major markets, and executive-level managers or partners develop new business through industry associations, business associations, and chambers of commerce and industry, etc., even in some cases social associations such as country clubs. The medium-level houses are generally area-specific or function specific, and are not easily able to leverage their business through distribution.

Our Human Resources Consulting Services will be sold and purchased mainly on a word-of-mouth basis, with prior relationships being the most important factor. New business will be developed through networking activities at industry, business and social associations. Our clients will primarily purchase our HR products and consulting services by mail, phone, fax, sales reps and via our e-commerce website.

Our clients will have the following access points:
1. **Order by Phone**
   Clients can contact us 24 hours a day, 7days a week at _____.
   Our Client Service Representatives will be available to assist clients
   Monday through Friday from ____ a.m. to ____ p.m. EST.
2. **Order by Fax**
   Clients may fax their orders to _____ anytime.
   They must provide: Account number, Billing and shipping address, Purchase order number, if applicable, Name and telephone number, Product number/description, Unit of measure and quantity ordered and Applicable sales

promotion source codes.
3. **Order Online**
Clients can order online at www._____.com. Once the account is activated, clients will be able to place orders, browse the catalog, check stock availability and pricing, check order status and view both order and transaction history.
4. **In-person**
All clients can be serviced in person at our facilities Monday through Friday from ___ a.m. to ___ p.m. EST.

We will utilize the following distribution channels:
1. Retail — via our offices selling to final business buyers.
2. Wholesale — selling through jobbers to our commercial accounts.
3. Direct Mail — using catalogs and flyers to sell directly to business buyers at retail prices plus shipping.
4. Telemarketing — selling directly to business buyers at retail via phones.
5. Cybermarketing — selling directly to business buyers via computer networks
6. Sales Force — using independent commissioned representatives to sell products and HR consulting services.

6.1.6 Sales Rep Plan

The following parameters will help to define our sales rep plan:

1.	In-house or Independent	_____
2.	Salaried or Commissioned	_____
3.	Salary or Commission Rate	_____
4.	Salary Plus Commission Rate	_____
5.	Special Performance Incentives	_____
6.	Negotiating Parameters	Price Breaks/Added Services/ _____
7.	Performance Evaluation Criteria	No. of New Clients/Sales
8.	Number of Reps	_____
9.	Sales Territory Determinants	Geography/Demographics/ _____
10.	Sales Territories Covered	_____
11.	Training Program Overview	_____
12.	Training Program Cost	_____
13.	Sales Kit Contents	_____
14.	Primary Target Market	_____
15.	Secondary Target Market	_____

Rep Name   Compensation Plan   Assigned Territory

6.2 Competitive Advantages

A **competitive advantage** is the thing that differentiates a business from its competitors. It is what separates our business from everyone else. It answers the questions: "Why do clients buy from us versus a competitor?", and "What do we offer clients that is unique?". We will use the following competitive advantages to set us apart from our competitors. The distinctive competitive advantages which _____ (company name) brings to the marketplace are as follows: (Note: Select only those you can support)

A key competitive edge will be our compensation flexibility from clients. Most or all other companies require compensation to be in the form of cash, because for them 'cash is king'. But, _____ (company name) will be able to take stock options in lieu of some cash. While our consultancy needs some cash to float the business, it can take up to _____% of its fees in equity. We will be able to do this because we have secured an office space that is low in cost and fully equipped with _____, helping to significantly reduce our overhead expenses. This will allow our company to accept options as payment in the expectation of an upside to come several years from now.

Our firm will provide human resource solutions that align with the client's business strategies and optimize their human capital to create a sustainable competitive advantage. We will have the flexibility to work with smaller organizations to act as their "Human Resources Department", working with them on a continuing basis rather than forcing them to hire a full-time employee. For larger organizations we will work on outsourced HR projects and program development basis. If they have an HR question, we will provide the client with the answer virtually, by enabling usage of our HR consult/advice services over the phone or via e-mail.

Other competitive advantages include:
1. The delivery of whole, end-to-end HR solutions.
2. We partner with our clients to provide customized HR solutions that are needs-based.
3. Our Value Pricing = High Quality/ Low price
   Our rates are below others in the market, while the quality of our HR Management Services exceeds client expectations.
4. By keeping overhead low, we will be able to funnel profits back into operations and thus avoid high debt and lost sales opportunities.
5. We are locally owned and operated, and remain focused on our client needs.
6. Outstanding client service and the making of client satisfaction a top priority will give our company an additional edge in the competitive local market, and the ability to develop long-term relationships with our clients.
7. All orders for "In Stock" products are subject to our "No Hassle" return policy

9. Secure Online Ordering.
10. About 98% of orders for books and articles leave our warehouse within 24 hours.
11. Convenient hours of operation: Open 363 days a year/7-days a week.
13. Our commitment to superior client service.
15. Educational seminars related to developing a personnel plan that can jump start company sales.
16. Referral program incentives
17. Preferred Client Club Membership Benefits.
18. Online order status checking/ Email order status notifications.
20. Comprehensive and continuous sales associate/consultant training programs.
21. Stay abreast of latest business marketing trends.
22. Better understanding of the needs of our target market niche.
24. Our 110% Guarantee states that if the client is not delighted with our HR management services, they do not have to pay our invoice until we remedy the situation.

6.2.1   Branding Strategy

Our branding strategy involves what we do to shape what the client immediately thinks our business offers and stands for. The purpose of our branding strategy is to reduce client perceived purchase risk and improve our profit margins by allowing us to charge a premium for our Human Resources Consulting Services.

We will invest $____ every year in maintaining our brand name image, which will differentiate our HR consulting business from other companies. The amount of money spent on creating and maintaining a brand name will not convey any specific information about our products, but it will convey, indirectly, that we are in this market for the long haul, that we have a reputation to protect, and that we will interact repeatedly with our clients. In this sense, the amount of money spent on maintaining our brand name will signal to consumers that we will provide products and services of consistent quality.

We will use the following ways to build trust and establish our personal brand:
1. Build a consistently published blog and e-newsletter with informational content.
2. Create comprehensive social media profiles.
3. Contribute articles to related online publications.
4. Earn Career Certifications

Resources:
https://www.abetterlemonadestand.com/branding-guide/

Our key to marketing success will be to effectively manage the building of our brand platform in the market place, which will consist of the following elements:
   Brand Vision - our envisioned future of the brand is to be the national source for HR

management solutions to manage the complications of employee relations and performance incentives.

Brand Attributes - Partners, problem solvers, responsive, HR experts, flexible and easy to work with.

Brand Essence - the shared soul of the brand, the spark of which is present in every experience a client has with our products, will be "HR Problem Solving" and "Good Value." This will be the core of our organization, driving the type of people we hire and the type of behavior we expect.

Brand Image - the outside world's overall perception of our organization will be that we are HR management pros who are alleviating the effects of poor employee relationships.

Brand Promise - our concise statement of what we do, why we do it, and why clients should do business with us will be, "To help take the business to the next level"

We will use the following methodologies to implement our branding strategy:
1. Develop processes, systems and quality assurance procedures to assure the consistent adherence to our quality standards and mission statement objectives.
2. Develop business processes to consistently deliver upon our value proposition.
3. Develop training programs to assure the consistent professionalism and responsiveness of our employees.
4. Develop marketing communications with consistent, reinforcing message content.
5. Incorporate testimonials into our marketing materials that support our promises.
6. Develop marketing communications with a consistent presentation style. (Logo design, company colors, slogan, labels, packaging, stationery, etc.)
7. Exceed our brand promises to achieve consistent client loyalty.
8. Use surveys, focus groups and interviews to consistently monitor what our brand means to our clients.
9. Consistently match our brand values or performance benchmarks to our client requirements.
10. Focus on the maintenance of a consistent number of key brand values that are tied to our company strengths.
11. Continuously research industry trends in our markets to stay relevant to client needs and wants.
12. Attach a logo-imprinted product label and business card to all products, marketing communications and invoices.
13. Develop a memorable and meaningful tagline that captures the essence of our brand.
14. Prepare a one-page company overview and make it a key component of our sales presentation folder.
15. Hire and train employees to put the interests of clients first.
16. Develop a professional website that is updated with fresh content on a regular basis.
17. Use our blog to circulate content that establishes our niche expertise and opens a two-way dialogue with our clients.
18. Create an effective slogan with the following attributes:
    a. Appeals to clients' emotions.

    b.   Shows off how our service benefits clients by highlighting our client service or care.
    c.   Has 8 words or less and is memorable
    d.   Can be grasped quickly by our audience.
    e.   Reflects our business' personality and character.
    f.   Shows sign of originality.

The communications strategy we will use to build our brand platform will include the following items:

- Website - featuring product line information, research, testimonials, cost benefit analysis, frequently asked questions, and policy information. This website will be used as a tool for both our sales team and our clients.
- Presentations, brochures and mailers geared to the consumer, explaining the benefits of our product line as part of a comprehensive HR servicing plan.
- Presentations and brochures geared to the family decision maker explaining the benefits of our HR programs in terms of positive outcomes, reduced cost from workforce complications, and reduced risk of lawsuits or negative survey events.
- A presentation and recruiting brochure geared to prospective sales people that emphasizes the benefits of joining our organization.
- Training materials that help every employee deliver our brand message in a consistent manner.

6.2.2 Brand Positioning Statement

We will use the following brand positioning statement to summarize what our brand means to our targeted market:

To _____ (target market) _____ (company name) is the brand of _____ (product/service frame of reference) that enables the client to _____ (primary performance benefit) because ____ (company name) _____ (products/services) _____ (are made with/offer/provide) the best _____ (key attributes)

6.3 Business SWOT Analysis

Definition: SWOT Analysis is a powerful technique for understanding your Strengths and Weaknesses, and for looking at the Opportunities and Threats faced.

Strategy: We will use this SWOT Analysis to uncover exploitable opportunities and carve a sustainable niche in our market. And by understanding the weaknesses of our business, we can manage and eliminate threats that would otherwise catch us by surprise. By using the SWOT framework, we will be able to craft a strategy that distinguishes our business from our competitors, so that we can compete successfully in the market and turn strengths into opportunities.

Strengths
What Human Resources Consulting Services are we best at providing?
What unique resources can we draw upon?
1. Experienced HR consulting team from the _____ industry with experience and technical know-how in many areas.
2. Strong networking relationships with many different organizations.
3. Excellent sales staff who are experienced, highly trained and very client attentive.
4. Wide diversity of HR product/service bundled offerings targeted at several market segments.
5. High client loyalty.
6. Remarkable introduction of creativity into the marketing plan process.
7. Knowledge of networking, public relations and database management.
8. Direct sales staff is skilled at relationship and consultative selling.
9. Strategic allies allow us to leverage our HR capabilities.
10. Expert skills in marketing and communications.
11. Local presence and direct touch points in a major market.
12. _____ (Start-up/Mid-sized) Biz orientation and focus.
13. Flexible compensation plans.
14. _____

Weaknesses
In what areas could we improve?
Where do we have fewer resources than others?
1. New comer to the area.
2. Lack of marketing experience.
3. The struggle to build brand equity.
4. A limited marketing budget to develop brand awareness.
5. Finding dependable and people oriented staff.
6. A focus on one HR Audit system, not commonly used by businesses.
9. Integrating new organizational practices and personnel is a challenge.
10. A limited financial base to support growth plans.
11. Management expertise gaps.
12. Inadequate monitoring of competitor reviews, strategies and responses.
13. _____

Opportunities
What opportunities are there for new and/or improved services?
What HR management trends could we take advantage of?
1. Could take market share away from existing competitors.
2. Greater need for mobile services by time starved executives.
3. Growing market with a significant percentage of the target market still not aware that _____ (company name) exists.

4. The ability to develop many long-term client relationships.
5. Expanding the range of HR product/service packaged offerings.
6. Greater use of direct advertising to promote our HR consulting services.
7. Establish referral relationships with local businesses serving the same target market segment.
8. Networking with non-profit organizations.
9. Unwillingness of competitor to take on new accounts.
10. Competitors offer slow client response times.
11. Could help clients to realize greater web-based sales.
12. Use of our level of HR consulting services as a differentiating factor.
13. The rate of new product introduction presents an unexplored opportunity.
14. The ability to get cutting edge experience by helping start-up companies transform themselves into seasoned companies.
15. The market trend toward outsourcing.
16. _____

Threats

What trends or competitor actions could hurt us?
What threats do our weaknesses expose us to?

1. Another Human Resources Consulting business could move into this area.
2. Further declines in the economic forecast.
3. Inflation affecting operations for gas, labor, and other operating costs.
4. Keeping trained efficient staff and key personnel from moving on or starting their own business venture.
5. Imitation competition from similar indirect service providers.
6. Price differentiation is a significant competition factor.
7. Innovation shorten new service and product lifecycles, and time to market become a critical factor.
8. Greater apprehension about internet security measures.
9. Global recession slows the pace of new technology adoption.
10. Must continuously stay at the forefront of new technology introductions.
11. Barriers to entry in this market are extremely low.
12. _____

Recap:

We will use the following strengths to capitalize on recognized opportunities:
1. _____
2. _____

We will take the following actions to turn our weaknesses into strengths and prepare to defend against known threats.
1. _____
2. _____

6.4.0   Marketing Strategy

Our marketing message will emphasize the following benefits of our services:
1. Knowledgeable and friendly consultants
2. Guaranteed Client Satisfaction Policy.
3. Niche Specialty: _____

The marketing strategy will revolve around two different types of media, sales brochures and a website. These two tools will be used to make clients aware of our broad range of marketing service and product offerings. The company will also rely heavily on word-of-mouth referrals for business.

One focus of our internet marketing strategy will be to drive clients to our website for lead generation, HR seminar registration and book order submissions. Additionally, orders placed via the website will be rewarded with a ___ % discount.

A combination of local media and event marketing will be utilized. _____ (company name) will create an identity oriented marketing strategy with executions particularly in the local media. Our marketing strategy will utilize prime time radio spots, print ads, press releases, yellow page ads, flyers, and e-newsletter distribution. We will make effective use of direct response advertising, and include coupons in all print ads for HR Audits.

We will use comment cards, newsletter sign-up forms and surveys to collect client email addresses and feed our client relationship management (CRM) software system. This system will automatically send out, on a predetermined schedule, follow-up materials, such as article reprints, seminar invitations, email messages, surveys and e-newsletters. We will offset some of our advertising costs by asking our suppliers and other local merchants to place ads in our newsletter.

Current Situation
We will study the current marketing situation on a weekly basis to analyze trends and identify sources of business growth. As onsite owners, we will be on hand daily to insure client service. Our services include report products of the highest quality and a prompt response to feedback from clients. Our extensive and highly detailed financial statements, will enable us to stay competitive and exploit presented opportunities.

Marketing Budget
Our marketing budget will be a flexible $_____ per quarter. The marketing budget can be allocated in any way that best suits the time of year.

Marketing budget per quarter:

Newspaper Ads	$_____	Radio advertisement	$_____
Web Page	$_____	client contest	$_____
Direct Mail	$_____	Sales Brochure	$_____
Trade Shows	$_____	Seminars	$_____
Superpages	$_____	Google Adwords	$_____
Giveaways	$_____	Vehicle Signs	$_____

Business Cards	$ _____	Flyers	$ _____
Labels/Stickers	$ _____	Videos/DVDs	$ _____
Samples	$ _____	Newsletter	$ _____
Bandit Signs	$ _____	Email Campaigns	$ _____
Sales Reps Comm.	$ _____	Restaurant Placemats	$ _____
Press Releases	$ _____	Billboards	$ _____
Movie Theater Ads	$ _____	Fund Raisers	$ _____
Infomercials	$ _____	Speeches	$ _____
Postcards	$ _____	Proof Books	$ _____
Social Networking	$ _____	Charitable Donations	$ _____
Other	$ _____		

Total: $ _____

Our objective in setting a marketing budget has been to keep it between ____ (5?) and ____ (7?) percent of our estimated annual gross sales.

The following represents a recap of our marketing programs:
- Promotion expenses (free gifts for allowing an HR Audit)
- Printed materials (sales brochures, pamphlets, fliers, postcards)
- Media advertisements (radio, newspapers, outdoor billboards)
- Bartering (exchanging our services for ad placement)
- Donations (door prizes, charities)
- Referral Program Brochure
- Website Development

Marketing Schedule
Our research indicates that sales and marketing efforts are best carried out in the fall, from early September until Thanksgiving in late November. These ten to fourteen weeks are the time to follow up on all consulting leads, make sales calls, generate proposals and try to get definite commitments from people about projects. The period from early July until Labor Day is a bad time for any decisions from clients or prospective clients

Marketing Mix
Clients will primarily come from word-of-mouth and our referral program. The overall market approach involves creating brand awareness through targeted advertising, public relations, co-marketing efforts with select alliance partners, direct mail, email campaigns (with constant contact.com), seminars and a website.

Advertising
_____ (company name) will rely on the recommendations of satisfied clients and preferred vendors as a means of attracting clients away from the competition. Past experience has also proven that many clients come on the recommendations of others. Although word-of-mouth is an effective way of increasing market share, it is also extremely slow. To accelerate the process of expanding the client base, the business will maintain an advertising budget of $_____ for the first year. The bulk of this budget will be spent on listings in online directories, complimentary discount coupons, and direct

mailings to ad respondents.

Pro Bono Work
We will perform pro bono work for non-profits and community groups to increase our visibility, network with other professional contacts, build our brand with people in our community and possibly enhance our human resources consulting skills.

Teaching Programs
We will attempt to secure a part-time marketing teaching position at the local university or community college, in an effort to share our HR expertise, improve visibility and make contacts.

Video Marketing Clips
We will link to our website a series of YouTube.com based video clips that talk about our range of Human Resources Consulting Services. We will create business marketing videos for our HR Consulting firm that are both entertaining and informational.

The video will include:
- **Client testimonials** - We will let our best clients become our instant sales force because people will believe what other clients say about us more readily than what we say about ourselves.
- **Product Demonstrations** - Train and pre-sell our potential clients on our most popular services just by talking about and showing them. Often, our potential clients don't know the full range and depth of our services because we haven't taken the time to show and tell them.
- **Include Business Website Address**
- **Owner Interview:** Explanation of mission statement and unique selling proposition.
- **Frequently Asked Questions** - We will answer questions that we often get, and anticipate rejections we might get and give great reasons to convince potential clients that we are the best Human Resources Consulting Service in the area.
- **Include a Call to Action** - Ex: We have the experience and the know-how to improve your profitability. So call us, right now, and let's get started.
- **Seminar** - Include a portion of a seminar on 'How to Develop a Cost-effective Personnel Plan".
- **Comment on industry trends and product news** - We will appear more in-tune and knowledgeable in our market when we can talk about what's happening in our consulting industry and marketplace.

Resources: www.businessvideomarketing.tv
             www.hotpluto.com
             www.hubspot.com/video-marketing-kit
             www.youtube.com/user/mybusinessstory

Analytics Report
http://support.google.com/youtube/bin/static.py?hl=en&topic=1728599&guide=1714169&page=guide.cs

Note: Refer to Video Marketing Tips in rear marketing worksheets section.

Example:
https://www.youtube.com/watch?v=nAE1MLZvq9k

Top 12 places where we will share our marketing videos online:

YouTube   www.youtube.com

This very popular website allows you to log-in and leave comments and ratings on the videos. You can also save your favorite videos and allows you to tag posted videos. This makes it easier for your videos to come up in search engines.

Google Video   http://video.google.com/

A video hosting site. Google Video is not just focused on sharing videos online, but this is also a market place where you can buy the videos you find on this site using Google search engine.

Yahoo! Video   http://video.yahoo.com/

Uploading and sharing videos is possible with Yahoo Video!. You can find several types of videos on their site and you can also post comments and ratings for the videos.

Revver   http://www.revver.com/

This website lets you earn money through ads on your videos and you will have a 50/50 profit split with the website. Another great deal with Revver is that your fans who posted your videos on their site can also earn money.

Blip.tv   http://blip.tv/

Allows viewers to stream and download the videos posted on their website. You can also use Creative Commons licenses on your videos posted on the website. This allows you to decide if your videos should be attributed, restricted for commercial use and be used under specific terms.

Vimeo   http://www.vimeo.com/

This website is family safe and focuses on sharing private videos. The interface of the website is similar to some social networking sites that allow you to customize your profile page with photos from Flickr and embeddable player. This site allows users to socialize through their videos.

Metacafe   http://www.metacafe.com/

This video sharing site is community based. You can upload short-form videos and share it to the other users of the website. Metacafe has its own system called VideoRank that ranks videos according to the viewer reactions and features the most popular among the viewers.

ClipShack   http://www.clipshack.com/

Like most video sharing websites, you can post comments on the videos and even tag some as your favorite. You can also share the videos on other websites through the html code from ClipShack and even sending it through your email.

Veoh   http://www.veoh.com/

You can rent or sell your videos and keep the 70% of the sales price. You can upload a range of different video formats on Veoh and there is no limit on the size and length of the file. However, when your video is over 45 minutes it has to be downloaded before the viewer can watch it.

Jumpcut   http://download.cnet.com/JumpCut/3000-18515_4-10546353.html

Jumpcut allows its users to upload videos using their mobile phones. You will have to attach the video captured from your mobile phone to an email. It has its own movie making wizard that helps you familiarize with the interface of the site.

DailyMotion   **www.dailymotion.com**

As one of the leading sites for sharing videos, Dailymotion attracts over 114 million unique monthly visitors (source: comScore, May 2014) 1.2 billion videos views worldwide (source: internal). Offers the best content from users, independent content creators and premium partners. Using the most advanced technology for both users and content creators, provides high-quality and HD video in a fast, easy-to-use online service that also automatically filters infringing material as notified by content owners.

Offering 32 localized versions, their mission is to provide the best possible entertainment experience for users and the best marketing opportunities for advertisers, while respecting content protection.

CitySquares

A leader in video marketing and advertising solutions for local businesses working to expand their online exposure and generate new prospective clients. Building innovative video applications that deliver the best ways for local businesses to connect with clients. Their full-service video marketing platform makes it easy and affordable for any small or medium sized business to utilize video to grow their online brand. Services include Video Creation and Online Distribution, YouTube In-Stream Advertising, Facebook Advertising and Lead Capturing, and CitySquares Local Business Directory, which is fast becoming the largest video business directory on the web.

Trade Shows

We will exhibit at as many local trade shows per year that the meet the following criteria:
1. Provide opportunities to market our consulting products and services.
2. Provides opportunities to engage in distinctive learning programs.
3. Participants are able to forge fruitful connections with their peers.
4. The location is accessible and affordable.

Best Practices Resources:
www.shrm.org/resourcesandtools/hr-topics/behavioral-competencies/consultation/pages/tradeshowbestpractices.aspx
http://augustafreepress.com/trade-show-booth-ideas-rock-show/

We will exhibit at as many local trade shows per year as possible. These include Business Trade Shows and Exhibitions, Business Expos, business spot-lights with our local Chamber of Commerce, and more. The objective is to get our company name and service out to as many potential clients as possible. When exhibiting at a trade show, we will put our best foot forward and represent ourselves as professionals. We will be open, enthusiastic, informative and courteous. We will exhibit our services with sales brochures, logo-imprinted giveaways, sample products, a portfolio for people to browse through and a computer to run our video presentation through. We will use a 'free drawing' for a free Business Audit and a sign-in sheet to collect names and email addresses. We will also develop a questionnaire or survey that helps us to assemble an ideal client profile and qualify the leads we receive. We will train our booth attendants to answer all type of questions and to handle objections. We will also seek to present educational seminars at the show to gain increased publicity, and name and expertise recognition. Most importantly, we will develop and implement a follow-up program to stay-in-touch with prospects.

Resources: www.tsnn.com
www.expocentral.com
www.acshomeshow.com

Business Expos
The goal of Business Expos are to create environments that enable companies to market directly to their target audience and network with businesses who have like interests and initiatives. Business Expos coordinate events specifically designed to encourage networking and develop a client base in all types of industry.

Directory of HR Conferences   https://hr-guide.com/HR/Conferences.htm
Examples:
www.employeebenefitadviser.com/news/benefits-forum-expo-2018
https://www.hrssoutsourcing.com/

Resources:
http://www.eventmanagement.org/newyork/demographics.php
http://www.floridabusinessexpo.com/

Business Card

Our business card will include our company logo, complete contact information, name and title, association logos, slogan or markets serviced, and certifications. The center of our bi-fold card will contain a listing of the services we offer. We will give out multiple business cards to friends, family members, and to each client, upon the completion of the service. We will also distribute business cards in the following ways:
1. Attached to invoices, surveys, flyers and door hangers.
2. Included in client product packages.
3. We will leave a stack of business cards in a Lucite holder with the local Chamber of Commerce and any other businesses offering free counter placement.

We will use fold-over cards because they will enable us to list all our services and complete contact instructions on the inside of the card. We will also give magnetic business cards to new clients for posting on the refrigerator door.

We will place the following referral discount message on the back of our business cards:
- Our business is very dependent upon referrals. If you have associates who could benefit from our quality foodservices, please write your name at the bottom of this card and give it to them. When your friend presents this card at their first appointment, he or she will be entitled to 10% off discount. And, on your next invoice, you will also get a 10% discount as a thank you for your referral. The card will feature our 'free sampling program' and info about our specialty service.

Resource:
www.vistaprint.com

Direct Mail Package

To build name recognition and to announce the opening of our human resources consulting practice, we will offer a mail package consisting of a tri-fold brochure containing a coupon for a 50% discount on a HR Performance Audit to encourage new clients to sample our Human Resources Consulting Services. From those self-identified local clients, we shall ask them to complete a survey that will further the opening of a dialogue. Those clients returning completed surveys will receive a gift or discount.

We will use direct mail to send out non-salesy offers for white papers or case studies, which HR and Management people appreciate. We will ensure our mailings are clean and professionally done, have little "glitz" and offer practical information an HR professional can use. We will not make over-the-top claims that HR professionals are known to instantly trash. We will feature compelling offers like a free white paper with solutions to up-to-the-minute industry challenges.

Resource:
https://www.entrepreneur.com/article/233303

Our direct mail program will feature the following key components:
1. A call to action.
2. Test marketing using a limited 100-piece mailing.
3. A defined set of target markets.
4. A follow up phone call.
5. A personalized cover-letter.
7. A special trial offer with an expiration date.

Resources:
www.directmailquotes.com/rfq/quote1.cfm?affiliate=14
http://www.listgiant.com/

Online Directory Listings

The following directory listings use proprietary technology to match clients with industry professionals in their geographical area. The local search capabilities for specific niche markets offer an invaluable tool for the client. These directories help member businesses connect with purchase-ready buyers, convert leads to sales, and maximize the value of client relationships. Their online and offline communities provide a quick and easy no-cost solution for clients to find a marketing consultant quickly. We intend to sign-up with all no cost directories and evaluate the ones that charge a fee.

SHRM	http://vendordirectory.shrm.org/GetListed.aspx
DMOZ	www.dmoz.org/Business/Human_Resources/Consulting/
Consultants Registrar	www.consultantsregistrar.com/
Consulting Bench	www.consultingbench.com/consulting-firms/human-resources-consulting-firms
Inc Rankings	www.inc.com/inc5000/list/2014/industry/human-resources/
HR.com	www.hr.com/buyersguide/company

We will make certain that our listings contain the following information:

- Business Name
- Phone number
- Email address
- Contact Person: name, phone #, email
- Company logo
- Short Business description
- Specialties
- Twitter Business Page Link
- Address
- Days and Hours of operation
- Website URL
- Facility Photos
- Products/ Services offered
- Affiliations
- Facebook Business Page Link
- LinkedIn Business Page Link

Other General Directories Include:

Listings.local.yahoo.com	Switchboard Super Pages
YellowPages.com	MerchantCircle.com
Bing.com/businessportal	Local.com
Yelp.com	BrownBook.com
InfoUSA.com	iBegin.com
Localeze.com	Bestoftheweb.com
YellowBot.com	HotFrog.com
InsiderPages.com	MatchPoint.com
CitySearch.com	YellowUSA.com
Profiles.google.com/me	Manta.com
Jigsaw.com	LinkedIn.com
Whitepages.com	PowerProfiles.com
Judysbook.com	Company.com
Google.com	Yahoo.com
SuperPages.com	TrueLocal.com
ExpressUpdate.com	Citysquares.com
MojoPages.com	DMOZ
BOTW	Business.com

Get Listed — http://getlisted.org/enhanced-business-listings.aspx
Universal Business Listing — https://www.ubl.org/index.aspx
www.UniversalBusinessListing.org

Universal Business Listing (UBL) is a local search industry service dedicated to acting as a central collection and distribution point for business information online. UBL provides business owners and their marketing representatives with a one-stop location for broad distribution of complete, accurate, and detailed listing information.

Networking

Networking will be a key to success, because referrals and alliances formed can help keep our business growing. This will be an effective way to increase our client base. We will participate as a volunteer in civic and professional organizations whose membership includes our target client profile. This will help us to hear about new projects and companies getting under way in our business community. We will get to know the people likely to send us referrals. We understand that the key to making this strategy work, is to make a real contribution to the organization.

We will strive to build long-term mutually beneficial relationships with our networking contacts and join the following types of organizations:
1. We will form a LeTip Chapter to exchange business leads.
2. We will join the local BNI.com referral exchange group.
3. We will join the Chamber of Commerce to further corporate relationships.
4. We will join the Rotary Club, Kiwanis Club, Church Groups, etc.
5. We will become an active member of the local business community.
6. We will join Entrepreneurial Development Groups and Venture Capitalists Associations.
7. We will join American Society of Training and Development, National Speakers Association, and the Society of Human Resources Management.

These types of memberships will be respected by employers and may assist us in finding clients, because many human resource professionals join these types of organizations to network and learn emerging trends in the industry. We will talk to human resources professionals within these types of organizations to start networking. This will assist us in recruiting candidates who have the required skills we are offering to clients.

Chamber of Commerce
We will use our metropolitan _____ (city) Chamber of Commerce to target prospective corporate contacts. We will mail letters to each prospect describing our HR products and consulting services. We will follow-up with phone calls. We will hold a Chamber business mixer in our _____ offices. This popular networking event will offer the following two benefits:
1. Many business colleagues will visit our new offices.
2. Some attendees may want to purchase our consulting services.
Resource: http://www.uschamber.com/chambers/directory/default

Cambridge Who's Who   www.cambridgeregistry.com
A powerful networking resource that enables professionals to outshine their competition through effective branding and marketing. Cambridge Who's Who employs public relations techniques for members who seek to take advantage of its career enhancement and business advancement services. Cambridge Who's Who membership provides individuals with a valuable third-party endorsement of their accomplishments and gives them the tools needed to brand themselves and their businesses effectively. In addition to publishing biographies in print and electronic form, it offers an online networking platform where members can establish new professional relationships.

Consultant Brokers
We will work with brokers to make them exactly understand our technical strengths and weaknesses and only accept interviews where there is a perfect match.

Certified Professional Employer Organization (CPEO)

This designation is part of the federal regulatory environment for PEOs created by the Small Business Efficiency Act (SBEA) in 2014. To become and remain certified under the new voluntary IRS program, CPEOs must meet tax compliance, background, experience, business location, financial reporting, bonding, and other requirements. PEOs handle various payroll administration and tax reporting responsibilities for their business clients and are typically paid a fee based on payroll costs. A CPEO establishes a co-employment relationship with its clients. In it, the CPEO assumes many of the employee-related employer responsibilities, while the customer continues to manage and run the business.

Resources:
https://www.irs.gov/tax-professionals/certified-professional-employer-organization
https://www.insperity.com/blog/what-is-a-certified-peo/

Newsletters

We will develop a monthly e-newsletter to stay in touch with our clients and use it to market to local businesses. We will include the following types of information:

1. Success case studies
2. New Product/Service Introductions
3. Featured employee/client of month
4. Human resources consulting trends.
5. client endorsements/testimonials.
6. Classified ads from sponsors/suppliers.
7. Consulting Project Story
8. Polled survey results report.
9. Editorial Comments
10. Client contributed articles

Examples:
www.silvershr.com/topics/articles/newsletters/spring-2017-newsletters/

Resource:
http://www.shrm.org/publications/e-mailnewsletters/pages/default.aspx

We will adhere to the following newsletter writing guidelines:
1. We will provide content that is of real value to our subscribers.
2. We will provide solutions to our subscriber's HR problems or questions.
3. We will communicate regularly on a weekly basis.
4. We will create HTML Messages that look professional and allow us to track how many people click on our links and/or open our emails.
5. We will not pitch our business opportunity in our Ezine very often.
6. We will focus our marketing dollars on building our Ezine subscriber list.
7. We will focus on relationship building and not the conveying of a sales message.
8. We will vary our message format with videos, articles, checklists, quotes, pictures and charts.
9. We will recommend occasionally affiliate products in some of our messages to help cover our marketing costs.
10. We will consistently follow the above steps to build a database of qualified prospects and clients.

Resources:

www.mailchimp.com
www.constantcontact.com/email-templates/newsletter-templates
http://lmssuccess.com/10-reasons-online-business-send-regular-newsletter-clients/
www.smallbusinessmiracles.com/how/newsletters/
www.fuelingnewbusiness.com/2010/06/01/combine-email-marketing-and-social-media-for-ad-agency-new-business/

Example:
Each month you can expect:
- A helpful message about what you should be doing to better your business.
- A spotlight featuring one of our team members
- HR Alerts to keep you on top of changes in HR Laws, all in one simple place, straight from a trusted resource.
- The HR "Topic of the Month" – our take on a current HR issue and what steps you need to take to be compliant.

In addition to the email newsletter, you will also receive:
- Exclusive Access to instant blog updates and summaries only available to our newsletter subscribers.
- First Access to Upcoming Events at Integrity HR so you'll be sure not to miss your seat.
- Helpful toolkits, videos, podcasts, and whitepapers that keep you up to speed with the ever-changing world of HR.

Source:
https://integrityhr.com/newsletter/

Vehicle Signs
We will place magnetic signs on all our vehicles and include our company name, phone number, company slogan and website address, if possible.

DVD Presentation
We plan to create a DVD version of our video clips, which include a modified seminar presentation and client testimonials. We will include this DVD in our sales presentation folder and direct mail package.

Up-selling and Reselling
We plan to develop a broad range of HR product and consulting service programs in various price categories, so that we up-sell to current clients and re-sell to inactive accounts.

Advertising Wearables
We will give all preferred club members an eye-catching T-shirt or sweatshirt with our company name and logo printed across the garment to wear about town. We will also give them away as a thank you for client referral activities. We will also ask all employees to wear our logo-imprinted shirts at sponsored events. We will also sell the

garments via our website.

Sampling Program
We will give away a sampling of our Human Resources Consulting expertise in the form of a complementary seminar, a research report or a discounted human resources management audit to move a client relationship forward.

Testimonial Marketing
We will either always ask for testimonials immediately after a completed project or contact our clients once a quarter for them. We will also have something prepared that we would like the client to say that is specific to a service we offer, or anything relevant to advertising claims that we have put together. For the convenience of the client we will assemble a testimonial letter that they can either modify or just sign off on. Additionally, testimonials can also be in the form of audio or video and put on our website or mailed to potential clients in the form of a DVD or Audio CD. A picture with a testimonial is also excellent. We will put testimonials directly on a magazine ad, slick sheet, brochure, or website, or assemble a complete page of testimonials for our sales presentation folder. We will provide testimonial writing guidance so they include not just name and company, but also information about the type of service provided and the measurable outcomes of those services.

Examples:
www.hrconsultingpartners.net/testimonials/
http://www.hrconsults.com/about-us/testimonials

We will collect customer testimonials in the following ways:
1. Our website – A page dedicated to testimonials (written and/or video).
2. Social media accounts – Facebook fan pages offer a review tab, which makes it easy to receive and display customer testimonials.
3. Google+ also offers a similar feature with Google+ Local.
4. Local search directories – Ask clients to post more reviews on Yelp and Yahoo Local.
5. Customer Satisfaction Survey Forms

We will pose the following questions to our clients to help them frame their testimonials:
1. What was the obstacle that would have prevented you from buying this product?
2. "What was your main concern about buying this product?"
3. What did you find as a result of buying this product?
4. What specific feature did you like most about this product?
5. What would be three other benefits about this product?
6. Would you recommend this product? If so, why?
7. Is there anything you'd like to add?

Resource:
https://smallbiztrends.com/2016/06/use-customer-testimonials.html

Reminder Service

We will use a four-tier reminder system in the following sequence: email, postcard, letter, phone call. We will stress the importance of staying in touch in our messages and keeping their profile updated with their activities. We will also try to determine the reason for the non-response or inactivity and what can be done to reactivate the client. The reminder service will also work to the benefit of regular clients, that want to be reminded of an agreed upon special date or coming event.

Resource:
http://www.easyivr.com/reminder-service.htm

Business Logo

Our logo will graphically represent who we are and what we do, and it will serve to help brand our HR consultancy image. It will also convey a sense of uniqueness and professionalism. The logo will represent our company image and the message we are trying to convey. Our business logo will reflect the philosophy and objective of the liquor store business. Our logo will incorporate the following design guidelines:

1. It will relate to our industry, our name, a defining characteristic of our company or a competitive advantage we offer.
2. It will be a simple logo that can be recognized faster.
3. It will contain strong lines and letters which show up better than thin ones.
4. It will feature something unexpected or unique without being overdrawn.
5. It will work well in black and white (one-color printing).
6. It will be scalable and look pleasing in both small and large sizes.
7. It will be artistically balanced and make effective use of color, line density and shape.
8. It will be unique when compared to competitors.
9. It will use original, professionally rendered artwork.
10. It can be replicated across any media mix without losing quality.
11. It appeals to our target audience.
12. It will be easily recognizable from a distance if utilized in outdoor advertising.

Examples:
https://99designs.com/logo-design/contests/logo-human-resources-consulting-business-171777
https://www.pinterest.com/artdivacreative/human-resources-logo/
https://logo.designcrowd.com/contest.aspx?id=2746171

The following gig-work networks match workers to projects:

Resources: www.freelogoservices.com/   www.hatchwise.com
            www.logosnap.com   www.99designs.com
            www.fiverr.com   www.freelancer.com
            www.upwork.com   www.workpop.com

Logo Design Guide:
www.bestfreewebresources.com/logo-design-professional-guide

www.creativebloq.com/graphic-design/pro-guide-logo-design-21221

Charitable Donations
We will use these coupon donation opportunities to demonstrate our new HR products and consulting services, meet and greet many new potential clients and distribute lots of sales brochures and business cards to event sponsors and attendees.

Corporate Promotional Kit
Our promotional sales presentation kit for commercial accounts will contain the following items:

- Owner/GM Resume
- Press Clippings
- DVD Presentation
- FAQs
- Press Releases
- Client List
- Article Reprints
- Sales Brochures
- Business Cards
- Testimonials

Stage External Events
We will stage external events to become known in our community. This is essential to attracting referrals. We will schedule regular external events, such as seminar talks, HR Conferences, Webinars, trade show appearances and fundraiser demonstrations. We will use event registration forms, our website and an event sign-in sheet to collect the names and email addresses of all attendees. This database will be used to feed our automatic client relationship follow-up program and newsletter service.
Resource:
www.eventbrite.com
Examples:
https://events.hrgirlfriends.com/
https://events.hrgirlfriends.com/#espresso_calendar

Practice Brochures
Our practice brochure will include the following contents and become a key part of our direct mail package:

- Contact Information
- Client Testimonials
- Competitive Advantages
- Free Consultation/Audit Offer
- Consultancy Mission Statement
- Company Description
- List of Services/Benefits
- Owner/Consultant Resumes
- Notable Client List

Examples:
www.hrpiinc.com/wp-content/uploads/2012/06/hrpi_brochure_vertical.pdf

Sales Brochure Design
1. Speak in Terms of Our Prospects Wants and Interests.

2. Focus on all the Benefits, not Just Features.
3. Put the company logo and Unique Selling Proposition together to reinforce the fact that your company is different and better than the competition.
4. Include a special offer, such as a discount, a free report, a sample, or a free trial to increase the chances that the brochure will generate sales.

We will incorporate the following Brochure Design Guidelines:
1. Design the brochure to achieve a focused set of objectives (marketing of programs) with a target market segment (residential vs. commercial).
2. Tie the brochure design to our other marketing materials with colors, logo, fonts and formatting.
3. List capabilities and how they benefit clients.
4. Demonstrate what we do and how we do it differently.
5. Define the value proposition of our engineering installing services
6. Use a design template that reflects your market positioning strategy.
7. Identify your key message (unique selling proposition)
8. List our competitive advantages.
9. Express our understanding of client needs and wants.
10. Use easy to read (scan) headlines, subheadings, bullet points, pictures, etc.
11. Use a logo to create a visual branded identity.
12. The most common and accepted format for a brochure is a folded A3 (= 2 x A4), which gives 4 pages of information.
13. Use a quality of paper that reflects the image we want to project.
14. Consistently stick to the colors of our corporate style.
15. Consider that colors have associations, such as green colors are associated with the environment and enhance an environmental image.
16. Illustrations will be appropriate and of top quality and directly visualize the product assortment, product application and production facility.
17. The front page will contain the company name, logo, the main application of your product or service and positioning message or Unique Selling Proposition.
18. The back page will be used for testimonials or references, and contact details.

Sales Presentation Folder Contents

1.	Resumes	2.	Management Team Photos
3.	Contract/Application	4.	Frequently Asked Questions
5.	Sales Brochure	6.	Business Cards
7.	Testimonials/References	8.	HR Program Descriptions
9.	Informative Articles	10.	Referral Program
11.	Company Overview	12.	Operating Policies
13.	Article Reprints	14.	Press Releases

Coupons

We will use coupons with limited time expirations to get prospects to try our HR products and audit programs. We will also accept the coupons of our competitors to help establish new client relationships. We will run ads directing people to our Web site for a

$___ gift certificate. This will help to draw in new business and collect e-mail addresses for the distribution of a monthly newsletter. We will offer a discounted HR performance audit.

Examples:
www.localsaver.com/columbia-md/professional-services/consulting/kjt-hr-concepts-llc-coupon?dsc=MYDS&bizid=52048845&cpnid=5723234
https://www.retailmenot.com/view/hrdirect.com

Cross-Promotions

We will contact local businesses with client profiles similar to ours, such as computer and office supply stores, and ask them to hand out discount HR Audit coupons to each of their business clients. This will get us access to that business's client base, as well as a personal recommendation from that business to try our services.

Bidding Lists

We will add our company name to the bidders' lists in government agencies, companies and associations who have a need for Human Resources Consulting Services and who invite bids and proposals. This will require the furnishing of an application to the central purchasing organization of the federal, state, county or city agency. We will also seek certification as either a women-owned or minority owned or veteran owned business to receive preferential treatment when submitting proposals.
Resource:
www.findrfp.com/Government_Contracting/Government_Bidder_List.aspx

Premium Giveaways

We will distribute logo-imprinted promotional products at events, also known as giveaway premiums, to foster top-of-mind awareness (www.promoideas.org). These items include logo-imprinted T-shirts, business cards with magnetic backs, mugs with contact phone number and calendars that feature important date reminders.

Newspaper Ads

We will place ads in local free newspapers as a very economical way to start our business, as the return is strong on a per dollar spent basis. We will include a discount coupon to track results in zoned editions. We will use print ads in targeted publications to promote our upcoming events, like seminars and workshops.

Our newspaper ads will utilize the following design tips:
1. We will start by getting a media kit from the publisher to analyze their demographic information as well as their reach and distribution.
2. Don't let the newspaper people have total control of our ad design, as we know how we want our company portrayed to the market.
3. Make sure to have 1st class graphics since this will be the only visual distinction we can provide the reader about our business.

4. Buy the biggest ad we can afford, with full-page ads being the best.
5. Go with color if affordable, because consumers pick color ads over black 82% of the time.
6. Ask the paper if they have specific days that more of our type of buyer reads their paper.
7. If we have a hit ad on our hands, we will make it into a circular or door-hanger to extend the life of the offer.
8. Don't change an ad because we are getting tired of looking at it.
9. We will start our headline by telling our story to pull the reader into the ad.
10. We will use "Act Now" to convey a sense of urgency to the reader.
11. We will use our headline to tell the reader what to do.
12. The headline is a great place to announce a free offer.
13. We will write our headline as if we were speaking to one person, and make it personal.
14. We will use our headline to either relay a benefit or intrigue the reader into wanting more information.
15. Use coupons giving a dollar amount off, not a percentage, as people hate doing the math.

Local Publications

We will place low-cost classified ads in neighborhood publications to advertise our HR consulting services. We will also submit public relations and informative articles to improve our visibility and establish our HR expertise and trustworthiness. These publications include the following:
1. Neighborhood Newsletters and Church Bulletins
2. Local Restaurant Association Newsletter
3. Local Chamber of Commerce Newsletter
4. Realtor Magazines
5. Homeowner Association Newsletters

Resources:
Hometown News   www.hometownnews.com
Pennysaver   www.pennysaverusa.com

Publication Type	Ad Size	Timing	Circulation	Section	Fee

Magazine Ads

We plan on purchasing the names of local subscribers to national business magazines such as Inc. and Forbes Magazine to build an interest in some of our HR products and consulting services. We will use these ads to get our name in front of our likely prospects and track the return on investment to determine if we should expand or restrict this marketing strategy.

Business Journal Display Ads

We will consider placing display ads in business journals read by professionals and possibly rent a list of their local subscribers for a planned direct mailing. The mailing will describe our HR consulting service programs and other resources. We will use empirical data to prove how our targeted marketing programs can actually save companies money, and help their sales force to be more cost-efficient.

Publication Type	Ad Size	Timing	Circulation	Section	Fee

Article Submissions

We will pitch articles to local newspapers, business magazines and internet articles directories to help establish our specialized expertise and improve our visibility.
We will publish informational HR articles and issue press releases to succeed in the HR marketplace and to stand apart from our competitors and "influence the influencers." This tactic will work because individuals at every level of HR respond to best-practice and thought-leadership information.

Hyperlinks will be placed within written articles and can be clicked on to take the client to another webpage within our website or to a totally different website. These clickable links or hyperlinks will be keywords or relevant words that have meaning to our Human Resources Consulting. We will create keyword-rich article titles that match the most commonly searched keywords for our topic. In fact, we will create a position whose primary function is to link our Human Resources Consulting with opportunities to be published in local publications.

Publishing requires an understanding of the following publisher needs:
1. Review of good work.
2. Editor story needs.
3. Article submission process rules
4. Quality photo portfolio
5. Exclusivity requirements.
6. Target market interests

Our Article Submission Package will include the following:
1. Well-written materials
2. Good Drawings
3. High-quality Photographs
4. Well-organized outline.

Examples of General Publishing Opportunities:
1. Document a new solution to old problem
2. Publish a research study
3. Mistake prevention advice
4. Present a different viewpoint
5. Introduce a local angle on a hot topic.
6. Reveal a new trend.
7. Share specialty niche expertise.
8. Share wine health benefits

Examples of Specific Article Titles:
1. The Importance of Leadership in Managing Change
2. New Trends in HR Management
3. How to Evaluate Qualified Human Resources Consultants

4. How to Develop a Personnel Plan to Jumpstart Sales
5. Management Fads: 10 Things You Should Know to Avoid Being Had
6. How to Beat the Recession with the Right Recruiting Strategy
7. How Big Data Will Transform the HR Department
8. What to Look for in an HR Consulting Firm
   Ex: https://www.bbgbroker.com/hr-consulting-firm/
9. How Employers Can Conduct a Great Job Interview
   www.hrconsults.com/the-employers-guide-to-conducting-a-great-job-interview
10. Understanding Why Talented People Quit Their Jobs
    Ex: http://inhisnamehr.com/category/blog/human-resources/

Write Articles with a Closing Author Resource Box or Byline

1. Author Name with credential titles.
2. Explanation of area of expertise.
3. Mention of a special offer.
4. A specific call to action
5. A Call to Action Motivator
6. All possible contact information
7. Helpful Links
8. Link to Firm Website.

Article Objectives:

Article Topic	Target Audience	Target Date

Article Tracking Form

Subject	Publication	Target Audience	Business Development	Resources Needed	Target Date

Possible Magazines to submit articles include:

1. Fast Company Magazine
2. Inc Magazine
3. Forbes Magazine
4. Fortune Magazine

Resources:
Writer's Market   www.writersmarket.com
Directory of Trade Magazines   www.techexpo.com/tech_mag.html

Internet article directories include:

http://ezinearticles.com/   http://www.mommyshelpercommunity.com
http://www.articlecity.com   http://www.amazines.com
http://www.articledashboard.com   http://www.submityourarticle.com/articles
http://www.webarticles.com   http://www.articlecube.com
http://www.article-buzz.com   http://www.free-articles-zone.com
www.articletogo.com   http://www.content-articles.com
http://article-niche.com   http://superpublisher.com
http://www.articlenexus.com   www.articlebin.com
http://www.articlefinders.com   www.articlesfactory.com

http://www.articlewarehouse.com
http://www.easyarticles.com
http://ideamarketers.com/
http://clearviewpublications.com/
http://www.goarticles.com/
http://www.connectionteam.com
http://www.MarketingArticleLibrary.com
http://www.allwomencentral.com
http://www.reprintarticles.com
http://www.articlestreet.com
http://www.articlepeak.com
http://www.simplysearch4it.com
http://www.valuablecontent.com
http://www.article99.com

www.buzzle.com
www.isnare.com
//groups.yahoo.com/group/article_announce
www.ebusiness-articles.com
www.authorconnection.com/
www.digital-women.com/submitarticle.htm
www.searchwarp.com
www.marketing-seek.com
www.articles411.com
www.articleshelf.com
www.articlesbase.com
www.articlealley.com
www.articleavenue.com
www.virtual-professionals.com

Seminars

Seminars will present the following marketing and bonding opportunities:
1. Signage and branding as a presenting sponsor.
2. Opportunity to distribute name and logo imprinted handouts.
3. Media exposure through advertising and public relations.
4. The opportunity for one-on-one interaction with a targeted group of consumers to demonstrate an understanding of their needs and our matching expert solutions.
5. Use of sign-in sheet to collect names and email addresses for database build.

Possible seminar funding sources:
1. Small registration fee to cover the cost of hand-outs and refreshments.
2. Get sponsorship funding from partner/networking organizations.
3. Sponsorship classified ads in the program guide or handouts.

We will establish our expertise and trustworthiness by offering free seminars on the following types of topics:
1. The Top 10 Secrets to Breakthrough Personnel Development
2. How to Grow Your Business During a Recession
3. How to Reduce Your Fixed HR Management Costs.
4. How to Develop and Execute a HR Process Improvement Plan
5. What is Value Based Management?
6. How to Best Develop Leadership Skills in Your Organization.
7. How to Develop a High-Performance Recruitment System
   Ex: http://inhisnamehr.com/category/blog/

Seminar Example:
"Managing Employees to Success"
http://inhisnamehr.com/managing-employees-to-success-seminar-october-28-2016-new-bloomfield-pa/

Seminar target groups include the following:

1. Entrepreneur Clubs
2. Venture Capitalists
3. Office Supply Stores
4. New Business Owners
5. Computer Supply Outlets
6. Trade Associations

Seminar marketing approaches include:
1. Posting to website and enabling online registrations.
2. Email blast using www.constantcontact.com
3. Include seminar schedule in newsletter.
4. Classified ads using craigslist.org

Seminar Objectives:

Seminar Topic	Target Audience	Handout	Target Date

Proprietary Research Surveys

We will conduct surveys and collect relevant data to reinforce our firm's expertise, bring new ideas to our targeted clients, generate leads for our business and expand our network of contacts. The publicity we receive from conducting surveys will help to establish our authority on the chosen HR topics. We will use the survey findings as source material for articles, speeches, press releases and related reports. We will also consider the selling of the report of findings to create a new revenue stream.

Online Classified Ad Placements

The following free classified ad sites, will enable our business to thoroughly describe the benefits of our Human Resources Consulting Services:

1. **Craigslist.org**
2. Ebay Classifieds
3. Classifieds.myspace.com
4. KIJIJI.com
5. //Lycos.oodle.com
6. Webclassifieds.us
7. USFreeAds.com
8. www.oodle.com
9. Backpage.com
10. stumblehere.com
11. Classifiedads.com
12. gumtree.com
13. Inetgiant.com
14. www.sell.com
15. Freeadvertisingforum.com
16. Classifiedsforfree.com
17. www.olx.com
18. www.isell.com
19. Base.google.com
20. www.epage.com
21. Chooseyouritem.com
22. www.adpost.com
23. Adjingo.com
24. Kugli.com

Sample Craigslist.org Classified Ad

Is Your Business in Need of Quality Human Resources Consulting Services at Reasonable Rates? _____ (company name) is the answer to your profitability problems. We are your human resources management experts and offer all our new clients a 10% introductory discount on the following services: Internet Database Techniques, HR Audits, Growth Strategies, Personnel Plan Development and

Implementation, Leadership Development Analysis, and Change Management.
Contact us today to schedule your FREE Consultation or HR Audit.
Phone: _____ Website: _____ Email: _____

Two-Step Direct Response Classified Advertising
We will use 'two-step direct response advertising' to motivate readers to take a step or action that signals that we have their permission to begin marketing to them in step two. Our objective is to build a trusting relationship with our prospects by offering a free unbiased, educational report in exchange for permission to continue the marketing process. This method of advertising has the following benefits:

1.	Shorter sales cycle.	2.	Eliminates need for cold calling.
3.	Establishes expert reputation.	4.	Better qualifies prospects
5.	Process is very trackable.	6.	Able to run smaller ads.

Sample Two Step Lead Generating Classified Ad:
FREE Report Reveals "What Your HR Consultant Has Not Been Telling You About Leadership Training" or… "How to Succeed at HR Project Management".
Call 24 hour recorded message and leave your name and address. Your report will be sent out immediately.

Note: The respondent has shown they have an interest in our Human Resources Consulting Services specialty. We will send this lead the report with excellent HR advice. We will also include a section in the report on our HR Consulting Services and our complete contact information, along with a coupon for a free initial consultation.

Yellow Page Ads
Research indicates that the use of the traditional Yellow Page Book is declining, but that new residents or people who don't have many personal acquaintances will look to the Yellow Pages to establish a list of potential businesses to call upon. Even a small 2" x 2" boxed ad can create awareness and attract the desired target client, above and beyond the ability of a simple listing. We will use the following design concepts:

1. We will use a headline to sell people on our profitability results.
2. We will include a service guarantee to improve our credibility.
3. We will include a coupon offer and a tracking code, or unique tracking URL or phone number to monitor the response rate and decide whether to increase or decrease our ad size in subsequent years.
4. We will choose an ad size equal to that of our competitors, and evaluate the response rate for future insertion commitments.
5. We will include our hours of operation, motto or slogan and logo.
6. We will list some of the most popular benefits of using our HR consulting services.
7. We will include our competitive advantages, specialties and years in business.

Resources: www.superpages.com   www.yellowpages.com
Example: http://www.yellowpages.com/miami-fl/human-resource-consultants

Ad Information:

Book Title: _____   Coverage Area: _____
Yearly Fee: $_____   Ad Size: _____ page
Renewal date: _____   Contact: _____

Cable Television Advertising

Cable television will offer us more ability to target certain market niches or demographics with specialty programming. We will use our marketing research survey to determine which cable TV channels our clients are watching. It is expected that many watch the Home & Garden TV channel, and that people with surplus money watch the Golf Channel and the CNBC Business Network. Our plan is to choose the audience we want, and to hit them often enough to entice them to take action. We will also take advantage of the fact that we will be able to pick the specific areas we want our commercial to air. Ad pricing will be dependent upon the number of households the network reaches, the ratings the particular show has earned, contract length and the supply and demand for a particular network.

Resources:
Spot Runner   www.spotrunner.com
Television Advertising   http://televisionadvertising.com/faq.htm

Comcast Spotlight   www.comcastspotlight.com/
An advertising sales company providing video solutions to local, regional and national businesses through television and digital advertising. Comcast Spotlight provides local market coverage across multiple platforms (cable TV, satellite, telco, online, VOD) and can target clients geographically, demographically and by message to more efficiently and effectively reach specific audience segments.

Ad Information:

Length of ad "spot": ___ seconds   Development costs: $____ (onetime fee)
Length of campaign: __ (#) mos.   Runs per month: Three times per day
Cost per month.: $_____   Total campaign cost: $_____.

Radio Advertising

We will use non-event based radio advertising. This style of campaign is best suited for non-promotional sales driven retail businesses, such as our Human Resources Consulting Service. We will utilize a much smaller schedule of ads on a consistent long-range basis (48 to 52 weeks a year) with the We will use non-event based radio advertising. This style of campaign is best suited for non-sales driven retail businesses, such as our company. We will utilize a much smaller schedule of ads on a consistent long-range basis (48 to 52 weeks a year) with the objective of continuously maintaining top-of-mind-awareness. This will mean maintaining a sufficient level of awareness to be either the number one or number two choice when a triggering-event, such as an _____, moves the consumer into the market for services and forces "a consumer choice" about which company in the consumer's perception might help them the most. This consistent approach will utilize only one ad each week day (260 days per year) and allow our company to cost-effectively keep our message in front of consumers once every week day. The ad copy for this non-event campaign, called a positioning message, will not be time-sensitive. It will define and differentiate our business' "unique market position", and will be repeated for a year.

Note: On the average, listeners spend over 3.5 hours per day with radio.

Radio will give us the ability to target our audience, based on radio formats, such as news-talk, classic rock and the oldies. Radio will also be a good way to get repetition into our message, as listeners tend to be loyal to stations and parts of the day.

1. We will use radio advertising to direct prospects to our Web site, advertise a limited time promotion or call for an informational brochure.
2. We will try to barter our services for radio ad spots.
3. We will use a limited-time offer to entice first-time clients to use our Human Resources Consulting Services.
4. We will explore the use of on-air community bulletin boards to play our public announcements about community sponsored events.
5. We will also make the radio station aware of our expertise in the HR management consulting field and our availability for on-air interviews.
6. Our choice of stations will be driven by the market research information we collect via our surveys.
7. We will capitalize on the fact that many stations now stream their programming on the internet and reach additional local and even national audiences, and if online listeners like what they hear in our streaming radio spot, they can click over to our website.
8. Our radio ads will use humor, sounds, compelling music or unusual voices to grab attention.
9. Our spots will tell success stories or present situations that our target audience can relate to.
10. We will make our call to action, a website address or vanity phone number, easy to remember and tie it in with our company name or message.
11. We will approach radio stations about buying their unsold advertising space for

deep discounts. (Commonly known at radio stations' as "Run of Station")
On radio, this might mean very early in the morning or late at night. We will talk to our advertising representatives and see what discounts they can offer when one of those empty spaces comes open.

Resources: Radio Advertising Bureau   www.RAB.com
             Radio Locator   www.radio-locator.com
             Radio Directory   www.radiodirectory.com

Ad Information:
Length of ad "spot": ___ seconds   Development costs: $____ (onetime fee)
Length of campaign: __ (#) mos.   Runs per month: Three times per day
Cost per month.: $_____   Total campaign cost: $_____ .

Script Resources:
https://voicebunny.com/blog/5-tips-make-radio-ads-grab-attention-sell/
www.voices.com/documents/secure/voices.com-commercial-scripts-for-radio-and-television-ads.pdf
http://smallbusiness.chron.com/say-30second-radio-advertising-spot-10065.html
https://voicebunny.com/blog/5-tips-make-radio-ads-grab-attention-sell/

Blog Talk Radio

National Public Radio (www.NPR.org) plays host to a radio program called _____. The program features _____ (type of HR experts) who talk and blog about _____ (benefit package?) tips. This will help to establish our _____ expertise and build the trust factor with potential clients. Even if we can't get our own nationally syndicated talk show, we will try to make guest appearances and try our hand with podcasting by using apps like Spreaker or joining podcasting communities like BlogTalkRadio.

Resources:
National Public Radio   www.npr.org
Spreaker   http://www.spreaker.com/
Blog Talk Radio   http://www.blogtalkradio.com/

With BlogTalkRadio, people can either host their own live talk radio show with any phone and a computer or listen to thousands of new shows created daily.

E-mail Marketing

We will use the following email marketing tips to build our mailing list database, improve communications, boost client loyalty and attract new and repeat business.

1. Define our objectives as the most effective email strategies are those that offer value to our subscribers: either in the form of educational content or promotions. To drive sales, a promotional campaign is the best format. To create brand recognition and reinforce our expertise in our industry we will use educational newsletters.
2. A quality, permission-based email list will be a vital component of our email marketing campaign. We will ask clients and prospects for permission to add them to our list at every touch-point or use a sign-in sheet.
3. We will listen to our clients by using easy-to-use online surveys to ask specific

questions about clients' preferences, interests and satisfaction.
4. We will send only relevant and targeted communications.
5. We will reinforce our brand to ensure recognition of our brand by using a recognizable name in the "from" line of our emails and including our company name, logo and a consistent design and color scheme in every email.

Resources:
https://cbtnews.com/8-tips-drive-successful-email-marketing-campaign/
https://www.inman.com/2018/06/05/4-tips-for-effective-email-marketing/
https://due.com/blog/ways-take-good-care-email-list/

Every ___ (five?) to ____ (six?) weeks, we will send graphically-rich, permission-based, personalized, email marketing messages to our list of clients who registered on our website or attended our seminars or responded to our classified ads. The emails will alert clients in a ___ (?)-mile radius to promotions as well as other local events sponsored by the company. This service will be provided by either ExactTarget.com or ConstantContact.com. The email will announce a special event or new product or service introduction and contain a short sales letter. The message will invite recipients to click on a link to our website to checkout more information about the event or introduction. The software offered by these two companies will automatically personalize each email with the client's name. The software also provides detailed click-through behavior reports that will enable us to evaluate the success of each message. The software will also allow our company to dramatically scale back its direct mail efforts and associated costs. We will send a promotional e-mail about a promotion that the client indicated was important to them in their registration application. Each identified market segment will get notified of new products, specials and offers based on past buying patterns and what they've clicked on in our previous e-newsletters or indicated on their surveys. The objective is to tap the right client's need at the right time, with a targeted subject line and targeted content. Our general e-newsletter may appeal to most clients, but targeted mailings that reach out to our various audience segments will build even deeper relationships, and drive higher sales.

Resources:
www.constantcontact.com/pricing/email-marketing.jsp
http://www.verticalresponse.com/blog/10-retail-marketing-ideas-to-boost-sales/

Google Reviews
We will use our email marketing campaign to ask people for reviews. We will ask people what they thought of our consulting business or HR services and encourage them to write a Google Review if they were impressed. We will incorporate a call to action (CTA) on our email auto signature with a link to our Google My Review page.
Source:
https://superb.digital/how-to-ask-your-clients-for-google-reviews/

Resources:
https://support.google.com/business/answer/3474122?hl=en
https://support.google.com/maps/answer/6230175?co=GENIE.Platform

%3DDesktop&hl=en
www.patientgain.com/how-to-get-positive-google-reviews

Example:
We will tell our clients to:
1. Go to https://www.google.com/maps
2. Type in your business name, select the listing
3. There's a "card" (sidebar) on the left-hand side. At the bottom, they can click 'Be the First to Write a Review' **or** 'Write a Review' if you already have one review.

Source:
https://www.reviewjump.com/blog/how-do-i-get-google-reviews/

Voice Broadcasting

A web-based voice broadcast system will provide a powerful platform to generate thousands of calls to clients and clients or create customizable messages to be delivered to specific individuals. Voice broadcasting and voice mail broadcast will allow our company to instantly send interactive phone calls with ease while managing the entire process right from the Web. We will instantly send alerts, notifications, reminders, GOTV - messages, and interactive surveys with ease right from the Web. The free VoiceShot account will guide us through the process of recording and storing our messages, managing our call lists, scheduling delivery as well as viewing and downloading real-time call and caller key press results. The voice broadcasting interface will guide us through the entire process with a Campaign Checklist as well as tips from the Campaign Expert. Other advanced features include recipient targeting, call monitoring, scheduling, controlling the rate of call delivery and customized text to speech (TTS).

Resource:
http://www.voiceshot.com/public/outboundcalls.asp

Facebook.com

We will use Facebook to move our businesses forward and stay connected to our clients in this fast-paced world. Content will be the key to staying in touch with our clients and keeping them informed. The content will be a rich mix of information, before and after photos, interactive questions, current trends and events, industry facts, education, promotions and specials, humor and fun. We will use the following step system to get clients from Facebook.com and establish a two-way dialogue:

1. We will open a free Facebook account at Facebook.com.
2. We will begin by adding Facebook friends. The fastest way to do this is to allow Facebook to import our email addresses and send an invite out to all our clients.
3. We will post a video to get our clients involved with our Facebook page. We will post a video called "How to Improve Business Profitability through Better HR Practices" The video will be first uploaded to YouTube.com and then simply be linked to our Facebook page. Video will be a great way to get people

active and involved with our Facebook page.
4. We will send an email to our client's base that encourages them to check out the new video and to post their feedback about it on our Facebook page. Then we will provide a link to drive clients to our Facebook page.
5. We will respond quickly to feedback, engage in the dialogue and add links to our response that direct the author to a structured mini-survey.
6. We will optimize our Facebook profile with our business keyword to make it an invaluable marketing tool and become the "go-to" expert in our HR consulting industry
7. On a monthly basis, we will send out a message to all Facebook fans with a special offer, as Fan pages are the best way to interact with clients and potential clients on Facebook,
8. We will use Facebook as a tool for sharing success stories and relate the ways in which we have helped our clients.
9. We will use Facebook Connect to integrate our Facebook efforts with our regular website to share our Facebook Page activity. This will also give us statistics about our website visitors, and add social interaction to our site.

Resources:
http://www.facebook.com/advertising/
http://www.socialmediaexaminer.com/how-to-set-up-a-facebook-page-for-business/

Examples:
https://www.facebook.com/pages/Human-Resources-Consulting-LLC/332778453471185

Facebook Profiles represent individual users and are held under a person's name. Each profile should only be controlled by that person. Each user has a wall, information tab, likes, interests, photos, videos and each individual can create events.

Facebook Groups are pretty similar to Fan Pages but are usually created for a group of people with a similar interest and they are wanting to keep their discussions private. The members are not usually looking to find out more about a business - they want to discuss a certain topic.

Facebook Fan Pages are the most viral of your three options. When someone becomes a fan of your page or comments on one of your posts, photos or videos, that is spread to all their personal friends. This can be a great way to get your information out to lots of people...and quickly! In addition, one of the most valuable features of a business page is that you can send "updates" about new products and content to fans and your home building brand becomes more visible.

Facebook Live lets people, public figures and Pages share live video with their followers and friends on Facebook.
Source:
https://live.fb.com/about/
Resources:

https://www.facebook.com/business/a/Facebook-video-ads
http://smartphones.wonderhowto.com/news/facebook-is-going-all-live-video-streaming-your-phone-0170132/

Facebook Business Page
Resources:
https://www.facebook.com/business/learn/set-up-facebook-page
https://www.pcworld.com/article/240258/how_to_make_a_facebook_page_for_your_small_business.html
https://blog.hubspot.com/blog/tabid/6307/bid/5492/how-to-create-a-facebook-business-page-in-5-simple-steps-with-video.aspx

Small Business Promotions
This group allows members to post about their products and services and is a public group designated as a Buy and Sell Facebook group.
Source: https://www.facebook.com/groups/smallbusinesspronotions/
Resource:
https://www.facebook.com/business/a/local-business-promotion-ads
https://www.facebook.com/business/learn/facebook-create-ad-local-awareness
www.socialmediaexaminer.com/how-to-use-facebook-local-awareness-ads-to-target-clients/

Facebook Ad Builder
https://waymark.com/signup/db869ac4-7202-4e3b-93c3-80acc5988df9/?partner=fitsmallbusiness

Facebook Lead Ads_   www.facebook.com/business/a/lead-ads
A type of sponsored ad that appears in your audience's timeline just like other Facebook ads. However, the goal with lead ads is literally to capture the lead's info without them leaving Facebook. These ads don't link to a website landing page, creating an additional step.

Best social media marketing practices:
1. Assign daily responsibility for Facebook to a single person on your staff with an affinity for dialoguing.
2. Set expectations for how often they should post new content and how quickly they should respond to comments – usually within a couple hours.
3. Follow and like your followers when they seem to have a genuine interest in your area of health and wellness expertise.
4. Post on the walls of not only your own Facebook site, but also on your most active, influential posters with the largest networks.
5. Periodically post a request for your followers to "like" your page.
6. Monitor Facebook posts to your wall and respond every two hours throughout your business day.

We will use Facebook in the following ways to market our Human Resources

Consulting Service:
1. Promote our blog posts on our Facebook page
2. Post a video of our service people in action.
3. Make time-sensitive offers during slow periods
4. Create a special landing page for coupons or promotional giveaways
5. Create a Welcome tab to display a video message from our owner.
	Resource: Pagemodo.
6. Support a local charity by posting a link to their website.
7. Thank our clients while promoting their businesses at the same time.
8. Describe milestone accomplishments and thank clients for their role.
9. Give thanks to corporate accounts.
10. Ask clients to contribute stories about _____ occurrences.
11. Use the built-in Facebook polling application to solicit feedback.
12. Use the Facebook reviews page to feature positive comments from clients, and to respond to negative reviews.
13. Introduce clients to our staff with resume and video profiles.
14. Create a photo gallery of unusual ____ (requests/jobs?) to showcase our HR consulting expertise.

We will also explore location-based platforms like the following:
- FourSquare
- Facebook Places
- GoWalla
- Google Latitude

As a Human Resources Consulting Service serving a local business community, we will appreciate the potential for hyper-local platforms like these. Location-based applications are increasingly attracting young, urban influencers with disposable income, which is precisely the audience we are trying to attract. People connect to geo-location apps primarily to "get informed" about local happenings.

Foursquare.com
A web and mobile application that allows registered users to post their location at a venue ("check-in") and connect with friends. Check-in requires active user selection and points are awarded at check-in. Users can choose to have their check-ins posted on their accounts on Twitter, Facebook, or both. In version 1.3 of their iPhone application, foursquare enabled push-notification of friend updates, which they call "Pings". Users can also earn badges by checking in at locations with certain tags, for check-in frequency, or for other patterns such as time of check-in.]
Resource: https://foursquare.com/business/
https://support.foursquare.com/hc/en-us/articles/201065050-How-do-I-add-create-a-place-

Instagram
Instagram.com is an online photo-sharing, video-sharing and social networking service that enables its users to take pictures and videos, apply digital filters to them, and share them on a variety of social networking services, such as
Facebook, Twitter, Tumblr and Flickr. A distinctive feature is that it confines photos to a

square shape, similar to Kodak Instamatic and Polaroid images, in contrast to the 16:9 aspect ratio now typically used by mobile device cameras. Users are also able to record and share short videos lasting for up to 15 seconds.

Resources:

http://www.wordstream.com/blog/ws/2015/01/06/instagram-marketing

We will use Instagram in the following ways to help amplify the story of our brand, get people to engage with our content when not at our store, and get people to visit our store or site:

1. Let our clients and fans know about specific HR product availability.
2. Tie into trends, events or holidays to drive awareness.
3. Let people know we are open and our selection of HR consulting services is spectacular.
4. Run a monthly contest and pick the winning hash-tagged photograph to activate our client base and increase our exposure.
5. Encourage the posting and collection of happy onsite or offsite client photos.

Examples:

https://www.instagram.com/explore/locations/1015029571/bromelin-hr-consulting/

Note: Commonly found in tweets, a hashtag is a word or connected phrase (no spaces) that begins with a hash symbol (#). They're so popular that other social media platforms including Facebook, Instagram and Google+ now support them. Using a hashtag turns a word or phrase into a clickable link that displays a feed (list) of other posts with that same hashtag. For example, if you click on #_____ in a tweet, or enter #_____ in the search box, you'll see a list of tweets all about _____.

LinkedIn.com

This social media platform is a network that brings professionals, businesses and jobseekers together in one place. In fact, it is considered the core and central hub for anyone looking to hire or be hired. From easy-to-read resumes and work histories to accolades, LinkedIn is truly a goldmine for all HR teams and perfectly designed for headhunting and talent recruitment. The platform will also help our HR company to sort the wheat from the chaff, and find desirable candidates for all our clients' projects and network partners.

LinkedIn also ranks high in search engines and will provide a great platform for sending event updates to business associates. To optimize our LinkedIn profile, we will select one core keyword. We will use it frequently, without sacrificing consumer experience, to get our profile to skyrocket in the search engines. Linkedin provides options that will allow our detailed profile to be indexed by search engines, like Google. We will make use of these options so our business will achieve greater visibility on the Web. We will use widgets to integrate other tools, such as importing your blog entries or Twitter stream into your profile, and go market research and gain knowledge with Polls. We will answer questions in Questions and Answers to show our expertise, and ask questions in Questions and Answers to get a feel for what clients and prospects want or think. We will

publish our LinkedIn URL on all our marketing collateral, including business cards, email signature, newsletters, and web site. We will grow our network by joining industry and alumni groups related to our business. We will update our status examples of recent work, and link our status updates with our other social media accounts. We will start and manage a group or fan page for our product, brand or business. We will share useful articles that will be of interest to clients, and request LinkedIn recommendations from clients willing to provide testimonials. We will post our presentations on our profile using a presentation application. We will ask our first-level contacts for introductions to their contacts and interact with LinkedIn on a regular basis to reach those who may not see us on other social media sites. We will link to articles posted elsewhere, with a summary of why it's valuable to add to our credibility and list our newsletter subscription information and archives. We will post discounts and package deals. We will buy a LinkedIn direct ad that our target market will see. We will find vendors and contractors through connections.
Examples:
https://www.linkedin.com/title/human+resources+consultant
https://www.linkedin.com/company/human-resources-consulting-inc-/

Podcasting

Our podcasts will provide both information and advertising. Our podcasts will allow us to pull in a lot of clients. Our monthly podcasts will be heard by ___ (#) eventual subscribers. Podcasts can now be downloaded for mobile devices, such as an iPod. Podcasts will give our company a new way to provide information and an additional way to advertise. Podcasting will give our company another connection point with clients. We will use this medium to communicate on important HR issues, what is going on with a planned event or HR consulting service introduction, and other things of interest to our clients. The programs will last about 10 minutes and can be downloaded for free on iTunes. The purpose is not to be a mass medium. It is directed at a niche market with an above-average educational background and very special interests. It will provide a very direct and a reasonably inexpensive way of reaching our targeted audience.

Resources:
www.apple.com/itunes/download/
www.cbc.ca/podcasting/gettingstarted.html
www.bizjournals.com/southflorida/blog/2014/11/south-florida-entrepreneurs-how-
   podcasting-helped.html
http://www.smarttimeonline.com/category/podcast/

Examples:
https://blog.capterra.com/top-5-hr-podcasts/
http://inhisnamehr.com/category/podcasts/

Blogging

We will use our blog to keep clients and prospects informed about products, events and services that relate to our Human Resources Consulting business. Our blog will show readers that we are a good source of expert information that they can count on. With our blog, we can quickly update our clients anytime our company releases a new product or service. We will use our blog to share client testimonials and meaningful success stories. We will use the blog to supply advice on management challenges. Our visitors will be able to subscribe to our RSS feeds and be instantly updated without any spam filters interfering. We will also use the blog to solicit future service addition suggestions. We will use Real Simple Syndication (RSS) to automatically post all content posted on our website blog to our social media sites, such as Facebook and Twitter. Additionally, blogs are free and will allow for constant ease of updating.

Our blog will give our company the following benefits:
1. A cost-effective marketing tool.
2. An expanded network.
3. A promotional platform for new HR consulting services.
4. An introduction to people with similar interests.
5. Builds credibility and expertise recognition.

We will use our blog for the following purposes:
1. To share client testimonials, experiences and meaningful success stories.
2. Update our clients anytime our company releases a new service.
3. Supply advice on HR Management options.
4. Discuss research findings.
5. To publish helpful content.
6, To welcome feedback in multiple formats.
7. Link together other social networking sites, including Twitter.
8. To improve Google rankings.
9. Make use of automatic RSS feeds.

We will adhere to the following blog writing guidelines:
1. We will blog at least 2 or 3 times per week to maintain interest.
2. We will integrate our blog into the design of our website.
3. We will use our blog to convey useful information and not our advertisements.
4. We will make the content easy to understand.
5. We will focus our content on the needs of our targeted audience.

Our blog will feature the following on a regular basis:
1. Useful articles and assessment coupons.
2. Give away of a helpful free report in exchange for email addresses
3. Helpful information for our professional referral sources, as well as clients, and online and offline community members.
5. Use of a few social media outposts to educate, inform, engage and drive people back to our blog for more information and our free report.

To get visitors to our blog to take the next action step and contact our firm we will do the following:
1. Put a contact form on the upper-left hand corner of our blog, right below the

header.
2. Put our complete contact information in the header itself.
3. Add a page to our blog and title it, "Become My Client.", giving the reader somewhere to go for the next sign-up steps.
4. At the end of each blog post, we will clearly tell the reader what to do next; such as subscribe to our RSS feed, or to sign up for our newsletter mailing list.

Resources: www.blogger.com   www.blogspot.com
             www.wordpress.com   www.tumblr.com
             www.typepad.com
http://www.bloggersideas.com/tips-for-small-business-blogging-success/
http://www.blogwritersbootcamp.com/

Examples:
http://www.hrconsults.com/hr-insights/blog
http://jumpstart-hr.com/blog/
http://options4growth.net/options4growth-blog/

Become a Guest Blogger
We will become a guest blogger to help establish our expertise and visibility.
Example:
https://hrgirlfriends.com/submit-a-blog/

Twitter
We will use 'Twitter.com' as a way to produce new business from existing clients and generate prospective clients online. Twitter is a free social networking and micro-blogging service that allows its users to send and read other users' updates (otherwise known as tweets), which are text-based posts of up to 140 characters in length. Updates are displayed on the user's profile page and delivered to other users who have signed up to receive them. The sender can restrict delivery to those in his or her circle of friends, with delivery to everyone being the default. Users can receive updates via the Twitter website, SMS text messaging, RSS feeds, or email. Twitter will give us the ability to have ongoing two-way conversations with our clients, which will allow us to get better at what we do and offer, while giving us the ability to express our own unique 'personality'. We will use our Twitter account to respond directly to questions, distribute news, solve problems, post updates, circulate information about fundraisers, and offer special discounts, known as 'Tweet Deals', on selected products and services. Our posts on Twitter will include our URL (address), our new offers, process improvement tips and new service offerings. On a long-term basis, using Twitter consistently and efficiently will help push our website up the rankings on Google. The intangible, that will only have a positive effect, are the hundreds of impressions that each tweet will get, not to mention the positive statements that will be posted about our service, staff, selection and product knowledge. Using TweetReach, we expect our special promotional offers to receive thousands of impressions. We will also add our website, company logo, personal photo and/or blog on our profile page.

We will provide the following instructions to register as a 'Follower' of _____ (company name) on Twitter:
1. In your Twitter account, click on 'Find People' in the top right navigation bar, which will redirect to a new page.
2. Click on 'Find on Twitter' which will open a search box that says 'Who are you looking for?'
3. Type '_____ (company name) / _____ (owner name)' and click 'search'. This will bring up the results page.
4. Click the blue '_____' name to read the bio or select the 'Follow' button.

Examples:
https://twitter.com/day9consulting
https://twitter.com/kona_hr

Press Release Overview:
We will use market research surveys to determine the media outlets that our demographic clients read and then target them with press releases. We will draft a cover letter for our media kit that explains that we would like to have the newspaper print a story about the start-up of our new local HR consulting business or a milestone that we have accomplished. And, because news releases may be delivered by feeds or on news services and various websites, we will create links from our news releases to content on our website. These links which will point to more information or a special offer, will drive our clients into the sales process. They will also increase search engine ranking on our site. We will follow-up each faxed package to the media outlet with a phone call to the business section editor.

Media Kit
We will compile a media kit with the following items:
1. A pitch letter introducing our company and relevant impact newsworthiness for their readership.
2. A press release with helpful newsworthy story facts.
3. Biographical fact sheet or sketches of key personnel.
4. Listing of product and service features and benefits to clients.
5. Photos and digital logo graphics
6. Copies of media coverage already received.
7. Frequently Asked Questions (FAQ)
8. Client testimonials
9. Sales brochure
10. Media contact information
11. URL links to these online documents instead of email attachments.
12. Our blog URL address.

Public Relations Opportunities
The following represents a partial list of some of the reasons we will issue a free press release on a regular basis:

1. Announce Grand Opening Event and the availability of HR consulting services.
2. Planned Open House Event for new office opening.
3. Addition of new product releases or service line.
4. Support for a Non-profit Cause or other local event.
5. Presentation of a free HR training seminar or workshop.
6. Report Survey Results
7. Publication of an article on HR consulting trends.
8. Addition of a new staff member.
9. Notable Successes/Case Studies
10. Other Milestone Accomplishments.
11. New Niche Penetration Strategy

Examples:
https://www.hr.com/en/about_us/hr_com_press_releases/

We will use the following techniques to get our press releases into print:
1. Find the right contact editor at a publication, that is, the editor who specializes in human resources issues.
2. Understand the target publication's format, flavor and style and learn to think like its readers to better tailor our pitch.
3. Ask up front if the journalist is on deadline.
4. Request a copy of the editorial calendar--a listing of targeted articles or subjects broken down by month or issue date, to determine the issue best suited for the content of our news release or article.
5. Make certain the press release appeals to a large audience by reading a couple of back issues of the publication we are targeting to familiarize ourselves with its various sections and departments.
6. Customize the PR story to meet the magazine's particular style.
7. Avoid creating releases that look like advertising or self-promotion.
8. Make certain the release contains all the pertinent and accurate information the journalist will need to write the article and accurately answer the questions "who, what, when, why and where".
9. Include a contact name and telephone number for the reporter to call for more information.

PR Distribution Checklist
We will send copies of our press releases to the following entities:
1. Send it to clients to show accomplishments.
2. Send to prospects to help prospects better know who you are and what you do.
3. Send it to vendors to strengthen the relationship and to influence referrals.
4. Send it to strategic partners to strengthen and enhance the commitment and support to our firm.
5. Send it to employees to keep them in the loop.
6. Send it to Employees' contacts to increase the firm's visibility exponentially.
7. Send it to elected-officials who often provide direction for their constituents.
8. Send it to trade associations for maximum exposure.

9. Put copies in the lobby and waiting areas.
10. Put it on our Web site, to enable visitors to find out who we are and what our firm is doing, with the appropriate links to more detailed information.
11. Register the Web page with search engines to increase search engine optimization.
12. Put it in our press kit to provide members of the media background information about our firm.
13. Include it in our newsletter to enable easy access to details about company activities.
14. Include it in our brochure to provide information that compels the reader to contact our firm when in need of legal counsel.
15. Hand-it out at trade shows and job fairs to share news with attendees and establish credibility.

Media List

Journalist	Interests	Organization	Contact Info

Distribution:
www.1888PressRelease.com www.ecomwire.com
www.prweb.com www.WiredPRnews.com
www.PR.com www.eReleases.com
www.24-7PressRelease.com www.NewsWireToday.com
www.PRnewswire.com www.onlinePRnews.com
www.PRLog.org **www.onlinepressreleases.com**
www.businesswire.com www.marketwire.com
www.primezone.com www.primewswire.com
www.xpresspress.com/ www.ereleases.com/index.html
www.Mediapost.com www.digitaljournal.com
www.falkowinc.com/inc/proactive_report.html

Journalist Lists: www.mastheads.org www.easymedialist.com
www.helpareporter.com

Media Directories
Bacon's – www.bacons.com/ AScribe – www.ascribe.org/
Newspapers – www.newspapers.com/ Gebbie Press – www.gebbieinc.com/

Support Services
PR Web - http://www.prweb.com
Yahoo News – http://news.yahoo.com/
Google News – http://news.google.com/

Media Resource Expert

We will send email and mail to local media outlets, like our local TV news stations, Local Newspapers, and News Radio Stations, to advise them that we are a readily available resource for liquor store related new stories. We will include our areas of specialty, and how we can contribute to media stories about _____ and home tasting and cocktail parties in general. We will also indicate our willingness to share our

knowledge on how the public can prevent from being scammed by unethical
_____. We will always be on the look-out for opportunities to interview with local and national reporters. We will sign up for the following services that notify companies of reporters looking for interviews:

Reporter Connection	http://reporterconnection.com/
ProfNet Connection	http://www.profnetconnect.com/
Muck Rack	https://muckrack.com/benefits
News Wise	www.newswise.com/
Pitch Rate	http://pitchrate.com/
Experts	www.experts.com
News Basis	http://newsbasis.com/

Help A Reporter Out   www.helpareporter.com/
An online platform that provides journalists with a robust database of sources for upcoming stories. It also provides business owners and marketers with opportunities to serve as sources and secure valuable media coverage.

Resources:
http://www.thebuzzfactoree.com/journalists-seeking-sources/
http://ijnet.org/en/blog/5-ways-find-sources-online

Sample Letter Template:
http://locksmithprofits.com/locksmith-guest-expert-marketing/

Direct Mail/Postcards

As direct mail can be expensive to use, with a traditionally low response rate of 1 to 2%, we will only mail to a highly targeted list that we have created in-house, and not rented.

1. We will send a letter of announcement and a sales brochure to all existing contacts and clients.
2. We will use personalized postcards to stay-in-touch with prior clients.
3. Postcards will offer cheaper mailing rates, staying power and attention-grabbing graphics, but require repetition, like most other advertising methods.
4. We will develop an in-house list of potential clients for routine communications from open house events, seminar registrations, direct response ads, etc.
5. We will use postcards to encourage users to visit our website, and take advantage of a special offer.
6. We will grab attention and communicate a single-focus message in just a few words.
7. The visual elements of our postcard (color, picture, symbol) will be strong to help get attention and be directly supportive of the message.
8. We will facilitate a call to immediate action by prominently displaying our phone number and website address.
9. We will include a clear deadline, expiration date, limited quantity, or consequence of inaction that is connected to the offer to communicate immediacy

and increase response.
Resource:
www.Postcardmania.com

Tear-off Flyers

We will print fliers with a more complete description of the Human Resources Consulting Services we offer and pass them out to businesses in the more affluent local areas. We will also do the following with our flyers:

1. We will seek permission to post flyers on the bulletin boards in local businesses, community centers, libraries and medical practices.
2. We will also insert flyers into our direct mailings.
3. We will use our flyers as part of a handout package at open house events.
4. We will print flyers with discount coupons with expiration dates to motivate interest and track response rates.
5. We will list all the services we offer, along with the benefits to be realized from those services to help prospects to understand what they need and decide what they want.

Resources:
www.mycreativeshop.com/hr-consulting-flyer-template.aspx
www.stocklayouts.com/Templates/Flyer/Professional-Services/Human-Resources/Template-Design-Library.aspx

Cold Calling

To succeed in cold calling, we will develop techniques for getting to the decision-makers. The key will be to research carefully the power structure of the organization, and get that appointment. We will prepare by practicing and harnessing our sales pitch and improving our closing techniques.

Resources:
http://www.recruitingblogs.com/profiles/blogs/the-secret-to-cold-calling
https://salesscripter.com/cold-calling-sample/

Public Speaking Engagements

As a Human Resources Consulting expert, we will need to be visible talking about our field of expertise. Public speaking will provide an excellent opportunity to present our expertise to an interested audience. We will volunteer to share our knowledge in forums held at public libraries. We will also contact organizations and clubs in our area to offer our expertise. We will build an impressive resume to get an agent to look for possible speaking engagements. We will use speaking engagements as opportunities establish our area of expertise and credibility, generate leads, network and exchange ideas with new people. We will draft and circulate articles based on our speeches and post them to our website. We will also create audio and video offerings from our speech presentations.

Our speaking engagement will embody the following qualities:

1. Enthusiasm
2. Expert Knowledge
3. Sharing of extensive experience and resulting insights.
4. Entertaining with humor and creativity of presentation methods.
5. Motivational and Inspirational

We will develop at least one core presentation and adapt it to each audience. We will consider a "problem/solution" format where we describe a challenge and tell how our expertise achieved an exceptional solution. We will use speaking engagements as an opportunity to expose our areas of expertise to prospective clients. By speaking at conferences and forums put together by professional and industry trade groups, we will increase our firm's visibility, and consequently, its prospects for attracting new business. Public speaking will give us a special status, and make it easier for our speakers to meet prospects. Attendees expect speakers to reach out to the audience, which gives speakers respect and credibility. We will identify speaking opportunities that will let us reach our targeted audience. We will designate a person who is responsible for developing relationships with event and industry associations, submitting proposals and, most importantly, staying in touch with contacts. We will tailor our proposals to the event organizers' preferences.

Example of Speaker Proposal:
https://hrgirlfriends.com/become-a-speaker/

Speaking Proposal Package:
1. Speech Topic/Agenda/Synopsis
2. Target Audience: Community and Civic Groups
3. Speaker Biography
4. List of previous speaking engagements
5. Previous engagement evaluations

Possible Targets:
1.	Trade Organizations	2.	Business Expos
4.	Chamber of Commerce	5.	JCC's
6.	Support Groups	8.	Corporations
9.	Booking Agents	10.	Business Owners
11.	Entrepreneur Groups	12.	Industry Associations
13.	Professional Associations	14.	Angel Investors Groups
15.	Venture Capitalists		

Possible Speech Topics:
1. How to Write Winning Proposals
2. How to Improve Your HR Management Skills
3. Strategies for Valuing HR Consulting Services
4. Proven Methods to Run Successful Retail Training Programs.
5. Seizing Globalization Outsourcing Opportunities.
6. The Importance of Doing Background Checks on Staff and Vendors

7. How to Prevent Financial Fraud.
8. What is Knowledge Management and Why is it So Important?
9. Top 10 Proven Creative Team Building Methods
10. What is HR Process Improvement and What Can It Achieve?

Speech Tracking Form

Group/Class	Subject/Topic	Business Development Potential	Resources Needed	Target Date

We will use the following techniques to leverage the business development impact of our speaking engagements:

1. Send out press releases to local papers announcing the upcoming speech. We will get great free publicity by sending the topic and highlights of the talk to the newspaper.
2. Produce a flyer with our picture on it, and distribute it to our network.
3. Send publicity materials to our prospects inviting them to attend our presentation.
4. Whenever possible, get a list of attendees before the event. Contact them and introduce yourself before the talk to build rapport with your audience. Arrive early and don't leave immediately after your presentation.
5. Always give out handouts and a business card. Include marketing materials and something of value to the recipient, so that it will be retained and not just tossed away. You might include tips or secrets you share in your talk.
6. Give out an evaluation form to all participants. This form should request names and contact information. Offer a free consultation if it's appropriate. Follow up within 72 hours with any members of the audience who could become ideal clients.
7. Have a place on the form where participants can list other groups that might need speakers, along with the name of the program chairperson or other contact person.
8. Offer a door prize as incentive for handing in the evaluation. When you have collected all the evaluations, you can select a winner of the prize.
9. Meet with audience members, answer their questions and listen to their concerns. Stay after your talk and mingle with the audience. Answer any questions that come up and offer follow-up conversations for additional support.
10. Request a free ad in the group's newsletter in exchange for your speech.
11. Send a thank-you note to the person who invited you to speak. Include copies of some of the evaluations to show how useful it was.

Speaking Engagement Package

1. Video or DVD of prior presentation.
2. Session Description
3. Learning Objectives
4. Takeaway Message
5. Speaking experience
6. Letters of recommendation
7. General Biography
8. Introduction Biography

Resource:
www.toastmasters.com
www.nationalspeakers.com

Webinars

A webinar is a presentation, lecture, workshop or seminar that is transmitted over the Web. A key feature of a Webinar is its interactive elements -- the ability to give, receive and discuss information. Webinars will be used as an effective vehicle for communicating a message, building awareness and buy-in about a particular topic, and offering an interactive educational experience.

Our Webinars will be educational in nature and allow our HR consultancy to demonstrate the value of our Human Resources Consulting Service expertise, directly to prospects or existing clients without spending money to meet with them. Webinars allow prospects to listen to experts discuss uses, benefits and demand for certain HR products and consulting services while gleaning insights about the unique benefits businesses provide. Webinars, like other forms of content marketing, should convey succinct messages and focus on one topic of interest. Webinars tend to run an hour, including Q&A time. Webinars are generally in the form of slide decks. While webinar marketing is a great tool for lead generation, the webinars, themselves, must be informative and cater to the learning needs of clients or prospects. Pairing webinars with blog posts and other website content, as well as placing calls to action at the end of the presentations, can direct prospects through conversion funnels.

Sample Webinar
Title: How to Evaluate the Quality of a Human Resources Consulting Service
As a result of the webinar participants will be able to:
                              Develop In-house Training Programs
Prerequisite: None
Target Audience: Start-up and Mid-Sized Business Owners
Resources: www.gotomeeting.com/fec/webinar/secure_webinar_software
            www.webex.com/WebEx-Meetings-Purchase-FAQ.html?TrackID=
            1030070&hbxref=&goid=webex-meetings-FAQ

Books and Articles

Getting published will greatly help our company to establish a reputation for excellence in our field. We will contact editors of both print and online publications in our field, and pitch story ideas to them. We will seek to submit regular articles, or even start a business journal column. Becoming an author of a book will make it easier to establish our HR credentials and secure new clients for our consulting business.

Google Maps

We will first make certain that our business is listed in Google Maps. We will do a search for our business in Google Maps. If we don't see our business listed, then we will add our business to Google Maps. Even if our business is listed in Google Maps, we will create a Local Business Center account and take control of our listing, by adding more relevant information. Consumers generally go to Google Maps for two reasons: Driving Directions and to Find a Business.

Resource: http://maps.google.com/

Bing Maps   www.bingplaces.com/
This will make it easy for clients to find our business.

Apple Maps
A web mapping service developed by Apple Inc. It is the default map system of iOS, macOS, and watchOS. It provides directions and estimated times of arrival for automobile, pedestrian, and public transportation navigation.
Resources:
ttps://mapsconnect.apple.com
 http://www.stallcupgroup.com/2012/09/19/three-ways-to-make-your-pawn-business-more-profitable-and-sellable/
http://www.apple.com/ios/maps/
https://en.wikipedia.org/wiki/Apple_Maps

Google Places
Google Places helps people make more informed decisions about where to go for professional Human Resources Consulting Services. Place Pages connect people to information from the best sources across the web, displaying photos, reviews and essential facts, as well as real-time updates and offers from business owners. We will make sure that our Google Places listing is up to date to increase our online visibility. Google Places is linked to our Google Maps listing, and will help to get on the first page of Google search page results when people search for a Human Resources Consulting in our area.
Resource: www.google/com/places

Yelp.com
We will use Yelp.com to help people find our local business. Visitors to Yelp write local reviews, over 85% of them rating a business 3 stars or higher In addition to reviews, visitors can use Yelp to find events, special offers, lists and to talk with other Yelpers. As business owners, we will setup a free account to post offers, photos and message our clients. We will also buy ads on Yelp, which will be clearly labeled "Sponsored Results". We will also use the Weekly Yelp, which is available in 42 city editions to bring news about the latest business openings and other happenings.
Examples:
http://www.yelp.com/biz/steinhart-human-resources-consulting-atherton

Manta.com
Manta is the largest free source of information on small companies, with profiles of more than 64 million businesses and organizations. Business owners and sales professionals use Manta's vast database and custom search capabilities to quickly find companies, easily connect with prospective clients and promote their own services. Manta.com, founded in 2005, is based in Columbus, Ohio.
Examples:

manta.com/mb_55_A62E605K_3BR/human_resource_consulting_services/tampa_fl

Pay-Per-Click Advertising

Google AdWords, Yahoo! Search Marketing, and Microsoft adCenter are the three largest network operators, and all three operate under a bid-based model. Cost per click (CPC) varies depending on the search engine and the level of competition for a particular keyword. Google AdWords are small text ads that appear next to the search results on Google. In addition, these ads appear on many partner web sites, including NYTimes.com (The New York Times), Business.com, Weather.com, About.com, and many more. Google's text advertisements are short, consisting of one title line and two content text lines. Image ads can be one of several different Interactive Advertising Bureau (IAB) standard sizes.

Through Google AdWords, we plan to buy placements (ads) for specific search terms through this "Pay-Per-Click" advertising program. This PPC advertising campaign will allow our ad to appear when someone searches for a keyword related to our business, organization, or subject matter. More importantly, we will only pay when a potential client clicks on our ad to visit our website. For instance, since we operate a Human Resources Consulting Service in ___ (city), _____ (state), we will target people using search terms such as "HR management consultant, personnel development, HR project management, leadership development and staff assessments, in ____ (city), ____ (state)". With an effective PPC campaign our ads will only be displayed when a user searches for one of these keywords. In short, PPC advertising will be the most cost-effective and measurable form of advertising for our Human Resources Consulting Service.
Resources:
http://adwords.google.com/support/aw/?hl=en
www.wordtracker.com
http://www.google.com/support/analytics/
http://www.wordstream.com/local-online-marketing
https://www.wordstream.com/keywords
https://adwords.google.com/KeywordPlanner

Yahoo Local Listings

We will create our own local listing on Yahoo. To create our free listing, we will use our web browser and navigate to http://local.yahoo.com. We will first register for free with Yahoo, and create a member ID and password to list our business. Once we have accessed http://local.yahoo.com, we will scroll down to the bottom and click on "Add/Edit a Business" to get onto the Yahoo Search Marketing Local Listings page. In the lower right of the screen we will see "Local Basic Listings FREE". We will click on the Get Started button and log in again with our new Yahoo ID and password. The form for our local business listing will now be displayed. When filling it out, we will be sure to include our full web address (http://www.companyname.com). We will include a description of our Human Resources Consulting Services in the description section, but avoid hype or blatant advertising, to get the listing to pass Yahoo's editorial review. We will also be sure to select the appropriate business category and sub categories.

Examples:
https://local.yahoo.com/info-193179780-bluefire-hr-consulting-llc-chicago?csz=Chicago%2C+IL&stx=Talent+Agencies

Sales Reps

_____ (company name) will use independent commissioned sales reps to penetrate markets outside of _____ (city/state). Management will work to keep in constant communication with the sales reps to ensure that their service is professional and timely. Independent sales representatives provide the best mode for distribution in order to maintain pricing controls and higher margins. Independent sales reps are not full-time employees, thus benefits are not necessary. Independent sales reps receive a flat commission based on gross sales. Our sales reps are set at a commission rate of __ (15?) % of gross sales. The average sales rep can service up to __ (#) accounts with the average location generating around $____ per year. In addition to field calls, sales reps will represent the product line at all regional tradeshows, with the marketing director attending all national tradeshows.

Examples:
https://www.indeed.com/q-HR-Solutions-Sales-Representative-jobs.html

Advertorials

An advertorial is an advertisement written in the form of an objective article, and presented in a printed publication—usually designed to look like a legitimate and independent news story. We will use quotes as testimonials to back up certain claims throughout our copy and break-up copy with subheadings to make the material more reader-friendly. We will include the "call to action" and contact information with a 24/7 voicemail number and a discount coupon. The advertorial will have a short intro about a client's experience with our Human Resources Consulting Services and include quotes, facts, and statistics. We will present helpful information about HR project planning.

Affiliate Marketing

We will create an affiliate marketing program to broaden our reach. We will first devise a commission structure, so affiliates have a reason to promote our business. We will give them ___ (10) % of whatever sales they generate. We will go after business bloggers or webmasters who get a lot of web traffic for our keywords. These companies would then promote our HR products and consulting services, and they would earn commissions for the sales they generated. We will work with the following services to handle the technical aspects of our program.

ConnectCommerce	https://www.connectcommerce.com/
Commission Junction	https://members.cj.com
ShareASale	http://www.shareasale.com/
Share Results	
LinkShare	https://cli.linksynergy.com/cli/publisher/registration/
Affiliate Scout	http://affiliatescout.com/
Affiliate Seeking	http://www.affiliateseeking.com/
Clix Galore	http://www.clixgalore.com/

Resources:
https://www.affilorama.com/
www.godaddy.com/garage/smallbusiness/market/share-love-create-affiliate-program/
www.google.com/affiliatenetwork/ntn.html?advid=223777

Examples:
www.operationsinc.com/about-us/human-resources-consulting-network/human-resources-consulting-partner-network/

HotFrog.com
HotFrog is a fast-growing free online business directory listing over 6.6 million US businesses. HotFrog now has local versions in 34 countries worldwide.
Anyone can list their business in HotFrog for free, along with contact details, and products and services. Listing in HotFrog directs sales leads and enquiries to your business. Businesses are encouraged to add any latest news and information about their products and services to their listing. HotFrog is indexed by Google and other search engines, meaning that clients can find your HotFrog listing when they use Google, Yahoo! or other search engines.
Resource:
http://www.hotfrog.com/AddYourBusiness.aspx

Local.com
Local.com owns and operates a leading local search site and network in the United States. Its mission is to be the leader at enabling local businesses and consumers to find each other and connect. To do so, the company uses patented and proprietary technologies to provide over 20 million consumers each month with relevant search results for local businesses, products and services on Local.com and more than 1,000 partner sites. Local.com powers more than 100,000 local websites. Tens of thousands of small business clients use Local.com products and services to reach consumers using a variety of subscription, performance and display advertising and website products.
Resource:
http://corporate.local.com/mk/get/advertising-opportunities

Autoresponder
An autoresponder is an online tool that will automatically manage our mailing list and send out emails to our clients at preset intervals. We will write a short article that is helpful to potential Human Resources Consulting clients. We will load this article into our autoresponder. We will let people know of the availability of our article by posting to newsgroups, forums, social networking sites etc. We will list our autoresponder email address at the end of the posting, so they can send a blank email to our autoresponder to receive our article and be added to our mailing list. We will then email them at the interval of our choosing with special offers. We will load the messages into our autoresponder and set a time interval for the messages to be mailed out.
Resource:

www.aweber.com

Database Marketing

Database marketing is a form of direct marketing using databases of clients or prospects to generate personalized communications in order to promote a product or service for marketing purposes. The method of communication can be any addressable medium, as in direct marketing. With database marketing tools, we will be able to implement client nurturing, which is a tactic that attempts to communicate with each client or prospect at the right time, using the right information to meet that client's need to progress through the process of identifying a problem, learning options available to resolve it, selecting the right solution, and making the purchasing decision. We will use our databases to learn more about clients, select target markets for specific campaigns, through client segmentation, compare clients' value to the company, and provide more specialized offerings for clients based on their transaction histories, demographic profile and surveyed needs and wants. This database will give us the capability to automate regular promotional mailings, to semi-automate the telephone outreach process, and to prioritize prospects as to interests, timing, and other notable delineators. The objective is to arrange for first meetings, which are meant to be informal introductions, and valuable fact-finding and needs-assessment events.

We will use sign-in sheets, coupons, surveys and newsletter subscriptions to collect the following information from our clients:
1. Name
2. Telephone Number
3. Email Address
4. Address
5. Birth Date
6. Industry SIC

We will utilize the following types of contact management software to generate leads and stay in touch with clients to produce repeat business and referrals:
1. Act — www.act.com
2. Front Range Solutions — www.frontrange.com
3. The Turning Point — www.turningpoint.com
4. Acxiom — www.acxiom.com/products_and_services/

We will utilize contact management software, such as ACT and Goldmine, to track the following:
1. Dates for follow-ups.
2. Documentation of prospect concerns, objections or comments.
3. Referral source.
4. Marketing Materials sent.
5. Log of contact dates and methods of contact.
6. Ultimate disposition.

Cause Marketing

Cause marketing or cause-related marketing refers to a type of marketing involving the cooperative efforts of a "for profit" business and a non-profit organization for mutual benefit. The possible benefits of cause marketing for business include positive public relations, improved client relations, and additional marketing opportunities.

Cause marketing sponsorship by American businesses is rising at a dramatic rate, because clients, employees and stakeholders prefer to be associated with a company that is considered socially responsible. Our business objective will be to generate highly cost-effective public relations and media coverage for the launch of a marketing campaign focused on _____ (type of cause), with the help of the _____ (non-profit organization name) organization.

Resources:
www.causemarketingforum.com/
www.cancer.org/AboutUs/HowWeHelpYou/acs-cause-marketing

Courtesy Advertising

We will engage in courtesy advertising, which refers to a company or corporation "buying" an advertisement in a nonprofit dinner program, event brochure, and the like. Our company will gain visibility this way while the nonprofit organization may treat the advertisement revenue as a donation. We will specifically advertise in the following non-profit programs, newsletters, bulletins and event brochures: _____

Speaking Engagements

We will consider a "problem/solution" format where we describe a challenge and tell how our HR expertise achieved an exceptional solution. We will use speaking engagements as an opportunity to expose our areas of expertise to prospective clients. By speaking at conferences and forums put together by professional and industry trade groups, we will increase our firm's visibility, and consequently, its prospects for attracting new business. Public speaking will give us a special status, and make it easier for our speakers to meet prospects. Attendees expect speakers to reach out to the audience, which gives speakers respect and credibility. We will identify speaking opportunities that will let us reach our targeted audience. We will designate a person who is responsible for developing relationships with event and industry associations, submitting proposals and, most importantly, staying in touch with contacts. We will tailor our proposals to the event organizers' preferences.

Examples:
http://www.silvershr.com/hr-keynote-speaker/

Speaking Proposal Package:
1. Speech Topic/Agenda/Synopsis
2. Target Audience: Community and Civic Groups
3. Speaker Biography
4. List of previous speaking engagements
5. Previous engagement evaluations

Possible Targets:
1. Entrepreneurs
2. Small Business Startups

3. Venture Capitalists
4. Non-profits
5. Investment Clubs
6. Chamber of Commerce Members

Possible Speech Topics:
1. How to Manage HR Software Development and Implementation
2. How to Evaluate the Services of a Human Resources Consulting Service
3. How to Reduce HR Operating Expenses in Recessionary Times
4. How to Manage an Overseas Recruiting Strategy
5. New HR Project Management Tools

Speech Tracking Form

Group/Class	Subject/Topic	Business Development Potential	Resources Needed	Target Date

We will use the following techniques to leverage the business development impact of our speaking engagements:

1. Send out press releases to local papers announcing the upcoming speech. We will get great free publicity by sending the topic and highlights of the talk to the newspaper.
2. Produce a flyer with our picture on it, and distribute it to our network.
3. Send publicity materials to our prospects inviting them to attend our presentation.
4. Whenever possible, get a list of attendees before the event. Contact them and introduce yourself before the talk to build rapport with your audience. Arrive early and don't leave immediately after your presentation.
5. Always give out handouts and a business card. Include marketing materials and something of value to the recipient, so that it will be retained and not just tossed away. You might include tips or secrets you share in your talk.
6. Give out an evaluation form to all participants. This form should request names and contact information. Offer a free consultation if it's appropriate. Follow up within 72 hours with any members of the audience who could become ideal clients.
7. Have a place on the form where participants can list other groups that might need speakers, along with the name of the program chairperson or other contact person.
8. Offer a door prize as incentive for handing in the evaluation. When you have collected all of the evaluations, you can select a winner of the prize.
9. Meet with audience members, answer their questions and listen to their concerns. Stay after your talk and mingle with the audience. Answer any questions that come up and offer follow-up conversations for additional support.
10. Request a free ad in the group's newsletter in exchange for your speech.
11. Send a thank-you note to the person who invited you to speak. Include copies of some of the evaluations to show how useful it was.

Speaking Engagement Package
1. Video or DVD of prior presentation.
2. Session Description

3. Learning Objectives
4. Takeaway Message
5. Speaking experience
6. Letters of recommendation
7. General Biography
8. Introduction Biography

Resources:
www.toastmasters.com
www.nationalspeakers.com

Meet-up Groups

We will form a meet-up group to encourage people to participate in our HR audit programs.

Resource:
http://www.meetup.com/create/

Examples:
www.meetup.com/topics/human-resource-consultants/
www.meetup.com/topics/human-resources-and-team-building/
www.meetup.com/topics/networking-with-hr-professionals/

Marketing Associations/Groups

We will set up a marketing association comprised of complementary businesses. We will market our Human Resources Consulting Service as a member of a group of complementary companies. Our marketing group will include a lawyer, an accountant, and an insurance broker. Any business that provides business services will be a likely candidate for being a member of our marketing group. The group will joint advertise, distribute joint promotional materials, exchange mailing lists, and develop a group website. The obvious benefit is that we will increase our marketing effectiveness by extending our reach.

BBB Accreditation

We will apply for BBB Accreditation to improve our perceived trustworthiness. BBB determines that a company meets BBB accreditation standards, which include a commitment to make a good faith effort to resolve any consumer complaints. BBB Accredited Businesses pay a fee for accreditation review/monitoring and for support of BBB services to the public. BBB accreditation does not mean that the business' products or services have been evaluated or endorsed by BBB, or that BBB has made a determination as to the business' product quality or competency in performing services. We will place the BBB Accreditation Logo in all of our ads.

Examples:
www.bbb.org/sdoc/business-reviews/human-resources/san-diego-employers-association-in-san-diego-ca-100197/

Sponsor Events

The sponsoring of events, such as HR Conferences and golf tournaments, will allow our company to engage in what is known as experiential marketing, which is the idea that the best way to deepen the emotional bond between a company and its clients is by creating a

memorable and interactive experience. We will ask for the opportunity to prominently display our company signage and the set-up of a booth from which to handout sample products and sales literature. We will also seek to capitalize on networking, speech giving and workshop presenting opportunities.
Examples:
http://www.kmaconsultingllc.com/category/events-sponsorships/
Resource:
https://www.cwcg.org/sponsorship

Sponsorships
We will sponsor a local team, such as our child's little league baseball team, the local soccer club or a bowling group. We will then place our company name on the uniforms or shirts in exchange for providing the equipment and/or uniforms.

Patch.com
A community-specific news and information platform dedicated to providing comprehensive and trusted local coverage for individual towns and communities. Patch makes it easy to: Keep up with news and events, Look at photos and videos from around town, Learn about local businesses, Participate in discussions and Submit announcements, photos, and reviews.
Examples:
https://patch.com/connecticut/norwalk/hr-consulting-firm-expands-hiring-trumbull-resident

Mobile iPhone Apps
We will use new distribution tools like the iPhone App Store to give us unprecedented direct access to consumers, without the need to necessarily buy actual mobile *ads* to reach people. Thanks to Apple's iPhone and the App Store, we will be able to make cool mobile apps that may generate as much goodwill and purchase intent as a banner ad. We will research Mobile Application Development, which is the process by which application software is developed for small low-power handheld devices, such as personal digital assistants, enterprise digital assistants or mobile phones. These applications are either pre-installed on phones during manufacture, or downloaded by clients from various mobile software distribution platforms. iPhone apps make good marketing tools. The bottom line is iPhones and smartphones sales are continually growing, and people are going to their phones for information. Apps will definitely be a lead generation tool because it gives potential clients easy access to our contact and business information and the ability to call for more information while they are still "hot". Our apps will contain: directory of staffers, publications on relevant issues, office location, videos, etc.

We will especially focus on the development of apps that can accomplish the following:
1. **Mobile Reservations:** Clients can use this app to access mobile reservations linked directly to your in-house calendar. They can browse open slots and book appointments easily, while on the go.

2. **Appointment Reminders:** You can send current clients reminders of regular or special appointments through your mobile app to increase your yearly revenue per client.
3. **Style Libraries**
   Offer a style library in your app to help clients to pick out a ____ (report) style. Using a simple photo gallery, you can collect photos of various styles, and have clients browse and select specific report formats.
4. **Client Photos**
   Your app can also have a feature that lets clients take photos and email them to you. This is great for creating a database of client photos for testimonial purposes, advertising, or just easy reference.
5. **Special Offers**
   Push notifications allow you to drive activity on special promotions, deals, events, and offers. If you ever need to generate revenue during a down time, push notifications allow you to generate interest easily and proactively.
6. **Loyalty Programs**
   A mobile app allows you to offer a mobile loyalty program (buy ten ____, get one free, etc.). You won't need to print up cards or track anything manually – it's all done simply through users' mobile devices.
7. **Referrals**
   A mobile app can make referrals easy. With a single click, a user can post to a social media account on Facebook or Twitter about their experience with your business. This allows you to earn new business organically through the networks of existing clients.
8. **Product Sales**
   You can sell _____ products through your mobile app. Clients can browse products, submit orders, and make payments easily, helping you open up a new revenue stream.

Resources: http://www.apple.com/iphone/apps-for-iphone/
http://iphoneapplicationlist.com/apps/business/
Software Development: http://www.mutualmobile.com/
http://www.avenuesocial.com/mob-app.php#
http://www.biznessapps.com/

HR App Directories:
www.softwareadvice.com/hr/mobile-app-comparison/
www.shrm.org/resourcesandtools/hr-topics/technology/pages/hrapps.aspx

Transit Ads

According to the Metropolitan Transportation Authority, MTA subways, buses and railroads provide billions of trips each year to residents. Marketing our Human Resources Consulting Service in subway cars and on the walls of subway stations will be a great way to advertise our business to a large, captive audience.

Restroom billboard advertising (Bathroom Advertising)

We will target a captive audience by placing restroom billboard advertising in select high-traffic venues with targeted demographics. A simple, framed ad on the inside of a bathroom stall door or above a urinal gets at least a minute of viewing, according to several studies. The stall door ads are a good choice for venues with shorter waiting times, such as small businesses, while large wall posters are well-suited to airports or movie theatres where people are more likely to be standing in line near the entrance or exit. Many new restroom based ad agencies that's specialize in restroom advertisement have also come about, such as; Zoom Media, BillBoardZ , Flush Media , Jonny Advertising, Insite Advertising, Inc, Wall AG USA, ADpower, NextMedia, and Alive Promo (American Restroom Association, 9/24/2009).
Resources:
http://www.indooradvertising.org/
http://www.stallmall.com/
http://www.zoommedia.com/

Tumblr.com
Tumblr will allow us to effortlessly share anything. We will be able to post text, photos, quotes, links, music, and videos, from our browser, phone, desktop, email, or wherever we happen to be. We will be able to customize everything, from colors, to our theme's HTML.
Examples:
https://www.tumblr.com/search/human%20resources%20consultants

thumbtack.com
A directory for finding and booking trustworthy local services, which is free to consumers.
Resource:	www.thumbtack.com/postservice
Examples:	www.thumbtack.com/nv/las-vegas/human-resources-services/

Publish e-Book
Ebooks are electronic books which can be downloaded from any website or FTP site on the Internet. Ebooks are made using special software and can include a wide variety of media such as HTML, graphics, Flash animation and video. We will publish an e-book to establish our Human Resources Consulting expertise, and reach people who are searching for ebooks on how to make better use our products and/or services. Included in our ebook will be links back to our website, product or affiliate program. Because users will have permanent access to it, they will use our ebook again and again, constantly seeing a link or banner which directs them to our site. The real power behind ebook marketing will be the viral aspect of it and the free traffic it helps to build for our website. ebook directories include:
	www.e-booksdirectory.com/
	www.ebookfreeway.com/p-ebook-directory-list.html
	www.quantumseolabs.com/blog/seolinkbuilding/top-5-free-ebook-directories-subscribers/
Resources:
www.free-ebooks.net/

http://successinhr.com/write-your-own-hr-book-fast

e-books are available from the following sites:
- Amazon.com
- Lulu.com
- BarnesandNoble.com
- AuthorHouse.com
- Createspace.com
- Kobobooks.com
- Scribd.com

Resource:
www.smartpassiveincome.com/ebooks-the-smart-way/

Business Card Exchanges

We will join our Chamber of Commerce or local retail merchants' association and volunteer to host a mixer or business card exchange. We will take the opportunity to invite social and business groups to our offices to enjoy wine tastings, and market to local businesses. We will also build our email database by collecting the business cards of all attendees.

Hubpages.com

HubPages has easy-to-use publishing tools, a vibrant author community and underlying revenue-maximizing infrastructure. Hubbers (HubPages authors) earn money by publishing their Hubs (content-rich Internet pages) on topics they know and love, and earn recognition among fellow Hubbers through the community-wide HubScore ranking system. The HubPages ecosystem provides a search-friendly infrastructure which drives traffic to Hubs from search engines such as Google and Yahoo, and enables Hubbers to earn revenue from industry-standard advertising vehicles such as Google AdSense and the eBay and Amazon Affiliates program. All of this is provided free to Hubbers in an open online community.

Resources:
http://hubpages.crabbysbeach.com/blogs/
http://hubpages.com/learningcenter/contents

Examples:
https://hubpages.com/business/How-To-Work-For-A-Company-That-Does-Not-Share-Your-Values

Pinterest.com

The goal of this website is to connect everyone in the world through the 'things' they find interesting. They think that a favorite book, toy, or recipe can reveal a common link between two people. With millions of new pins added every week, Pinterest is connecting people all over the world based on shared tastes and interests. What's special about Pinterest is that the boards are all visual, which is a very important marketing plus. When users enter a URL, they select a picture from the site to pin to their board. People spend hours pinning their own content, and then finding content on other people's boards to "re-pin" to their own boards. We will use Pinterest for remote personal shopping appointments. When we have a client with specific needs, we will create a board just for them with items we sell that would meet their needs, along with links to other tips and

content. We will invite our client to check out the board on Pinterest, and let them know we created it just for them.
Examples:
https://www.pinterest.com/hradvisorsinc/human-resources-consultant/

Pinterest usage recommendation include:
1. Conduct market research by showing photos of potential products or test launches, asking the client base for feedback.
2. Personalize the brand by showcasing style and what makes the brand different, highlighting new and exciting things through the use of imagery.
3. Add links from Pinterest photos to the company webstore, putting price banners on each photo and providing a link where users can buy the products directly.
4. Share high-quality pictures or property images and put links back to our blog/website.
5. Make Boards interesting with product label photos.
6. Showcase beautiful pictures of homes listed and include a link back to our website or blog.
7. Focus on educating followers and sharing what they would like to see, like images from a _____ company and _____ websites.
8. Ask happy clients to pin pictures of themselves in their new _____ (offices).
9. We will create a video and add a Call to Action in the description or use annotations, such as check my YouTube article, for the viewers to Pin videos or follow our Pins on Pinterest.
10. Encourage followers' engagement with a call to action, because 'likes', _____ questions, comments and 'repins' will help our pins get more authority and visibility.
11. Optimize descriptions with keywords that people might be looking for when searching Pinterest, as we can add as many hashtags as we want.
12. Be consistent by pinning regularly.
13. Let people know we are on Pinterest by adding "Pin it" and "follow" buttons to our blog and/or website.

Resources:
www.copyblogger.com/pinterest-marketing/
www.shopify.com/infographics/pinterest
www.pinterest.com/brettcarneiro/ecommerce/
www.cio.com/article/3018852/e-commerce/how-to-use-pinterest-to-grow-your-business.html

Topix.com
Topix is the world's largest community news website. Users can read, talk about and edit the news on over 360,000 of our news pages. Topix is also a place for users to post their own news stories, as well as comment about stories they have seen on the Topix site. Each story and every Topix page comes with the ability to add your voice to the conversation.
Examples:

http://www.topix.com/forum/business/human-resources

Survey Marketing

We will conduct a door-to-door survey of businesses in our target area to illicit opinions to our proposed business. This will provide valuable feedback, lead to prospective clients and serve to introduce our Human Resources Consulting Service business, before we begin actual operations. We will also survey our potential market beforehand so that we can establish what our clients are missing in their current HR management needs. We will want to know what they want in terms of special HR products and consulting services, and give it to them.

'Green' Marketing

We will target environmentally friendly clients to introduce new clients to our business and help spread the word about going "green". We will use the following 'green' marketing strategies to form an emotional bond with our clients:

1. We will use clearly labeled 'Recycled Paper' and Sustainable Packaging, such as receipts and storage containers.
2. We will use "green", non-toxic cleaning supplies.
3. We will install 'green' lighting and heating systems to be more eco-friendly.
4. We will use web-based Electronic Mail and Social Media instead of using paper advertisements.
5. We will find local suppliers to minimize the carbon footprint that it takes for deliveries.
6. We will use products that are made with organic ingredients and supplies.
7. We will document our 'Green' Programs in our sales brochure and website.
8. We will be a Certified Energy Star Partner.
9. We will install new LED warehouse lighting, exit signs, and emergency signs.
10. We will install motion detectors in low-traffic areas both inside and outside of warehouses.
11. We will implement new electricity regulators on HVAC units and compressors to lower energy consumption.
12. We will mount highly supervised and highly respected recycling campaigns.
13. We will start a program for waste product to be converted into sustainable energy sources.
14. We will start new company-wide document shredding programs.
15. We will use of water-based paints during the finishing process to reduce V.O.C.'s to virtually zero.
16. Use of solar panels for non-critical sections and facilities in the complex.
17. Use of only hybrid or electric vehicles.

Sticker Marketing

Low-cost sticker, label and decal marketing will provide a cost-effective way to convey information, build identity and promote our company in unique and influential ways. Stickers can be affixed to almost any surface, so they can go and stay affixed where other marketing materials can't; opening a world of avenues through which we can reach our target audience. Our stickers will be simple in design, and convey an impression quickly and clearly, with valuable information or coupon, printed optionally as part of its backcopy. Our stickers will handed-out at trade shows and special events, mailed as a postcard, packaged with product and/or included as part of a mailing package. We will insert the stickers inside our product or hand them out along with other marketing tools such as flyers or brochures. Research has found that the strongest stickers are usually less than 16 square inches, are printed on white vinyl, and are often die cut. Utilizing a strong design, in a versatile size, and with an eye-catching shape, that is, relevant to our business, will add to the perceived value of our promotional stickers.

We will adhere to the following sticker design tips:
1. We will strengthen our brand by placing our logo on the stickers and using company colors and font styles.
2. We will include our phone number, address, and/or website along with our logo to provide clients with a call to action.
3. We will write compelling copy that solicits an emotional reaction.
4. We will use die-cut stickers using unusual and business relevant shapes to help draw attention to our business.
5. We will consider that size matters and that will be determined by where they will be applied and the degree of desired visibility to be realized.
6. We will be aware of using color on our stickers as color can help create contrast in our design, which enables the directing of prospect eyes to images or actionable items on the stickers.
7. We will encourage clients to post our stickers near their phones, on yellow page book covers, on event invitations, on notepads, on book covers, on gift boxes and product packaging, etc.
8. We will place our stickers on all the products we sell.

USPS Every Door Direct Mail Program
Every Door Direct Mail from the U.S. Postal Service® is designed to reach every home, every address, every time at a very affordable delivery rate. Every business and resident living in the _____ zip code will receive an over-sized post card and coupon announcing the _____ (company name) grand opening 7-days before the grand opening:

Price – USPS Marketing Mail™ Flats up to 3.3 oz
EDDM Retail® USPS Marketing Flats $0.177 per piece
EDDM BMEU USPS Marketing Mail at $0.156 per piece

Resource:
https://www.usps.com/business/every-door-direct-mail.htm
https://eddm.usps.com/eddm/client/routeSearch.action

Google Calendar   www.google.com/calendar
We will use Google Calendar to organize our mobile Human Resources Consulting seminar schedule and share events with friends.

ZoomInfo.com
Their vision is to be the sole provider of constantly verified information about companies and their employees, making our data indispensible — available anytime, anywhere and anyplace the client needs it. Creates just-verified, detailed profiles of 65 million businesspeople and six million businesses. Makes data available through powerful tools for lead generation, prospecting and recruiting.
Example:
www.zoominfo.com/c/WATSON-Human-Resource-Consultant-Inc/359486835

Zipslocal.com
Provides one of the most comprehensive ZIP Code-based local search services, allowing visitors to access information through our online business directories that cover all ZIP Codes in the United States. Interactive local yellow pages show listings and display relevant advertising through the medium of the Internet, making it easy for everyone to find local business information.
Example:
http://www.zipslocal.com/85043/human-resources.html

Hold Biggest Fan Contest
Do you love _____ (company name)? Do you have a great story about how the team at ____ (company Name) helped you "get there" to achieve your goals? Well, then ____ (company name) wants to hear from you! _____ (company name) has launched the "Biggest Fan Contest" on its Facebook Page at the beginning of ____ (month), inviting current and former clients to share why they are _____'s (company name) "Biggest Fan." Participants are eligible to win a number of prizes including: _____.
To enter, visit www.facebook.com/_____ (company name), "like" the page, and click the "Biggest Fan Contest" tab on the righthand side. Participants are then asked to write a short blurb or upload a photo sharing why they love _____ (company name). If you have a story to tell or photo to share, enter today. Contest ends _____ (date).
See contest tab for full details.

Data.com/connect/index.jsp
A dynamic community with connections to millions of B2B decision makers. It's the fastest way to reach the right people, and never waste time hunting down the wrong person again.
Resource:
http://community.jigsaw.com/t5/How-to-Use-Jigsaw/bd-p/jigsawresourcecenter

BusinessVibes   www.businessvibes.com/about-businessvibes
A growing B2B networking platform for global trade professionals. BusinessVibes uses a social networking model for businesses to find and connect with international partner companies. With a network of over 5000+ trade associations, 20 million companies and 25,000+ business events across 100+ major industries and 175 countries, BusinessVibes is a decisive source to companies looking for international business partners, be they

clients, suppliers, JV partners, or any other type of business contact.
Examples:
https://www.businessvibes.com/companyprofile/Human-Consulting-Evolved-LLC

Yext.com
Enables companies to manage their digital presence in online maps, directories and apps. Over 400,000 businesses make millions of monthly updates across 85+ exclusive global partners, making Yext the global market leader. Digital presence is a fundamental need for all 50 million businesses in the world, and Yext's mission is perfect location information in every hand. Yext is based in the heart of New York City with 350 employees and was named to Forbes Most Promising Companies lists for 2014 and 2015, as well as the Fortune Best Places to Work 2014 list.

Google+
We will pay specific attention to Google+, which is already playing a more important role in Google's organic ranking algorithm. We will create a business page on Google+ to achieve improved local search visibility. Google+ will also be the best way to get access to Google Authorship, which will play a huge role in SEO.
Resources:
https://plus.google.com/pages/create
http://www.google.com/+/brands/
https://www.google.com/appserve/fb/forms/plusweekly/
https://plus.google.com/+GoogleBusiness/posts
http://marketingland.com/beyond-social-benefits-google-business-73460

Examples:
https://plus.google.com/+CpshrUs

Inbound Marketing
Inbound marketing is about pulling people in by sharing relevant HR consulting information, creating useful content, and generally being helpful. It involves writing everything from buyer's guides to blogs and newsletters that deliver useful content. The objective will be to nurture clients through the buying process with unbiased educational materials that turn consumers into informed buyers.
Resource:
https://www.hubspot.com/services/consulting

Google My Business Profile   www.google.com/business/befound.html
We will have a complete and active Google My Business profile to give our HR Consultancy company a tremendous advantage over the competition, and help potential clients easily find our company and provide relevant information about our business.

Google My Business will let us:
- Manage business listing info for search, maps and Google+
- Upload photos and/or a virtual tour of our business

- Share content and interacting with followers on Google+
- See reviews from across the web and responding to Google+ reviews
- Integrate with AdWords Express to create and track campaigns
- Access Insights reports, the new social analytics tool for Google+
- See information about our integrated YouTube and Analytics accounts
- Resource:
- https://www.wordstream.com/blog/ws/2014/06/12/google-my-business

Pro Bono Work: Sampling Program

We will give each sample software demonstration with a mini-survey to enable clients to rate the product and supply constructive feedback. We will also make certain to always trade free samples for the recipient's contact information. All samples will have a label with our complete contact information.

Additionally, each year, we will provide *pro bono* human resources consulting to a number of social services nonprofits that need, but cannot yet afford, consulting services. *Pro bono* service will be a part of our commitment to serving the nonprofit community and helping organizations serve their clients effectively. In addition, our team will serve our local communities as non-profit board members and through volunteer work and non-profit outreach.

Reddit.com

An online community where users vote on stories. The hottest stories rise to the top, while the cooler stories sink. Comments can be posted on every story, including stories about startup liquor store companies.

Example:
www.reddit.com/r/humanresources/comments/5dvf3n/how_to_get_into_hr_consulting/
https://www.reddit.com/r/human_resources/

6.2.1 Strategic Alliances

We will form strategic alliances to accomplish the following objectives:
1. To share marketing expenses.
2. To realize bulk buying power on wholesale purchases.
3. To engage in barter arrangements.
4. To collaborate with industry experts.
5. To set-up mutual referral relationships.

We will seek to form networking alliances with the following types of organizations to foster mutually beneficial referral relationships:
1. Venture Capitalists
2. Entrepreneur Associations and Clubs
3. Nonprofit Consulting Organizations
4. Government agencies supporting small businesses Ex: SBA and SCORE.
5. Financial Planners and Bankers
6. Other Niche Consultants
7. Lawyers and Accountants
8. Insurance and Real Estate Brokers
9. Office Supply and Computer Stores
10. Health Insurance Providers

Example:
Maxwell Health   www.maxwellhealth.com
An enrollment and administration platform. This benefits and HR technology platform and innovative marketplace combines the management of and enrollment in benefits into one experience. This online solution enables employees to seamlessly enroll in and manage their own benefits and allows the company to go completely paperless. Employees can use the mobile app to access their benefits and stay healthy throughout the year. The platform also offers an Integrated Concierge Service, which includes Health Advocate to help employees save money on out-of-pocket healthcare costs and navigate their benefits, and Teladoc, the first and largest telemedicine provider, to tackle the biggest problems in healthcare: access, quality, and cost.

We will assemble a sales presentation package that includes sales brochures, business cards, and a DVD seminar presentation. We will print coupons that offer a discount or other type of introductory deal. We will ask to set-up a take-one display for our sales brochures at the business registration counter. We will give the referring business any one

or combination of the following reward options:
1. Referral fees
2. Free services
3. Mutual referral exchanges

We will monitor referral sources to evaluate the mutual benefits of the alliance and make certain to clearly define and document our referral incentives prior to initiating our referral exchange program.

6.4.2   Monitoring Marketing Results

To monitor how well __ (company name) is doing, we will measure how well the advertising campaign is working. We will take random client surveys. What we would like to know is how they heard of us and how they like and dislike about our services. In order to get responses to the surveys, we will be give discounts as thank you rewards.

Response Tracking Methods
   Coupons: ad-specific coupons that easily enable tracking
   Landing Pages: unique web landing pages for each advertisement
   800 Numbers: unique 1-800-# per advertisement
   Email Service Provider: Instantly track email views, opens, and clicks

Our financial statements will offer excellent data to track all phases of sales. These are available for review on a daily basis. _____ (company name) will benchmark our objectives for sales promotion and advertising in order to evaluate our return on invested marketing dollars, and determine where to concentrate our limited advertising dollars to realize the best return. We will also strive to stay within our marketing budget.

Key Marketing Metrics
We will use the following two marketing metrics to evaluate the cost-effectiveness of our marketing campaign:
1. The cost to acquire a new client: The average dollar amount invested to get one new client. Example: If we invest $3,000 on marketing in a single month and end the month with 10 new clients, our cost of acquisition is $300 per new client.
2. The lifetime value of the average active client. The average dollar value of an average client over the life of their business with you. To calculate this metric for a given period of time, we will take the total amount of revenue our business generated during the time period and divide it by the total number of clients we had from the beginning of the time period.
3. We will track the following set of statistics on a weekly basis to keep informed of the progress of our business:
    A. Number of total referrals.
    B. Percentage increase of total referrals (over baseline).
    C. Number of new referral sources.
    D. Number of new clients/month.
    E. Number of Leads

Key Marketing Metrics Table

We've listed some key metrics in the following table. We will need to keep a close eye on these, to see if we meet our own forecasted expectations. If our numbers are off in too many categories, we may, after proper analysis, have to make substantial changes to our marketing efforts.

Key Marketing Metrics	2018	2019	2020
Revenue			
Leads			
Leads Converted			
Avg. Transaction per Client			
Avg. Dollars per Client			
Number of Referrals			
Number of PR Appearances			
Number of Testimonials			
Number of New Club Members			
Number of Returns			
Number of BBB Complaints			
Number of Completed Surveys			
Number of Blog readers			
Number of Twitter followers			
Number of Facebook Fans			

Metric Definitions

1. Leads: Individuals who step into the store to consider a purchase.
2. Leads Converted: Percent of individuals who actually make a purchase.
3. Average Transactions Per Client: Number of purchases per client per month. Expected to rise significantly as clients return for more and more ____ items per month
4. Average $ Per Client: Average dollar amount of each transaction. Expected to rise along with average transactions.
5. Referrals: Includes client and business referrals
6. PR Appearances: Online or print mentions of the business that are not paid advertising. Expected to be high upon opening, then drop off and rise again until achieving a steady level.
7. Testimonials: Will be sought from the best and most loyal clients. Our objective is ___ (#) per month) and they will be added to the website. Some will be sought as video testimonials.
8. New Loyalty Club Members: This number will rise significantly as more clients see the value in repeated visits and the benefits of club membership.
9. Number of Returns/BBB Complaints: Our goal is zero.
10. Number of Completed Surveys: We will provide incentives for clients to complete client satisfaction surveys.

6.4.3 Word-of-Mouth Marketing

We plan to make use of the following techniques to spur word-of-mouth advertising:
1. Repetitive Image Advertising
2. Provide exceptional client service.
3. Make effective use of loss leaders.
2. Schedule in-store activities, such as demonstrations or special events.
3. Make trial easy with a coupon or introductory discount.
4. Initiate web and magazine article submissions
5. Utilize a sampling program
6. Add a forward email feature to our website.
7. Share relevant and believable testimonial letters
8. Publish staff bios.
9. Make product/service upgrade announcements
10. Hold contests or sweepstakes
12. Have involvement with community events.
13. Pay suggestion box rewards
14. Distribute a monthly newsletter
15. Share easy-to-understand information (via an article or seminar).
16. Make personalized marketing communications.
17. Structure our referral program.
18. Sharing of Community Commonalities
19. Invitations to join our community of shared interests.
20. Publish Uncensored Client Reviews
21. Enable Information Exchange Forums
22. Provide meaningful comparisons with competitors.
23. Clearly state our user benefits.
24. Make and honor ironclad guarantees
25. Provide superior post-sale support
26. Provide support in the pre-sale decision making process.
27. Host Free Informational Seminars or Workshops
28. Get involved with local business organizations.
29. Issue Press Release coverage of charitable involvements.
30. Hold traveling company demonstrations/exhibitions/competitions.
31. Stay in touch with inactive clients.

6.4.4 Referral Marketing

We will make referrals a primary goal of our marketing plan and set the target line at 60% of new business. We understand the importance of setting up a formal referral program with the following characteristics:
1. Give a premium reward based simply on people giving referral names.
2. Send an endorsed testimonial letter from a loyal client to the referred prospect.
3. Include a separate referral form as a direct response device.

4. Provide a space on the response form for leaving positive comments that can be used to build a testimonial letter, that will be sent to each referral.
5. We will clearly state our incentive rewards, and terms and conditions.
6. We will distribute a newsletter to stay in touch with our clients and include articles about our referral program success stories.

We will work to secure more referral business by taking the following steps:

1. Study the client's business.
   We will do research to understand the business issues and challenges facing our client and the way in which our services can help the business to gain real competitive advantages.
2. Speak the client's language and avoid computer technical jargon.
   We will speak knowledgeably about our client business challenges and opportunities.
3. Solve the right problem.
   We will focus on the business process the client is trying to accomplish.
4. Improve questioning and listening skills.
   We will not be so quick to drive to a universal solution, but rather take the time to understand how we can add value to the client's business.
5. Develop good long-term relationships.
   We will seek to be consultative and supportive in all of our client meetings and establish an open channel for the two-way dialogue and exchange of ideas.
6. Keep in touch with clients.
   We will stay in touch by forwarding article reprints, newsletter copies, seminar invitations, holiday greetings and survey report results.
7. Tell the client how important referrals are to our business.
   We will impress upon the client that our best clients resulted from existing client referrals.
8. Define for the client the characteristics of the ideal referral candidate.
   We will build a profile of the ideal client and communicate those characteristics to our clients to serve as a reference guide.
9. Document our referral incentives.
   We will create a referral rewards schedule, along with terms and conditions, and promptly issue the published rewards.
10. Express our appreciation for all referrals.
    We will also express our appreciation with phone calls and handwritten notes.

Resources:
National Consultants Referral   www.4consulting-services.com/
National Consultants Referral Service   www.consultantsbureau.org/

6.4.5 Client Satisfaction Survey

We will design a client satisfaction survey to measure the "satisfaction quotient" of our Human Resources Consulting clients. By providing a detailed snapshot of our current client base, we will be able to generate more repeat and referral business and enhance the profitability of our HR Consulting company.

Our client Satisfaction Survey will include the following basics:
1. How do our clients rate our business?
2. How do our clients rate our competition?
3. How well do our clients rate the value of our products or services?
4. What new client needs and trends are emerging?
5. How loyal are our clients?
6. What can be done to improve client loyalty and repeat business?
7. How strongly do our clients recommend our business?
8. What is the best way to market our business?
9. What new value-added services would best differentiate our business from that of our competitors?
10. How can we encourage more referral business?
11. How can our pricing strategy be improved?

Our client satisfaction survey will help to answer these questions and more. From the need for continual new products and services to improved client service, our satisfaction surveys will allow our organization to quickly identify problematic and underperforming areas, while enhancing our overall client satisfaction.

Examples:
https://www.qualtrics.com/blog/customer-satisfaction-survey-questions/
http://smallbiztrends.com/2007/06/the-small-biz-7-survey.html

Resources:
www.thefusionfactor.com/media/HRConsultants_YourClientsSatisfied.pdf
www.surveymonkey.com/mp/human-resource-surveys/
www.survata.com/
www.google.com/insights/consumersurveys/use_cases
www.surveymonkey.com/mp/customer-satisfaction-survey-questions/
www.smetoolkit.org/smetoolkit/en/content/en/6708/Customer-Satisfaction-Survey-Template-
http://smallbusiness.chron.com/common-questions-customer-service-survey-1121.html
www.pwc.com/us/en/hr-management/people-analytics/workforce-customer-satisfaction-surveys.html

6.4.5 Marketing Training Program

Our Marketing Training Program will include both an initial orientation and training, as well as ongoing continuing education classes. Initial orientation will be run by the owner until an HR manager is hired. For one week, half of each day will be spent in training, and the other half shadowing the operations manager.

Training will include:

- Learning the entire selection of our Human Resources Consulting products and services.
- Understanding our Mission Statement, Value Proposition, Position Statement and Unique Selling Proposition.
- Appreciating our competitive advantages.
- Understanding our core message and branding approach.
- Learning our store's policies; returns processing, complaint handling, etc.
- Learning our client services standards of practice.
- Learning our client and business referral programs.
- Learning our Membership Club procedures, rules and benefits.
- Becoming familiar with our company website, and online ordering options.
- Service procedures specific to the employee's role.

Ongoing workshops will be based on client feedback and problem areas identified by mystery buyers, which will better train employees to educate clients. These ongoing workshops will be held ____ (once?) a month for ____ (three?) hours.

6.5 Sales Strategy

The development of our sales strategy will start by developing a better understanding of our client needs. To accomplish this task, we will pursue the following research methods:

1. Join the associations that our target clients belong to.
2. Contact the membership director and establish a relationship to understand their member's needs, challenges and concerns.
3. Identify non-competitive suppliers who sell to our client to learn their challenges and look for partnering solutions.
4. Work directly with our client and ask them what their needs are and if our business may offer a possible solution.

Our sales strategy will be targeted at obtaining both the individual business owners and commercial clients. We will need to sell our company, not necessarily the products. We will need to promote our human resources consulting services and ongoing support, monitoring and evaluation capabilities.

Our sales strategy will revolve around teaching businesses about the role of HR, and how our HR services can improve a company's bottom line. We will train our consultants to use our low-key and effective viral/educational sales approach that we will call Process-Oriented Selling program. Our consultants will learn how to use our products and services as part of a consultative approach to selling. They will be teaching prospects about how our HR systems can improve employee engagement, retention, performance and productivity.

Our marketing and sales will be done primarily through networking. This means the bulk of the leads will be developed through a personal/professional relationship that the owner has developed either in his previous professional work or through his activities with the _____ (state) Entrepreneurs Association and other similar associations. The sales message will be based on our experience in the HR field as well as our compensation flexibility. The owner will be able to explain to the prospective client the HR areas that he has experience in and the solutions that he can offer. The owner will also be able to speak about our firm's ability to accept options in lieu of cash. This will be appealing to companies, particularly in the current capital market which is quite scarce. Since capital has become difficult to come by, emerging companies will be excited about this option.

The individual clients will be primarily obtained through word-of-mouth referrals, but we will also advertise introductory offers to introduce people to the various HR management products and services we offer. The combination of the perception of higher HR support quality, exceptional technical support and the recognition of superior value should turn referral leads into satisfied clients.

The company's sales strategy will be based on the following elements:
- Advertising in the Yellow Pages - two inch by three-inch ads describing our services will be placed in the local Yellow Pages.
- Placing classified advertisements in the regional editions of business magazines, and craigslist.com.
- Word of mouth referrals - generating sales leads in the local community through client referrals.
- Subscribe to "Commerce Business Daily" to receive Federal Government announced procurements. Resource: http://cbdnet.gpo.gov/

We also plan to hire a local independent commissioned sales rep to sell our HR consulting products/services to local businesses. In addition, _____ (company name) plans to offer a Club Membership Card with different membership levels of benefits.

Our basic sales strategy is to:
- Develop a website for lead generation by _____ (date).
- Provide exceptional client service.
- Accept payment by all major credit cards, cash, PayPal and check.
- Survey our clients regarding services they would like to see added.
- Sponsor charitable and other community events.
- Motivate employees with a pay-for-performance component to their straight salary compensation package, based on profits and client satisfaction rates.
- Build long-term client relationships by putting the interests of clients first.
- Establish mutually beneficial relationship with all vendors.

Direct Sales
The company will develop a database of client names, addresses, email addresses,

key dates and personal preferences. This information will be used for email and direct mail efforts to build client loyalty. We will also use the services of independent commissions sales reps to approach small and mid-sized businesses. Their personal selling activities will be supported by regular advertising and lead generation programs.

Indirect Sales
We will establish a referral program for clients. We will start an affiliate program for strategic business alliance partners.

6.5.1　　Client Retention Strategies

We will use the following techniques to improve client retention and the profitability of our business:
1. Keep the offices sparkling clean and well-organized.
2. Use only well-trained salespersons, and the highest quality equipment.
3. Ask the clients for feedback and promptly act upon their inputs.
4. Tell clients how much you appreciate their business.
5. Call regular clients by their first names.
6. Send thank you notes.
7. Offer free new HR product and service samples.
8. Change sales presentations on a regular basis.
9. Practice good phone etiquette
10. Respond to complaints promptly.
11. Reward referrals.
12. Publish a monthly newsletter.
13. Develop and publish a list of frequently asked questions.
14. Issue Preferred Client Membership Cards.
15. Hold informational seminars and workshops.
16. Run contests.
17. Develop service contract programs.
18. Provide an emergency hotline number.
19. Publish code of ethics and our service guarantees.
20. Publish all client reviews.
21. Help clients to make accurate competitor comparisons.
22. Build a stay-in-touch (drip marketing) communications calendar.
23. Keep marketing communications focused on our competitive advantages.
24. Offer repeat user discounts and incentives.
25. Be supportive and encouraging, and not judgmental.
26. Measure client retention and look at recurring revenue and client surveys.

We will also consider the following client Retention Programs:

Type of Program	client Rewards
Frequency Purchase Loyalty Program	Special Discounts
	Free Product or Services

Rebate Loyalty Programs	Credit Based on Percent of Incremental Sales from Prior Period.
'Best client' Program	Special Recognition/Treatment/Offers
Affinity Programs	Sharing of Common Interests
	Accumulate Credit Card Points
client Community Programs	Special Event Participation
Auto-Knowledge Building Programs	Purchase Recommendations based On Past Transaction History
Profile Building Programs	Recommendations Based on Stated client Profile Information.

6.5.2 Sales Forecast

Our sales projections are based on the following:
1. Actual sales volumes of local competitors
2. Interviews with other Human Resources Consulting owners and managers
3. Observations of sales and traffic at competitor establishments.
4. Government and industry trade statistics
5. Local population demographics and projections.
6. Discussions with suppliers.

Our sales forecast is an estimated projection of expected sales over the next three years, based on our chosen marketing strategy and assumed competitive environment. It is calculated by multiplying the forecasted number of clients we plan to acquire by our average hourly rate and the estimated number of hours of service needed per client annually.

Sales are expected to be below average during the first year, until a regular client base has been established. It has been estimated that it takes the average Human Resources Consulting business a minimum of two years to establish a significant client base. After the client base is built, sales will grow at an accelerated rate from word-of-mouth referrals and continued networking efforts.

We expect sales to steadily increase as our marketing program and contact management system are executed. By using advertising, especially discounted introductory HR audit coupons, as a catalyst for this prolonged process, _____ (company name) plans to attract more clients sooner.

Throughout the first year, it is forecasted that sales will incrementally grow until profitability is reached toward the end of year _____ (one?). Year two reflects a conservative growth rate of ____ (15?) percent. Year three reflects a growth rate of _____ (15?) percent.

With our unique product and service offerings, along with our thorough and aggressive marketing strategies, we believe that the following sales forecasts are actually on the conservative side.

Table: Sales Forecast

	Annual Sales		
Sales Forecast			
Unit Sales	**2018**	**2019**	**2020**
Hourly Rate Consulting			
Retainer Consulting			
Project Consulting			
Market Research			
Strategic Reports			
Seminars/Workshops			
HR Audits			
Recruiting Commission			
Miscellaneous			
Total Unit Sales			
Unit Prices			
Hourly Rate Consulting			
Retainer Consulting			
Project Consulting			
Market Research			
Strategic Reports			
Seminars/Workshops			
HR Audits			
Recruiting Commission			
Miscellaneous			
Sales (Unit Sales x Unit Prices)			
Hourly Rate Consulting			
Retainer Consulting			
Project Consulting			
Market Research			
Strategic Reports			
Seminars/Workshops			
HR Audits			
Recruiting Commission			
Miscellaneous			
Total Sales			
Direct Unit Costs:			
Hourly Rate Consulting			
Retainer Consulting			
Project Consulting			
Market Research			

Strategic Reports _____
Seminars/Workshops _____
HR Audits _____
Recruiting Commission _____
Miscellaneous _____

Direct Cost of Sales
Hourly Rate Consulting _____
Retainer Consulting _____
Project Consulting _____
Market Research _____
Strategic Reports _____
Seminars/Workshops _____
HR Audits _____
Recruiting Commission _____
Miscellaneous _____
Subtotal Direct Cost of Sales _____
Note: The per-unit price of inventory purchases, includes cost of shipping.

6.6   Merchandising Strategy

Merchandising is that part of our marketing strategy that is involved with promoting the sales of our merchandise, as by consideration of the most effective means of selecting, pricing, displaying, and advertising items for sale in our computer consulting business. We will monitor our sales figures and data to confirm that products in demand are well-stocked and slow-moving products are phased-out. We will   improve telephone skills of employees to boost phone orders. We will attach our own additional business labels to all products to promote our line of services and location. We will make sure sales brochures and flyers are always available.

6.7   Pricing Strategy

___ (company name) will charge enough to reflect our expertise and value, because perception is important. Research indicates that fees much lower than clients are used to paying might set off warning signals, and fees that are much higher might create concern. We will seek to strike the right balance to ensure revenue generation and a steady stream of clients.

The following factors will go into establishing rates and project fees:

1. What other consultants are charging for similar services
2. The type of business or industry being targeted
3. The client's history with using consultants
4. Supply and demand
5. The consultant's level of experience and expertise.
6. Profit objectives

Fees for individual projects will be based on a number of factors, including project objectives, scope of services provided, success criteria, budget (if applicable) and timeline.

Note: The decision of whether to charge by the hour or by the project is an individual one and varies from one consultant to another; however, project-based billing seems to be most prevalent.
Source:
www.shrm.org/resourcesandtools/tools-and-samples/toolkits/pages/introductiontoconsulting.aspx

Consulting will be based on $_____ per day for project consulting, $_____ per day for market research, and $_____ per month and up for retainer consulting. Market research reports should be priced at $_____ per report, which will require that reports be very well planned, focused on very important HR topics, very well presented.

To simplify billing to clients, ___ (company name) will work on a fixed pricing structure. We will determine the standard pricing structure for each deliverable based on hourly estimates and fees. This will be expressed to the client as a per-deliverable fixed price in a quote. Clients can determine which deliverables they would like to purchase. We will charge the quoted price even if we have underestimated hours, to maintain credibility with budget-conscious small businesses. Pricing structure will be based on $____/hour multiplied by the number of hours that it would take our most experienced consultant to finish the project. If less experienced consultants participate on the project, it will likely take more time; however, the price of the deliverable to the client will not change.

In time, we may consider a cash-and-equity arrangement, or potentially all equity for specific projects. Before we can begin with this stage of pricing, we will need more experienced finance and accounting skills to determine proper equity stakes that should be requested, etc. Additionally, we will offer cost-effective Web-hosting services that will provide ongoing revenue streams. It is anticipated that most clients will sign-up for our one-year contracts requiring minimal accounting.

_____ (company name) will adopt the following pricing strategies:
1. Hourly Rate Pricing Average: $_____ (100?) per hour.
2. A Daily Rate of $ _____.
   We will typically use the daily or hourly rate for training or tasks that have a clearly defined time parameters and outcomes.
3. Annual Retainer Pricing: Based on the expected minimum number of hours per month, the average was $_____ (500?)
4. Fixed Price Project Pricing: Based on a daily rate (8 hours x $100/hour)
   Using this common method of pricing, specific results will be identified for the completion of the project.
5. Percentage Fee: When the outcome of the project is easily and clearly measurable, we will consider a percentage of the financial success of the project.

Note: Many HR consultants advise against using hourly rates exclusively—or at all in some cases, as an hourly billing structure gives clients too much leeway to determine the scope of work. That can be a problem when the HR consultant is better informed than the client about the amount of work that will be required to address the client's problem. Some HR consultants use a combination of monthly retainers for specified deliverables, project rates and hourly billing. Although project rates and monthly retainers may include a rough estimate of work hours, the reports generated for clients each month will focus entirely on what work has been accomplished.

Other Pricing Strategies:

1. We must insure that our price plus service equation is perceived to be an exceptional value proposition.
2. We must refrain from competing on price, but always be price competitive.
3. We must develop value-added services, and bundle those with our products to create offerings that cannot be easily price compared. This would include such services as free battery testing and installations.
4. We must focus attention on our competitive advantages, which include the diversity of our product line, the quality of our service offerings, the ready availability of our stock, our value pricing strategy, our client service and technical support.
5. Development of a pricing strategy based on our market positioning strategy, which is ____ (mass market value leadership/exceptional premium niche value?)
6. Our pricing policy objective, which is to _____ (increase profit margins/ achieve revenue maximization to increase market share/lower unit costs).
7. We will use marketplace intelligence and gain insights from competitor pricing strategy comparisons.
8. We will solicit pricing feedback from clients using surveys and informal interviews.
9. We will utilize limited time pricing incentives to penetrate niche markets.
10. We will conduct experiments at prices above and below the current price to determine the price elasticity of demand. (Inelastic demand or demand that does not decrease with a price increase, indicates that price increases may be feasible.)
11. We will keep our offerings and prices simple to understand and competitive, based on market intelligence.
12. We will consider the following Pricing Strategy Options:

Penetration Pricing	Temporary, artificially low prices to gain market share.
Economy Pricing	Everyday no frills low prices on basic offerings.
Loss Leader	Selling at or below cost to attract clients who might buy other profitable products/services.
Price Skimming	High prices due to temporary, but substantial competitive advantage.
Psychological Pricing	Book price point perspective (Ex: $19.99)
Grand Opening Pricing	Lower rate to build client database faster.
Optional Product	Optional extras increase overall sale price.

Product Bundle Pricing Combine several products/services into a package.
Value Pricing   Bundled packages resulting from increased competition.

Determining the costs of servicing business is the most important part of covering our expenses and earning profits. We will factor in the following pricing formula: Materials + Overhead + Labor + Profit = Price

We will develop a pricing strategy that will reinforce the perception of value to the client and manage profitability, especially in the face of rising inflation. To ensure our success, we will use periodic competitor and client research to continuously evaluate our pricing strategy. We intend to review our profit margins every six months.
Resources: www.dice.com / www.realrates.com

6.8   Differentiation Strategies

We will use differentiation strategies to develop and market unique products for different client segments. To differentiate ourselves from the competition, we will focus on the assets, creative ideas and competencies that we have that none of our competitors has. The goal of our differentiation strategies is to be able to charge a premium price for our unique Human Resources Consulting Services.

Differentiation in our HR Consultancy will be achieved in the following types of ways, including:

                                          Explanation
- ☐ Product features   _____
- ☐ Complementary services   _____
- ☐ Technology embodied in design   _____
- ☐ Location   _____
- ☐ Service innovations   _____
- ☐ Superior service   _____
- ☐ Creative advertising   _____
- ☐ Better supplier relationships   _____

Source: http://scholarship.sha.cornell.edu/cgi/viewcontent.cgi?article=1295&context=articles

Differentiating will mean defining who our perfect target market is and then catering to their needs, wants and interests better than everyone else. It will be about using surveys to determine what's most important to our targeted market and giving it to them consistently.   It will not be about being "everything to everybody"; but rather, "the absolute best to our chosen targeted group".

In developing our differentiation strategy will we use the following form to help define our differences:

1.   Targeted client segments   _____
2.   Client characteristics   _____

3. Client demographics _____
4. Client behavior _____
5. Geographic focus _____
6. Ways of working _____
7. Service delivery approach _____
8. Client problems/pain points _____
9. Complexity of clients' problems _____
10. Range of services _____

We will use the following approaches to differentiate our products and services from those of our competitors to stand apart from standardised offerings:

1. Superior quality
2. Unusual or unique product features
3. More responsive client service
4. Rapid product or service innovation
5. Advanced technological features
6. Engineering design or styling
7. Additional product features
8. An image of prestige or status

Specific Differentiators will include the following:
1. Being a Specialist in one procedure
2. Utilizing advanced/uncommon technology
3. Possessing extensive experience
4. Building an exceptional facility
5. Consistently achieving superior results
6. Having a caring and empathetic personality
7. Giving client s WOW experience, including a professional client welcome package.
8. Enabling convenience and 24/7 online accessibility
9. Calling clients to express interest in their challenges.
10. Keeping to the appointment schedule.
11. Remembering client names and details like they were family
12. Assuring client fears.
13. Building a visible reputation and recognition around our community
14. Acquiring special credentials or professional memberships
15. Providing added value services, such as taxi service, longer hours, financing plans, and post-sale services.

Primary Differentiation Strategies:
1. We will offer a 24/7 on-call (help desk) service as a way to build client satisfaction, bring in more word-of-mouth business and secure premium hourly rate pricing for this service.
2. Clients will be able to check their page on our company web site to see the status of any pending problems and resolutions.

3. We will locate and resell marketing software that is not commercially available and we have the right to modify the source code to suit the client's specific needs.
4. We intend to sell our company as a strategic partner.
5. We will use lower pricing to penetrate new mid-level markets and premium pricing in the case of upper-end market segments.
6. To deliver a superior client experience we will deliver on the following key initiatives:
   - Development of client satisfaction and team member engagement surveys.
   - Examination of all standard operating procedures.
   - Improve team member recruitment, training and retention
7. We will develop a referral program to turn clients into commissioned sales agents
8. We plan to develop alternative revenue streams as listed in the services section of this business plan.
9. We will seek to differentiate our company by its dedication to service, ease of ordering, and knowledgeable, friendly sales force as well as its ability to provide one-stop shopping for all marketing and growth consulting needs.
10. We plan to publish a monthly newsletter and use classified advertising revenues from suppliers and local merchants to partially fund the newsletter.
11. We will promote our "green" practices.
12. We will customize our offerings according to the cultural influences, customs, interests and tastes of our local market to create loyalty and increase sales.
13. We will issue a satisfaction guarantee in exchange for the right to ask for additional fees if our results exceed expectations.
14. We will impress clients with the simplicity with which we convey our brilliant, innovative and creative ideas.
15. Our undisputed niche expertise.
16. We offer our clients an ironclad guarantee that is tangible and quantifiable.
17. We will reduce client perceived risk with a "100 percent money-back guarantee".
18. We will giveaway complementary seminars and research reports to demonstrate our expertise in a particular industry field.
19. We will incorporate our Code of Ethics into our presentation folder to build trust.
20. We will incorporate highly recognized, third party testimonials into our marketing materials.
21. A laser focus on small business
22. We will target new regions with local consultants, allowing us to personally interact with small businesses without needing to bring consultants to the region.
23. By relying on a nationally distributed talent base coordinated to work together remotely, we will be able to bring together a variety of skills to meet the needs of our clients.

6.9 Milestones

The Milestones Chart is a timeline that will guide our company in developing and growing our business. It will list chronologically the various critical actions and events that must occur to bring our business to life. We will make certain to assign real, attainable dates to each planned action or event. _____ (company name) has identified several specific milestones which will function as goals for the company. The milestones will provide a target for achievement as well as a mechanism for tracking progress. The dates were chosen based on realistic delivery times and necessary construction times. All critical path milestones will be completed within their allotted time frames to ensure the success of contingent milestones. The following table will provide a timeframe for each milestone.

Table: Milestones

Milestones	Start Date	End Date	Budget	Responsibility
Business Plan Completion				
Incorporate Business Form				
Secure Permits/Licenses				
Locate & Secure Space				
Obtain Insurance				
Establish Bank Relationship				
Secure Additional Financing				
Get Start-up Cost Quotes				
Establish Vendor Accounts				
Purchase Office Equipment				
Renovate Space				
Define Marketing Programs				
Install Equipment/Systems				
Set-up Accounting System				
Finalize Media Plan				
Create Facebook Brand Page				
Open Twitter Account				
Conduct Blogger Outreach				
Develop Personnel Plan				
Hire sales rep				
Personnel Training Program				
Implement Marketing Plan				
Get Website Live				
Conduct SEO Campaign				
Form Strategic VC Alliances				
Purchase Inventory/Supplies				
Press Release Announcements				
Check All Systems				
Secure First Clients				
Advertise Grand Opening				
Full Time Work Threshold				
Kickoff Advertising Program				
Join Community Orgs./Network				
Conduct Satisfaction Surveys				
Monitor Social Media Networks				
Respond Positively to Reviews				

Measure Return on Marketing $$$ _____
Service Expansion Strategy   _____
Revenues Exceed $_____   _____
Profitability   _____
Geographic Expansion   _____
Totals: _____

7.0 Website Plan Summary

_____ (company name) is currently developing a website at the URL address www. (company name).com. We will primarily use the website to advertise our services and special seminar events, provide content-rich articles that stimulate client interest and to post a catalog of our hardware and software products. We will use email to communicate with clients wishing to sign-up for email specials and our newsletter.

The website will be developed to offer clients a product catalog for online orders and appointment setting. The overriding design philosophy of the site will be ease of use. We want to make the process of placing an order as easy and fast as possible thereby encouraging increased sales. We will incorporate special features such as a section that is specific to each client so the client can easily make purchases of repeat items. Instead of going through the website every month and locating their monthly needs, the site will capture regularly ordered items for that specific client, significantly speeding up the ordering process. This ease-of-use feature will help increase sales as clients become more and more familiar with the site and appreciate how easy it is to place an order.

We will also provide multiple incentives to sign-up for various benefits, such as our newsletters and promotional sale notices. This will help us to build an email database, which will supply our automated client follow-up system. We will create a personalized drip marketing campaign to stay in touch with our clients and prospects.

We will develop our website to be a resource for web visitors who are seeking knowledge and information about HR Audit procedures, with a goal to service the knowledge needs of our clients and generate leads. Our home page will be designed to be a "welcome mat" that clearly presents our service offerings and provides links through which visitors can gain easy access to the information they seek. We will use our website to match the problems our clients face with the solutions we offer.

We will use the free tool, Google Analytics (http://www.google.com/analytics), to generate a history and measure our return on investment. Google Analytics is a free tool that can offer insight by allowing the user to monitor traffic to a single website. We will just add the Google Analytics code to our website and Google will give our firm a dashboard providing the number of unique visitors, repeat traffic, page views, etc. This will help to stop wasting our company's money on inefficient marketing. Using an analytic program will show exactly which leads are paying off, and which ones to do without. We will find out what's bringing our site the most traffic and how to improve upon that.

This website will serve the following purposes:

About Us	Company history
How We Work/Our Philosophy	
HR Consulting Services	
Contact Us	Client service contact info
Ask the Expert	
Frequently Asked Questions	FAQs
Principals/Consultant Staff	Resumes
Newsletter Sign-up	Mailing List
Newsletter Archives	Helpful articles
Catalog of Products	
Catalog of Training Programs	Workshops
Product Catalog	Publications/Affiliate Program
Upcoming Events	Seminar/Webinar/Conference/Forum
HR Articles	Download White Papers
Portfolio Samples	Brochures/PR/Website/Ads
Testimonials	With Client Photos
Case Studies	Monthly Client Spotlight
Referral Program	Details
Directions	Location directions.
Client Satisfaction Survey	Feedback
Press Releases	In the News Archive
Strategic Alliance Partners	Links
Privacy Policy	
Favorite Links	Professional Associations
Our Blog	Office diary/Accept comments
Refer-a-Friend	Viral marketing
Video Clips	Seminar Presentation/Testimonials
LinkedIn/Facebook Links	
Guarantees/Code of Ethics	
Mission Statement	
Career Opportunities	
Client List	
Classified Ads	

Classified Ads
By joining and incorporating a classified ad affiliate program into our website, we will create the ultimate win-win-win. We will provide our guests with a free benefit, increase our rankings with the search engines by incorporating keyword hyperlinks into our site, attract additional markets to expose to our product, create an additional income source as they upgrade their ads, and provide our prospects a reason to return to our web site again and again

Resources:
    App Themes   www.appthemes.com/themes/classipress/

e-Classifieds	http://www.e-classifieds.net/
Noah's Classifieds	http://www.noahsclassifieds.org/
Joom Prod	http://www.joomprod.com/

7.1 Website Marketing Strategy

Our online marketing strategy will employ the following distinct mechanisms:

1. Search Engine Submission

    This will be most useful to people who are unfamiliar with ___(company name), but are looking for a Human Resources Consulting Service. There will also be searches from clients who may know about us, but who are seeking additional information.

    Search Engine Optimization (SEO)
    SEO is a very important digital marketing strategy because search engines are the primary method of finding information for most internet users. SEO is simply the practice of improving and promoting a website in order to increase the number of visitors a site receives from search engines. Basic SEO techniques will range from the naming of webpages to the way that other websites link to our website. We will also need to get our business listed on as many relevant online directories as possible, such as Google, Yelp, Kudzu and Yahoo Local, write a blog that solicit comments and be active on social media sites.
    We will also try to incorporate local terms potential clients would use, such as "_____ (city) human resource consulting firm." This will make it more likely that local clients will find us close to the top of their search.
    Resource;
    www.officerreports.com/blog/wp-content/uploads/2014/11/SEOmoz-The-Beginners-Guide-To-SEO-2012.pdf

2. Website Address (URL) on Marketing Materials

    Our URL will be printed on all marketing communications, business cards, letterheads, faxes, and invoices and product labels. This will encourage a visit to our website for additional information

3. Online Directories Listings

    We will list our website on relevant, free and paid online directories and manufacturer website product locators.
    The good online directories possess the following features:
    Free or paid listings that do not expire and do not require monthly renewal.
    Ample space to get your advertising message across.
    Navigation buttons that are easy for visitors to use.
    Optimization for top placement in the search engines based on keywords that people typically use to find Human Resources Consulting Services.

Direct links to your website, if available.

An ongoing directory promotion campaign to maintain high traffic volumes to the directory site.

4. Strategic Business Partners

   We will use a Business Partners page to cross-link to prominent _____ (city) area dance web sites as well as the city Web sites and local recreational sites. We will also cross-link with brand name suppliers.

5. YouTube Posting

   We will produce a video of testimonials from several of our satisfied clients and educate viewers as to the range of our services and products. Our research indicates that the YouTube video will also serve to significantly improve our ranking with the Google Search Engine.

6. Exchange of links with strategic marketing partners.

   We will cross-link to non-profit businesses that accept our gift certificate donations as in-house run contest prize awards.

7. E-Newsletter

   Use the newsletter sign-up as a reason to collect email addresses and limited profiles, and use embedded links in the newsletter to return readers to website.

8. Create an account for your photos on flickr.com

   We will use the name of our site on flickr so we have the same keywords.
   To take full advantage of Flickr, we will use a JavaScript-enabled browser and install the latest version of the Macromedia Flash Player.

9. Geo Target Pay Per Click (PPC) Campaign

   Available through Google Adwords program. Example keywords include management consultant, business analyst, business plan, business profitability audit, business performance analysis….. and _____ (city).

10. Post messages on Internet user groups and forums.

    Get involved with consulting related discussion groups and forums and develop a descriptive signature paragraph.
    Examples: http://managementconsultant.blogsome.com/
                http://forum.top-consultant.com/US/list.aspx

11. Write up your own LinkedIn.com and Facebook.com profiles.

    Highlight your background and professional interests.

12. Blog to share our success stories and latest trends.
    We will use our blog to post positions on industry trends, announcements, activities, seminars and accomplishments. We will also use it to post controversial articles, ask for feedback, conduct online surveys, solicit suggestions and encourage direct contact.   Resource: www.blogger.com

13. Really Simple Syndication (RSS)
    Headlines are picked up by news syndication services and delivered to readers who have requested information on specific topics.
    Resource: www.newsgator.com / www.bloglines.com

7.2 Development Requirements

A full development plan will be generated as documented in the milestones. Costs that ____ (company name) will expect to incur with development of its new website include:

Development Costs
    User interface design $_____.
    Site development and testing $_____
    Site Implementation $._____

Ongoing Costs
    Website name registration $_____ per year.
    Site Hosting $_____ or less per month.
    Site design changes, updates and maintenance are considered part of Marketing.

The site will be developed by _____ (company name), a local start-up company. The user interface designer will use our existing graphic art to come up with the website logo and graphics. We have already secured hosting with a local provider, _____ (business name). Additionally, they will prepare a monthly statistical usage report to analyze and improve web usage and return on investment.

The plan is for the website to be live by _____ (date).
Basic website maintenance, including update and data entry will be handled by our staff. Site content, such as images and text will be maintained by _____ (owner name).

In the future, we may need to contract with a technical resource to build the trackable article download and newsletter capabilities.
Resource: www.godaddy.com

7.3 Frequently Asked Questions

We will use the following guidelines when developing the frequently asked questions for the ecommerce section of the website:

1. Use a Table of Contents: Offer subject headers at the top of the FAQ page with a hyperlink to that related section further down on the page for quick access.
2. Group Questions in a Logical Way and group separate specific questions related to a subject together.
3. Be Precise with the Question: Don't use open-ended questions.
4. Avoid Too Many Questions: Publish only the popular questions and answers.
5. Answer the Question with a direct answer.
6. Link to Resources When Available: via hyperlinks so the client can continue with self-service support.
7. Use Bullet Points to list step-by-step instructions.
8. Focus on Client Support and Not Marketing.
9. Use Real and Relevant Frequently Asked Questions from actual clients.
10. Update Your FAQ Page as clients continue to communicate questions.

The following frequently asked questions will enable us to convey a lot of important information to our clients in a condensed format. We will post these questions and answers on our website and create a hardcopy version to be included on our sales presentation folder.

Why should we use your HR Consulting Firm?
We are a highly knowledgeable and experienced Human Resources Team. With over ____ (#) years of combined HR experience we have the depth and knowledge to help partner with your management team. We have created HR departments in many organizations that are true strategic business partners.

How are you paid for your services?
We are paid for our time. We provide a proposal before we begin any project.

How do we get started on a project?
An initial meeting is held, free of charge, to determine the issues your company must consider when dealing with HR issues. Once determined we provide you with a proposal for the work we could undertake.

Who works on my file?
As our Senior Consultant, _____ oversees all projects and works directly with every client. Additional support is provided by members of our consulting team. This collaborative approach allows us to draw on each other's strengths to reach the best solution for our clients.

How do I know if _____ (company name) is a good match for my business?
We can work with almost any legitimate, sustainable business that has the potential to

grow their annual revenues to at least ____ (five?) million dollars. We will be happy to discuss your situation confidentially, and will immediately let you know whether or not we think we are a good fit for your business.

Do you work with businesses that do not involve a lot of technology?
Although most of our client businesses are technology focused, we also work with clients in other areas.

How much do you charge for your services?
As a Human Resources Consulting Service, most of our services are customized for each specific client. Our hourly rates start as low as $____ (250?) per hour. The actual rate we charge depends on the type of engagement, the scope of the project, the client industry, the complexity of the work, the specific skill sets required, and other factors.

Do you provide client references?
We are happy to provide client references to serious prospects once we have held initial discussions and have tentatively agreed on the scope and structure of an engagement.

I need help with my business, but the services I need do not neatly fit into any of the categories listed in your website. Can you still help me?
If your company can benefit from a team of senior HR experts, then we are likely to be a good fit. Give us a call during business hours and we will be happy to discuss your situation at no charge.

My company has very proprietary information which I do not want to leak out. Do you sign non-disclosure agreements?
Once we have determined that there is a good match between your needs and our capabilities, we can send you a mutual non-disclosure agreement. This agreement protects both parties from disclosure of confidential information. And, if you become a client our standard contract provides ample protection that covers most circumstances.

Why don't you list more of your clients' names on your website?
Most of our clients insist on strict confidentiality, so we cannot divulge any information about them beyond their industry and a general description of the type of services we provided them.

Do you work with non-profit organizations?
Although most of our clients are small or mid-size businesses, we also work with other entities. As long as we are a good fit in terms of skills and expertise we are happy to work with non-profit organizations.

How will a HR Audit benefit my company?
An HR Audit will benefit your company in the following ways:
1. Identifies opportunities to align HR initiatives with business strategies
2. Identifies HR metrics that are meaningful indicators to employee engagement
3. Identifies compliance concerns for current and pending laws and regulations

4. Enhances effective utilization of the human resource function
5. Establishes a baseline to ensure continuous improvement
6. Performs due diligence for shareholders, owners, and potential investors

How do we improve our employee turnover rate?
Hire the right people, give them the tools they need to do their job and make them feel appreciated and valued. Communication is critical. Employees do NOT leave for money —- they leave because they do not feel engaged or respected.

Examples:
http://www.silvershr.com/hr-frequently-asked-questions/
https://hrgirlfriends.com/category/real-talk/

7.4 Website Performance Summary

We will use web analysis tools to monitor web traffic, such as identifying the number of site visits. We will analyze client transactions and take actions to minimize problems, such as incomplete sales and abandoned shopping carts. We will use the following table to track the performance of our website:

Category	2018 Fcst	2018 Act	2019 Fcst	2019 Act	2020 Fcst	2020 Act
No. of Clients						
New Newsletter Subscribers						
Unique Visitors						
Avg. Time on Site						
Pages per Visit						
Percent New Visits						
Bounce Rate						
No. of Products						
Product Categories						
Number of Incomplete Sales						
Conversion Rate						
Affiliate Sales						
Client Satisfaction Score						

7.5 Website Retargeting/Remarketing

Research indicates that for most websites, only 2% of web traffic converts readers on the first visit. Retargeting will keep track of people who have visited our website and displays our ads to them as they browse online. This will bring back 98% of users who don't convert right away by keeping our brand at the top of their mind. Setting up a remarketing tracking code on our website will allow us to target past visitors who did not convert or take the desired action on our site. After people have been to our website and are familiar with our brand, we will market more aggressively to this 'warm traffic.'

Resource:
www.marketing360.com/remarketing-software-retargeting-ads/

8.0 Operations Plan

Operations include the business aspects of running our business, such as conducting quality assessment and improvement activities, auditing functions, cost-management analysis, and client service. Our operations plan will present an overview of the flow of the daily activities of the business and the strategies that support them. It will focus on the following critical operating factors that will make the business a success:

1. We will enjoy the following advantages in the sourcing of our inventory: _____

2. We will utilize the following technological innovations in the client relationship management (CRM) process: _____

3. We will make use of the following advantages in our distribution process: _____

4. We will develop the following in-house training program to improve staff productivity: _____

5. We will utilize the following system to better control inventory carrying costs. _____

6. We will implement the following quality control plan: _____

Quality Control Plan
Our Quality Control Plan will include a review process that checks all factors involved in our operations. The main objectives of our quality control plan will be to uncover defects and bottlenecks, and reporting to management level to make the decisions on the improvement of the whole production process. Our review process will include the following activities:
    Quality control checklist
    Finished report review
    Structured walkthroughs
    Statistical sampling

Testing process

Operations Planning

We will use Microsoft Visio to develop visual maps, which will piece together the different activities in our organization and show how they contribute to the overall "value stream" of our business. We will rightfully treat operations as the lifeblood of our business. We will develop a combined sales and operations planning process where sales and operations managers will sit down every month to review sales, at the same time creating a forward-looking 12-month rolling plan to help guide the product development and manufacturing processes, which can become disconnected from sales. We will approach our operations planning using a three-step process that analyzes the company's current state, future state and the initiatives it will tackle next. For each initiative, such as launching a new product or service, the company will examine the related financials, talent and operational needs, as well as target client profiles. Our management team will map out the cost of development and then calculate forecasted return on investment and revenue predictions.

We plan to submit business proposals that utilize the following outline:
1. Opening: A recap of prior discussions.
2. Statement of Client Objectives/Project Scope
3. Sequential Action Steps
4. Progress Report Timetable
5. Client Expected Project Benefit Results
6. Client Responsibilities
7. Time and Costs/Staffing Requirements
8. Summary Conclusions
9. Consultant Qualifications, Credentials and References

We will get all agreements with clients in writing and have the document signed by both parties.

We will use the Client Needs Analysis Worksheet, as provided in the appendix, to precisely document client needs and specifications, style preferences, and time and budget constraints.

We also plan to develop a list of specific interview questions and a worksheet to evaluate, compare and pre-screen potential suppliers. We will also check vendor references and their rating with the Hoovers.com.

We plan to write and maintain an Operations Manual and a Personnel Policies Handbook. The Operating Manual will be a comprehensive document outlining virtually every aspect of the business. The operating manual will include management and accounting procedures, hiring and personnel policies, and daily operations procedures, such as opening and closing the store, and how to _____. The manual will cover the following topics:

- Community Relations   - Client Relations

- Media Relations
- Vendor Relations
- Competition Relations
- Environmental Concerns
- Intra Company Procedures
- Banking and Credit Cards
- Computer Procedures
- Quality Controls
- Open/Close Procedures
- Software Documentation

- Employee Relations
- Government Relations
- Equipment Maintenance Checklist
- Inventory Controls
- Accounting and Billing
- Financing
- Scheduling Procedures
- Safety Procedures
- Security Procedures
- Contracts/Forms Management

We plan to create the following business manuals:

	Manual Type	Key Elements
1.	Operations Manual	Process flowcharts
2.	Employee Manual	Benefits/Appraisals/Practices
3.	Managers Manual	Job Descriptions
4.	Client Service Policies	Inquiry Handling Procedures

Model Employee Handbook

We will develop a model employee handbook that can be easily customized to match a client company's culture and specific needs. The many benefits of creating a comprehensive model employee handbook will include:

1. Providing employees with vital information, such as company history, traditions, growth, mission, values, and vision.
2. Providing a resource that answers many recurring questions employees have about company policies.
3. Setting guidelines for performance and stating the potential consequences of behavior, both positive and negative, in the workplace.
4. Eliminating gray areas so that everyone has a clear understanding of the rules and can expect to be treated fairly and equally.
5. Informing employees of company benefits, such as holidays, vacation, personal days, and health insurance

Our plan is to automate our sales process, by developing an online job cost calculator. We plan to adapt Quickbooks to track product inventory and sales. The plan is to place special emphasis on using technology to make the transaction with clients more efficient and to accept a wide range of credit and debit card options. All systems are computer based and allow for accurate off-premises control of all aspects of our service business.

Software Options
Quickbooks //quickbooks.intuit.com/product/accounting-software/

9.0 Management Summary

The Management Plan will reveal who will be responsible for the various management functions to keep the business running efficiently. It will further demonstrate how that individual has the experience and/or training to accomplish each function. It will address who will do the planning function, the organizing function, the directing function, and the controlling function. We will also develop an employee retention plan because there are distinct cost advantages to retaining employees. It costs a lot to recruit and train a new employee, and in the early days, new employees are a lot less productive. We will need to make sure that our employees are satisfied in order to retain them and, in turn, create satisfied clients.

At the present time _____ (owner name) will run all operations for _____ (company name). _____ (His/Her) background in _____ (business management?) indicates an understanding of the importance of financial control systems. Other key personnel are the project managers. There is not expected to be any shortage of qualified staff from local labor pools in the market area.

_____ (owner name) will be the owner and operations manager of _____ (company name). His/her general duties will include the following:
1. Oversee the daily operations
2. Ordering inventory and supplies.
3. Develop and implementing the marketing strategy
4. Purchasing equipment.
5. Arranging for the routine maintenance and upkeep of the facility.
7. Hiring, training and supervision of new staff.
8. Scheduling and planning special events.
9. Creating and pricing service programs and packages.
10. Managing events.
12. Managing the accounting/financial aspect of the business.
13. Bookkeeping and payroll
14. Contract negotiation/vendor relations.

The operations manager will take a monthly draw of $_____ month.

9.1 Owner Personal History

The owner has been working in the _____ (auto) industry for over ____ (#) years, gaining personal knowledge and experience in all phases of the industry. _____ (owner name) is the founder and operations manager of _____ (company name). He/she began his/her career as a _____.

Over the last ____ (#) years, _____ (owner name) became quite proficient in a wide range of management activities and responsibilities, becoming an operations manager for _____ (former employer name) from _____ to _____ (dates). There he/she was able to achieve _____.

_____, owner of _____ (company name), has a ____ degree in _____.
For ____ years he/she has managed a business similar to _____ (company name).
_____ (His/her) duties included _____.

Specifically, the owner brings _____ (#) years of experience as a _____ , as well as certification as a _____ from the _____ (National _____ Association). He/she is an experienced entrepreneur with ____ years of small business accounting, finance, marketing and management experience. Education includes college course work in business administration, banking and finance, investments, and commercial credit management.

The owner will draw an annual salary of $_____ from the business although most of this goes to repay loans to finance business start-up costs. These loans will be paid-in-full by _____ (month) of _____ (year).

9.2 Organizational Structure

The structure of the company is defined below. Only managers have voting rights in the company while all members are given equity stakes. Consultants have neither an equity stake nor voting rights. They are compensated for the work they perform on behalf of the firm.

Executive director managers	Managing director
Members	Principal consultants
Managing consultants	Senior consultants
Non-managers	Consultants

9.3 Management Compensation

Managers will be compensated on the profit of the firm based on equity percentages. Consultants will be paid according to the deliverables that they create.

9.4 Management Team Gaps

Despite the owner's and manager's experience in the _____ (auto?) industry, the company will also retain the consulting services of _____ (consultant company name). This company has over _____ (#) years of experience in the _____ industry, and has successfully opened dozens of Human Resources Consulting businesses across the country. The Consultants will be primarily used for market research, client satisfaction surveys and to provide additional input in the evaluation of new business opportunities. The company also expects to retain the services of a local CPA. Additionally, the business will make use of the following advisory board to provide support for strategic planning and human resource related issues.

The Board of Advisors will provide continuous mentoring support on business matters. Expertise gaps in legal, tax, marketing and personnel will be covered by the Board of

Advisors. The owner will actively seek free business advice from SCORE, a national non-profit organization with a local office. This is a group of retired executives and business owners who donate their time to serve as business counselors to new business owners.

Advisory Resources Available to the Business Include:

	Name	Address	Phone
CPA/Accountant			
Attorney			
Insurance Broker			
Banker			
Business Consultant			
Wholesale Suppliers			
Trade Association			
Realtor			
SCORE.org			
Other			

Management Matrix

Note: See appendix for attached management resumes.

Name	Title	Functions	Responsibilities

Outsourcing Matrix

Company Name	Functions	Responsibilities	Cost

Note: Marketing and public relations will be handled mainly by the owner. If there is a greater need, a marketing consultant will be hired to help issue press releases and generate seminar and website content.

9.5 Personnel Plan

Employee Requirements:
1. **Skills and Abilities**
   Suitable consultant candidates will include those with some experience in the energy industry and who have degrees in business or engineering education. Candidates must be self-motivating, and have strong client service skills. Previous experience as a programmer is preferred.

2. **Recruitment**

   We will recruit by asking friends in the energy industry for recommendations or placing ads in energy-related media. We will attend energy events, such as conferences, to meet people in person. Experience suggests that personal referrals are an excellent source for experienced consultants.

   Resources:

   https://jobs.hrgirlfriends.com/

3. **Training and Supervision**

   Training is largely accomplished through hands-on experience with supplemental instruction given on more complicated projects. Additional knowledge is gained through trade shows, and industry books, magazines, production manuals, and promotional materials. We will foster professional development and independence in all phases of our business. Supervision is task-oriented and the quantity is dependent on the complexity of the job assignment. Employees are called team members because they are part of Team _____ (company name). They will also participate in our written training modules.

4. **Salaries and Benefits**

   Employees will be basically paid a minimum wage plus commission. Good training and incentives, such as cash bonuses handed out monthly to everyone from managers to drivers for reaching sales goals, will serve to retain good employees. An employee discount of ____ percent on personal sales is offered. As business warrants, we hope to put together a benefit package that includes insurance, and paid vacations. The personnel plan also assumes a 5% annual increase in salaries.

5. **Incentive Plan**

   All employees will qualify for a quarterly bonus (equal to as much as ____ (10)% of their salary) based on several performance measures, including input from clients. In fact, ____(40) % of the potential bonus is tied to client feedback. Four times a year, as well as at the conclusion of major projects, management will call ____ (25) or so active clients. clients will be asked if they're satisfied with their assigned team's ability to communicate, solve problems, and respond to their needs, and, if so, would they be willing to serve as a reference? After talking to clients, the manager rates employees on a scale of one to five for each area of client service. Dissatisfied clients are weighed more heavily.

6. **Feedback Mechanism**

   We will provide incentives for employees to provide improvement suggestions and enhance our innovativeness and productivity.

Personnel Plan

1. We will develop a system for recruiting, screening and interviewing employees.
2. Criminal background checks and drug testing will be performed, as well as reference checks, because most organizations require these types of testing for human resources

professionals due to the sensitivity and confidentiality related to this type of work..
3. We will develop a consultant training course.
4. We will keep track of staff scheduling.
5. We will develop client satisfaction surveys to provide feedback and ideas.
6. We will develop and perform semi-annual employee evaluations.
7. We will "coach" all our employees to improve their abilities and range of skills.
8. We will employ temp employees to assist with one-time big projects.
9. Each employee will be provided a detailed job description and list of business policies, and be asked to sign these documents as a form of employment contract.

Resource:
http://www.jobhero.com/resume-samples/human-resource-consultant

9.6 Job Description Format

Our job descriptions will adhere to the following format guidelines:

1. Job Title
2. Reports to:
3. Pay Rate
4. Job Responsibilities
5. Travel Requirements
5. Supervisory Responsibilities
6. Qualifications
7. Work Experience
8. Required Skills
10. Salary Range
11. Benefits
12. Opportunities

The following table summarizes our personnel expenditures for the first three years, with salaries increasing from $_____ in the first year to about $_____ in the third year.

Job Description -- Human Resources Consultant

Responsible for providing human capital management advisory services to businesses. Helps companies develop and communicate policies, train employees, and implement a recruitment process. A professional level human resources position that provides advice, assistance, and training to client company personnel on human resources policies and procedures regarding the recruitment and hiring processes, performance management, legal compliance, labor issues and disciplinary procedures.

PRIMARY RESPONSIBILITIES

Advise companies on best human capital management practices.
Helps clients strategically integrate effective HR processes, programs and practices into their daily operations.
Perform internal reviews and audit of current systems and policies.
Perform quality assurance checks.
Deliver surveys to employees.
Conduct investigations and research into reclassification and classification.
Match job seekers to employers.
Ensure business practices are in accordance with human resource policies and labor laws.
Help train managers and HR employees.
Provide company with updated salary and job description information.
Help implement applicant tracking systems.

Provide consultation and guidance to senior management and organizational partners in the interpretation of human resource management policies, procedures, programs and application of related government laws and regulations.
Lead HR-related projects.
Provide advice on discipline process, conduct disciplinary review conferences and advise on appropriate outcomes.
Develop employee restructuring plans.
Devise severance packages.
Participate in the design, development and implementation of innovative workforce retention programs.
Provide review and approval of requests for reduction-in-force, reorganizations/realignments.

Resource: https://www.humanresourcesedu.org/hr-consultant/

Job Description: Human Resources Specialist

A term used to define an individual who has expertise and responsibility for a specific area or function in the field of Human Resources (i.e. compensation, benefits, employee relations, etc.)

Key Responsibilities:
1. Define the nature and extent of the problem that they have been asked to solve.
2. Analyze relevant data—which may include annual revenues, employment, or expenditures
3. Interview managers and employees while observing their operations.
4. Develop solutions to the problem.
5. Decided on a course of action
6. Report their findings and recommendations to the client.
7. Help implement suggestions.

Table: Personnel Plan

	Number of Employees	Hourly Rate	Annual Salaries 2018	2019	2020
Ops Manager/Owner					
Office Manager					
VP Marketing					
Editorial/Graphics					
Human Resources Consultants					
Human Resources Specialist					
Phone Sales					
Secretarial					
Bookkeeper					
P/T Janitorial					
Other					
Total People: Headcount					
Total Annual Payroll					

Payroll Burden (Fringe Benefits)   (+)   _____
Total Payroll Expense   (=)   _____

Salary Notes:
In its 2012 Occupational Outlook Handbook, the U.S. Bureau of Labor and Statistics (BLS) listed the median salary for human resource managers as $99,180 per year with a projected job outlook of 13 percent growth over the next decade. Suffice it to say, the median salary and job growth expectations look promising for HR consultants. As professionals who perform high-stress jobs in HR departments, their pay is commensurate with the experience and qualifications necessary for the job.

According to the Georgetown University Career Development Center, analysts with Human Resources Consulting Services can expect an annual starting salary of approximately $60,000 with a signing bonus in the area of $10,000. Associates have a wide range of salaries, with highly-paid consultants earning $130,000 per year. Partners in a Human Resources Consulting Service have the potential to earn even more money, as their salary is based on the success of the firm.

According to the IbisWorld research, the average wage for an HR consultant, regardless of company size, was projected to be $81,913 in 2013, up from $79,016 in 2004. HR consultants say their hourly fee typically ranges from $90 to $225.

According to the Bureau of Labor Statistics (BLS), the annual, mean salary for consultants was $90,860, as of May 2014, thereby revealing that companies

8.0   Risk Factors

Risk management is the identification, assessment, and prioritization of risks, followed by the coordinated and economical application of resources to minimize, monitor, and control the probability and/or impact of unfortunate events or to maximize the realization of opportunities. For the most part, our risk management methods will consist of the

following elements, performed, more or less, in the following order.
1. Identify, characterize, and assess threats
2. Assess the vulnerability of critical assets to specific threats
3. Determine the risk (i.e. the expected consequences of specific types of attacks on specific assets)
4. Identify ways to reduce those risks
5. Prioritize risk reduction measures based on a strategy

Types of Risks:

_____ (company name) faces the following kinds of risks:

1. **Financial Risks**

    Our quarterly revenues and operating results are difficult to predict and may fluctuate significantly from quarter to quarter as a result of a variety of factors. Among these factors are:
    - Changes in our own or competitors' pricing policies.
    - Recession pressures.
    - Fluctuations in expected revenues from advertisers, sponsors and strategic relationships.
    - Timing of costs related to acquisitions or payments.

2. **Legislative / Legal Landscape.**

    Our participation in the consulting arena presents unique risks:
    - Service/Product and other related liability.
    - State regulations on licensing, certification, privacy and insurance.

3. **Operational Risks**

    For the past __ (#) years the owner has been dealing with computers, so he is comfortable with technology and understands a wide array of software applications. However, the biggest potential problem will be equipment malfunction. To minimize the potential for problems, the owner will be taking equipment repair training from the manufacturer and will deal with basic troubleshooting and minor repairs. Beyond that, we have identified a service technician who is located close-by.

    To attract and retain client to the _____ (company name) community, we must continue to provide differentiated and quality services. This confers certain risks including the failure to:
    - Anticipate and respond to consumer preferences for partnerships and service.
    - Attract, excite and retain a large audience of clients to our community.
    - Create and maintain successful strategic alliances with quality partners.
    - Deliver high quality, client service.
    - Build our brand rapidly and cost-effectively.
    - Compete effectively against better-established HR consulting firms.

4. **Human Resource Risks**

   The most serious human resource risk to our business, at least in the initial stages, would be my inability to operate the business due to illness or disability. The owner is currently in exceptional health and would eventually seek to replace himself on a day-to-day level by developing systems to support the growth of the business.

5. **Marketing Risks**

   Advertising is our most expensive form of promotion and there will be a period of testing headlines and offers to find the one that works the best. The risk, of course, is that we will exhaust our advertising budget before we find an ad that works. Placing greater emphases on sunk-cost marketing, such as our office set-up and on existing relationships through direct selling will minimize our initial reliance on advertising to bring in a large percentage of business in the first year.

6. **Business Risks**

   A major risk to retail service businesses is the performance of the economy and the small business sector. Since economists are predicting this as the fastest growing sector of the economy, our risk of a downturn in the short-term is minimized. The entrance of one of the major consultancies into our marketplace is a risk. They offer more of the latest equipment, provide a wider array of products and services, competitive prices and 24-hour service. This situation would force us to lower our prices in the short-term until we could develop an offering of higher margin, value-added services not provided by the large chains. It does not seem likely that the relative size of our market today could support the overhead of one of those operations. Projections indicate that this will not be the case in the future and that leaves a window of opportunity for ___ (company name) to aggressively build a loyal client base. We will also not pursue big-leap, radical change misadventures, but rather strive to hit stepwise performance benchmarks, with a planned consistency over a long period of time.

The Company's start-up quarterly revenues and operating results are difficult to predict and may fluctuate from quarter to quarter as a result of a variety of factors, including changes in pricing to accommodate local market conditions, recession pressures and seasonal patterns of spending.

To combat the usual start-up risks we will do the following:
1. Utilize our industry experience to quickly establish desired strategic relationships.
2. Pursue business outside of our immediate market area.
3. Diversify our range of product and service offerings.
4. Develop multiple distribution channels.
5. Monitor our competitor actions.
6. Stay in touch with our clients and suppliers.
7. Watch for trends which could potentially impact our business.
8. Continuously optimize and scrutinize all business processes.

9. Institute daily financial controls using Business Ratio Analysis.
10. Create pay-for-performance compensation and training programs to reduce employee turnover.
11. Break the project into discrete parts and bid on one part at a time.
12. Request progress payments in all contracts.
13. Clearly define the limits of what we are responsible for by stating assumptions.
14. Raise our price to cover overruns.
15. Create a detailed specification for the project.
16. Update the specification after testing and evaluating the Phase I results.
17. We will build a contingency fund into the project price as a safety cushion.
18. Develop a methodology for evaluating project results.
19. Develop a definition for project success.
20. Develop a precise project plan for every project.

Further, to attract and retain clients the Company will need to continue to expand its market offerings, utilizing third party strategic relationships. This could lead to difficulties in the management of relationships, competition for specific services and products, and/or adverse market conditions affecting a particular partner.

The Company will take active steps to mitigate risks. In preparation of the Company's pricing, many factors will be considered. The Company will closely track the activities of all third parties, and will hold monthly review meetings to resolve issues and review and update the terms associated with strategic alliances.

Additionally, we will develop the following kinds of contingency plans:
Disaster Recovery Plan
Business Continuity Plan
Business Impact and Gap Analysis
Testing & Maintenance

The Company will utilize marketing and advertising campaigns to promote brand identity and will coordinate all expectations with internal and third-party resources prior to release. This strategy should maximize client satisfaction while minimizing potential costs associated with unplanned expenditures and quality control issues.

8.1   Reduce New Business Risk Tactics

We plan to use the following tactics to reduce our new business risk:
1. Implement your business plan based on go, no-go stage criteria.
2. Develop employee cross-training programs.
3. Regularly back-up all computer files/Install ant-virus software.
4. Arrange adequate insurance coverage with higher deductibles.
5. Develop a limited number of prototype samples.
6. Test market offerings to determine level of market demand and appropriate pricing strategy.

7. Thoroughly investigate and benchmark to competitor offerings.
8. Research similar franchised businesses for insights into successful prototype business/operations models.
9. Reduce operation risks and costs by flowcharting all structured systems & standardized manual processes.
10. Use market surveys to listen to client needs and priorities.
11. Purchase used equipment to reduce capital outlays.
12. Use leasing to reduce financial risk.
13. Outsource manufacturing to job shops to reduce capital at risk.
14. Use subcontractors to limit fixed overhead salary expenses.
15. Ask manufacturer about profit sharing arrangement.
16. Pay advertisers with a percent of revenues generated.
17. Develop contingency plans for identified risks.
18. Set-up procedures to control employee theft.
19. Do criminal background checks on potential employees.
20. Take immediate action on delinquent accounts.
21. Only extend credit to established account with D&B rating
22. Get regular competitive bids from alternative suppliers.
23. Check that operating costs as a percent of rising sales are lower as a result of productivity improvements.
24. Request bulk rate pricing on fast moving supplies.
25. Don't be tempted to tie up cash in slow moving inventory to qualify for bigger discounts.
26. Reduce financial risk by practicing cash flow policies.
27. Reduce hazard risk by installing safety procedures.
28. Use financial management ratios to monitor business vitals.
29. Make business decisions after brainstorming sessions.
30. Focus on the products/services with biggest return on investment.
31. Where possible, purchase off-the-shelf components.
32. Request manufacturer samples to build your prototype.
33. Design your production facilities to be flexible and easy to change.
34. Develop a network of suppliers with outsourcing capabilities.
35. Analyze and shorten every cycle time, including product development.
36. Develop multiple sources for every important input.
37. Treat the business plan as a living document and update it frequently.
38. Conduct a SWOT analysis and use determined strengths to pursue opportunities.
39. Conduct regular client satisfaction surveys to evaluate performance.
40. Develop clear and rigorously pursued performance mechanisms and standards to keep a steady pace of growth on track and avoid the penalty for over-extension.

8.2 Reduce Client Perceived Risk Tactics

We will utilize the following tactics to help reduce the new client's perceived risk of starting to do business with our company.

                                                                                                     Status

1. Publish a page of testimonials. _____
2. Secure Opinion Leader written endorsements. _____

3. Offer an Unconditional Satisfaction Money Back Guarantee. _____
4. Long-term Performance Guarantee (Financial Risk). _____
5. Guaranteed Buy Back (Obsolete time risk) _____
6. Offer free trials and samples. _____
7. Brand Image (consistent marketing image and performance) _____
8. Patents/Trademarks/Copyrights _____
9. Publish case studies _____
10. Share your expertise (Articles, Seminars, etc.) _____
11. Get recognized Certification _____
12. Conduct responsive client service _____
13. Accept Installment Payments _____
14. Display product materials composition or ingredients. _____
15. Publish product test results. _____
16. Publish sales record milestones. _____
17. Foster word-of-mouth by offering an unexpected extra. _____
18. Distribute factual, pre-purchase info. _____
19. Reduce consumer search costs with online directories. _____
20. Reduce client transaction costs. _____
21. Facilitate in-depth comparisons to alternative services. _____
22. Make available prior client ratings and comments. _____
23. Provide customized info based on prior transactions. _____
24. Become a Better Business Bureau member. _____
25. Publish overall client satisfaction survey results. _____
26. Offer plan options that match niche segment needs. _____
27. Require client sign-off before proceeding to next phase. _____
28. Document procedures for dispute resolution. _____
29. Offer the equivalent of open source code. _____
30. Stress your compatibility features (avoid lock-in fear). _____
31. Create detailed checklists & flowcharts to show processes _____
32. Publish a list of frequently asked questions/answers. _____
33. Create a community that enables clients to connect with
    each other and share common interests. _____
34. Inform clients as to your stay-in-touch methods. _____
35. Conduct and handover a detailed needs analysis worksheet. _____
36. Offer to pay all return shipping charges and/or refund all
    original shipping and handling fees. _____
37. Describe your product testing procedures prior to shipping. _____
38. Highlight your competitive advantages in all marketing materials. _____

9.0 Financial Plan

The over-all financial plan for growth allows for use of the significant cash flow generated by operations. We are basing projected sales on the market research, industry analysis and competitive environment.

_____ (company name) expects a profit margin of over ____ (60?) % starting with year one. By year two, that number should slowly increase as the law of diminishing costs takes hold, and the day-to-day activities of the business become less expensive.

Sales are expected to grow at ____ % per year, and level off by year _____.
The initial investment in _____ (company name) will be provided by _____ (owner name) in the amount of $ _____. The owner will also seek a ___ (#) year bank loan in the amount of $ _____ to provide the remainder of the required initial funding.

The funds will be used to renovate the space and to cover initial operating expenses.
The owner financing will become a return on equity, paid in the form of dividends to the owner. We expect to finance slow and steady growth through cash flow. Salaries and rent are the two major expenses. The owners do not intend to take any profits out of the business until the long-term debt has been satisfied.

Our financial plan includes:
Moderate growth rate with a steady cash flow.
Investing residual profits into company expansion.
Company expansion will be an option if sales projections are met and/or exceeded.
Marketing costs will remain below ___ (5?) % of sales.
Repayment of our loan calculated at a high A.P.R. of ___ (10?) percent and at a 10-year-payback on our $_____ loan.

Revenue Assumptions:

	Year	Sales/Month	Growth Rate
1.			
2.			
3.			

Resource:
www.score.org/resources/business-plans-financial-statements-template-gallery

9.1 Break-even Analysis

Fixed costs are based on running costs estimated by the owner(s) of the company and include payroll for all employees. Variable costs are based on a _____% estimate of the average sales per unit. The average revenue estimate is based on the judgment of the owner(s) who have had many years of experience in the industry and on the realistic assumption of the types of contracts the company will get in the beginning and the requirements needed to complete such commitments.

Definition: Break-Even Is the Volume Where All Fixed Expenses Are Covered. Based on projections, we will need an average of __ clients each month to breakeven.

Three important definitions used in break-even analysis are:
- **Variable Costs** (Expenses) are costs that change directly in proportion to changes in activity (volume), such as raw materials, labor and packaging.
- **Fixed Costs** (Expenses) are costs that remain constant (fixed) for a given time period despite wide fluctuations in activity (volume), such as rent, loan payments, insurance, payroll and utilities.
- **Unit Contribution Margin** is the difference between your product's unit selling price and its unit variable cost.
  Unit Contribution Margin = Unit Sales Price - Unit Variable Cost

For the purposes of this breakeven analysis, the assumed fixed operating costs will be approximately $ _____ per month, as shown in the following table.

Averaged Monthly Fixed Costs:
Payroll   _____
Rent   _____
Insurance   _____
Utilities   _____
Security.   _____
Legal/Technical Help _____
Other   _____
Total: _____

Variable Costs:
Cost of Inventory Sold   _____
Labor   _____
Supplies   _____
Direct Costs per Client   _____
Other   _____

Total   _____

A break-even analysis table has been completed on the basis of average costs/prices. With monthly fixed costs averaging $_____ , $____ in average sales and $_____ in average variable costs, we need approximately $_____ in sales per month to break-even. Based on our assumed ___ % variable cost, we estimate our breakeven sales volume at around $ _____ per month. We expect to reach that sales volume by our _____ month of operations. Our break-even analysis is shown in further detail in the following table.

Breakeven Formulas:
  Break Even Units = Total Fixed Costs / (Unit Selling Price - Variable Unit Cost)
  _____ = _____ / (_____ - _____)

  BE Dollars = (Total Fixed Costs / (Unit Price – Variable Unit Costs))/ Unit Price
  _____ = (_____ / (_____ - _____)) / _____

  BE Sales = Annual Fixed Costs / (1- Unit Variable costs / Unit Sales Price)
  _____ = _____ / (1 - _____ / _____)

Table: Break-even Analysis

Monthly Units Break-even   _____
Monthly Revenue Break-even $ _____
Assumptions:
Average Per-Unit Revenue $ _____
Average Per-Unit Variable Cost $ _____
Estimated monthly Fixed Cost $ _____

Ways to Improve Breakeven Point:
1. Reduce Fixed Costs via Cost Controls
2. Raise unit sales prices.
3. Lower Variable Costs by improving employee productivity or getting lower competitive bids from suppliers.
4. Broaden product/service line to generate multiple revenue streams.

9.2 Projected Profit and Loss

Pro forma income statements are an important tool for planning our future business operations. If the projections predict a downturn in profitability, we can make operational changes such as increasing prices or decreasing costs before these projections become reality.

Our monthly profit for the first year varies significantly, as we aggressively seek improvements and begin to implement our marketing plan. However, after the first ___ months, profitability should be established.

We predict advertising costs will go down in the next three years as word-of-mouth about our Human Resources Consulting company gets out to the public and we are able to find what has worked well for us and concentrate on those advertising methods, and corporate affiliations generate sales without the need for extra advertising.

Our net profit/sales ratio will be low the first year. We expect this ratio to rise at least _____ (15?) percent the second year. Normally, a startup concern will operate with negative profits through the first two years. We will avoid that kind of operating loss on our second year by knowing our competitors and having a full understanding of our target markets.

Our projected profit and loss is indicated in the following table. From our research of the consulting industry, our annual projections are quite realistic and conservative, and we prefer this approach so that we can ensure an adequate cash flow.

Key P & L Formulas:
Gross Margin = Total Sales Revenue - Cost of Goods Sold
Gross Margin % = (Total Sales Revenue - Cost of Goods Sold) / Total Sales Revenue
This number represents the proportion of each dollar of revenue that the company retains as gross profit.
EBITDA =Revenue - Expenses (exclude interest, taxes, depreciation & amortization)
PBIT = Profit (Earnings) Before Interest and Taxes = EBIT
A profitability measure that looks at a company's profits before the company has to pay corporate income tax and interest expenses. This measure deducts all operating expenses from revenue, but it leaves out the payment of interest and tax. Also referred to as "earnings before interest and tax ".
Net Profit = Total Sales Revenues - Total Expenses

Pro Forma Profit and Loss

	Formula	2018	2019	2020
Revenue:				
Human Resources Consulting				
Training Programs				
Seminars/Workshops				
Project Management Services				
Software Sales				

Other Product Sales
Other Consulting Income
Total Sales Revenue A

Direct Costs B
Other Costs of Goods C
Total Costs of Goods Sold B+C=D

Gross Margin A-D=E
Gross Margin % E / A

Expenses
Payroll
Payroll Taxes
Delivery Labor
Sales & Marketing
Portfolio Materials
Conventions/Trade Shows
Depreciation
License/Permit Fees
Entertainment
Travel
Dues and Subscriptions
Rent
Utilities
Deposits
Interest
Repairs and Maintenance
Janitorial Supplies
Office Supplies
General Supplies
Leased Equipment
Insurance
Bad Debts
Miscellaneous
Total Operating Expenses F

Profit Before Int. & Taxes E - F = G
Interest Expenses H
Taxes Incurred I
Net Profit G - H - I = J

Net Profit / Sales J / A = K

9.4 Projected Cash Flow

The Cash Flow Statement shows how the company is paying for its operations and future growth, by detailing the "flow" of cash between the company and the outside world. Positive numbers represent cash flowing in, negative numbers represent cash flowing out.

The first year's monthly cash flows are will vary significantly, but we do expect a solid cash balance from day one. We expect that the majority of our sales will be done in cash or by credit card and that will be good for our cash flow position. Additionally, we will stock only slightly more than one month's inventory at any time. Consequently, we do not anticipate any problems with cash flow, once we have obtained sufficient start-up funds.

A __ year commercial loan in the amount of $_____, sought by the owner will be used to cover our working capital requirement. Our projected cash flow is summarized in the following table, and is expected to meet our needs. In the following years, excess cash will be used to finance our growth plans.

Cash Flow Management:
We will use the following practices to improve our cash flow position:
1. Become more selective when granting credit.
2. Seek deposits or multiple stage payments.
3. Reduce the amount/time of credit given to clients.
4. Reduce direct and indirect costs and overhead expenses.
5. Use the 80/20 rule to manage inventories, receivables and payables.
6. Invoice as soon as the service has been performed.
7. Generate regular reports on receivable ratios and aging.
8. Establish and adhere to sound credit practices.
9. Use more pro-active collection techniques.
10. Add late payment fees where possible.
11. Increase the credit taken from suppliers.
12. Negotiate extended credit terms from vendors.
13. Use some barter arrangements to acquire goods and service.
14. Use leasing to gain access to the use of productive assets.
15. Covert debt into equity.
16. Regularly update cash flow forecasts.
17. Defer projects which cannot achieve acceptable cash paybacks.
18. Require a 50% deposit upon the signing of the contract and the balance in full, due five days before the event.

Cash Flow Formulas:
Net Cash Flow = Incoming Cash Receipts - Outgoing Cash Payments
Equivalently, net profit plus amounts charged off for depreciation, depletion, and amortization. (also called cash flow).

Cash Balance = Opening Cash Balance + Net Cash Flow
We are positioning ourselves in the market as a medium risk concern with steady cash flows. Accounts payable is paid at the end of each month, while sales are in cash, giving our company an excellent cash structure.

Pro Forma Cash Flow

	Formula	2018	2019	2020
Cash Received				
Cash from Operations				
Cash Sales	A			
Cash from Receivables	B			
Subtotal Cash from Operations	A + B = C			

Additional Cash Received
Non-Operating (Other) Income
Sales Tax, VAT, HST/GST Received
New Current Borrowing
New Other Liabilities (interest fee)
New Long-term Liabilities
Sales of Other Current Assets
Sales of Long-term Assets
New Investment Received
Total Additional Cash Received   D
Subtotal Cash Received   C + D = E

Expenditures
Expenditures from Operations
Cash Spending   F
Payment of Accounts Payable   G
Subtotal Spent on Operations   F+G = H

Additional Cash Spent
Non-Operating (Other) Expenses
Sales Tax, VAT, HST/GST Paid Out
Principal Repayment Current Borrowing
Other Liabilities Principal Repayment
Long-term Liabilities Principal Repayment
Purchase Other Current Assets
Dividends
Total Additional Cash Spent   I
Subtotal Cash Spent   H + I = J
Net Cash Flow   **E - J = K**
Cash Balance

9.5   Projected Balance Sheet

Pro forma Balance Sheets are used to project how the business will be managing its assets in the future. As a pure start-up business, the opening balance sheet may contain no values. The projected balance sheets must link back into the projected income statements and cash flow projections.

_____ (company name) does not project any real trouble meeting its debt obligations, provided the revenue predictions are met. We are very confident that we will meet or exceed all of our objectives in the Business Plan and produce a slow but steady increase in net worth.

All of our tables will be updated monthly to reflect past performance and future assumptions. Future assumptions will not be based on past performance but rather on economic cycle activity, regional industry strength, and future cash flow possibilities. We expect a solid growth in net worth by the year _____.

The Balance Sheet table for fiscal years 2018, 2019, and 2020 follows. It shows managed but sufficient growth of net worth, and a sufficiently healthy financial position.

Excel Resource:
www.unioncity.org/ED/Finance%20Tools/Projected%20Balance%20Sheet.xls

Key Formulas:

Paid-in Capital = Capital contributed to the corporation by investors on top of the par value of the capital stock.

Retained Earnings = The portion of net income which is retained by the corporation rather than distributed to the owners as dividends.

Earnings = Revenues - (Cost of Sales + Operating Expenses + Taxes)

Net Worth = Total Assets - Total Liabilities   Also known as 'Owner's Equity'.

Pro Forma Balance Sheet

	Formulas	2018	2019	2020
Assets				
Current Assets				
Cash				
Accounts Receivable				
Inventory				

Other Current Assets		_____
Total Current Assets	A	_____
Long-term Assets		
Long-term Assets	B	_____
Accumulated Depreciation	C	_____
Total Long-term Assets	B - C = D	_____
Total Assets	**A + D = E**	_____

Liabilities and Capital
Current Liabilities

Accounts Payable		_____
Current Borrowing		_____
Other Current Liabilities		_____
Subtotal Current Liabilities	F	_____
Long-term Liabilities		
Notes Payable		_____
Other Long-term Liabilities		_____
Subtotal Long-term Liabilities	G	_____
Total Liabilities	**F + G = H**	_____
Capital		
Paid-in Capital	I	_____
Retained Earnings	J	_____
Earnings	K	_____
Total Capital	I - J + K = L	_____
Total Liabilities and Capital	**H + L = M**	_____
Net Worth	E - H = N	_____

9.6   Business Ratios

Key Business Ratio Formulas:

EBIT = Earnings Before Interest and Taxes
EBITA = Earnings Before Interest, Taxes & Amortization. (Operating Profit Margin)

Sales Growth Rate =((Current Year Sales - Last Year Sales)/(Last Year Sales)) x 100

Ex: Percent of Sales = (Advertising Expense / Sales) x 100

Net Worth = Total Assets - Total Liabilities

Acid Test Ratio = Liquid Assets / Current Liabilities
Measures how much money business has immediately available. A ratio of 2:1 is good.

Net Profit Margin = Net Profit / Net Revenues
The higher the net profit margin is, the more effective the company is at converting revenue into actual profit.

Return on Equity (ROE) = Net Income / Shareholder's Equity
The ROE is useful for comparing the profitability of a company to that of other firms in the same industry. Also known as "return on net worth" (RONW).

Current Ratio = Current Assets / Current Liabilities
The higher the current ratio, the more capable the company is of paying its obligations. A ratio under 1 suggests that the company would be unable to pay off its obligations if they came due at that point.

Quick Ratio = Current Assets - Inventories / Current Liabilities
The quick ratio is more conservative than the current ratio, because it excludes inventory from current assets.

Pre-Tax Return on Net Worth = Pre-Tax Income / Net Worth
Indicates stockholders' earnings before taxes for each dollar of investment.

Pre-Tax Return on Assets = (EBIT / Assets) x 100
Indicates much profit the firm is generating from the use of its assets.

Accounts Receivable Turnover = Net Credit Sales / Average Accounts Receivable
A low ratio implies the company should re-assess its credit policies in order to ensure the timely collection of imparted credit that is not earning interest for the firm.

Net Working Capital = Current Assets - Current Liabilities
Positive working capital means that the company is able to pay off its short-term liabilities. Negative working capital means that a company currently is unable to meet its short-term liabilities with its current assets (cash, accounts receivable and inventory).

Interest Coverage Ratio = Earnings Before Interest & Taxes /Total Interest Expense
The lower the ratio, the more the company is burdened by debt expense. When a company's interest coverage ratio is 1.5 or lower, its ability to meet interest expenses may be questionable. An interest coverage ratio below 1 indicates the company is not generating sufficient revenues to satisfy interest expenses.

Collection Days = Accounts Receivables / (Revenues/365)
A high ratio indicates that the company is having problems getting paid for services.

Accounts Payable Turnover = Total Supplier Purchases/Average Accounts Payable
If the turnover ratio is falling from one period to another, this is a sign that the company is taking longer to pay off its suppliers than previously. The opposite is true when the turnover ratio is increasing, which means the firm is paying of suppliers at a faster rate.

Payment Days = (Accounts Payable Balance x 360) / (No. of Accounts Payable x 12)
The average number of days between receiving an invoice and paying it off.

Total Asset Turnover = Revenue / Assets
Asset turnover measures a firm's efficiency at using its assets in generating sales or revenue - the higher the number the better.

Sales / Net Worth = Total Sales / Net Worth

Dividend Payout = Dividends / Net Profit

Assets to Sales = Assets / Sales

Current Debt / Totals Assets = Current Liabilities / Total Assets

Current Liabilities to Liabilities = Current Liabilities / Total Liabilities

Business Ratio Analysis

	2018	2019	2020	Industry
Sales Growth				
Percent of Total Assets				
Accounts Receivable				21.50%
Inventory				3.50%
Other Current Assets				46.40%
Total Current Assets				71.40%

Long-term Assets		28.60%
Total Assets		100.00%
Current Liabilities		51.20%
Long-term Liabilities		19.50%
Total Liabilities		71.70%
Net Worth		29.30%

Percent of Sales

Sales		100.00%
Gross Margin		0.00%
Selling G&A Expenses		80.60%
Advertising Expenses		1.40%
Profit Before Interest & Taxes		1.70%

Main Ratios

Current		1.23
Quick		1.01
Total Debt to Total Assets		70.70%
Pre-tax Return on Net Worth		3.50%
Pre-tax Return on Assets		11.60%

Additional Ratios

Net Profit Margin
Return on Equity

Activity Ratios

Accounts Receivable Turnover
Collection Days
Inventory Turnover
Accounts Payable Turnover
Payment Days
Total Asset Turnover
Inventory Productivity
Sales per sq/ft.
Gross Margin Return on Inventory (GMROI)

Debt Ratios

Debt to Net Worth
Current Liabilities to Liabilities

Liquidity Ratios

Net Working Capital
Interest Coverage

Additional Ratios

Assets to Sales   _____
Current Debt / Total Assets   _____
Acid Test   _____
Sales / Net Worth   _____
Dividend Payout   _____

Business Vitality Profile
Sales per Employee   _____
Survival Rate   _____

Helpful Resources:

Associations:
Institute of -Human Resources Consultants   www.imcusa.org

Professional and Technical Consultants Association	www.patca.org/
Institute of Human Resources Consultants USA	www.imcusa.org
National Speakers Association	www.nsaspeaker.org
American Society for Training and Development	www.astd.org
Institute for the Certification of Computing Professionals	www.iccp.org
Association of Human Resources Consulting Services	www.amcf.org/amcf/

Miscellaneous:

Vista Print Free Business Cards	www.vistaprint.com
Free Business Guides	www.smbtn.com/businessplanguides/
Open Office	http://download.openoffice.org/
US Census Bureau	www.census.gov
Federal Government	www.business.gov
US Patent & Trademark Office	www.uspto.gov
US Small Business Administration	www.sba.gov
National Association for the Self-Employed	www.nase.org
International Franchise Association	www.franchise.org
Center for Women's Business Research	www.cfwbr.org

Advertising Plan Worksheet

Ad Campaign Title: _____

Ad Campaign Start Date: _____ End Date: _____

What are the features (what product has) and hidden benefits (what product does for consumer) of my products/services?

Who is the targeted audience?

What problems are faced by this targeted audience?

What solutions do you offer?

Who is the competition and how do they advertise?

What is your differentiation strategy?

What are your bullet point competitive advantages?

What are the objectives of this advertising campaign?

What are your general assumptions?

What positioning image do you want to project?
- ___ Exclusiveness
- ___ Low Cost
- ___ High Quality
- ___ Speedy Service
- ___ Convenient
- ___ Innovative

What is the ad headline?

What is the advertising budget for this advertising campaign?

What advertising methods will be used?
- ___ Radio
- ___ TV/Cable
- ___ Yellow Pages
- ___ Coupons
- ___ Telemarketing
- ___ Flyers
- ___ Direct Mail
- ___ Magazines
- ___ Newspapers
- ___ Press Release
- ___ Brochures
- ___ Billboards
- ___ Other

When will each advertising method start and what will it cost?

Method	Start Date	Frequency	Cost

Indicate how you will measure the cost-effectiveness of the advertising plan?
Formula: Return on Investment (ROI) = Generated Sales / Ad Costs.

Marketing Action Plan

Month: _____

Target Market: _____

Responsibilities: _____

Allocated Budget: _____

Objectives _____

Strategies _____

Implementation _____

Tactics _____

Results Evaluation _____

_____

Lessons Learned:

_____

Viral Marketing

Definition: Also known as word-of-mouth advertising.
Objective: To prompt your clients to deliver your sales message to others.
Strategy: Encourage and enable communication recipients to pass the offer

> or message along to others.

Benefit: Provides an excellent advertising return on investment and builds the trust factor.

Methodologies:
1. Encourage blog comments and two-way dialogue.
2. Use surveys to solicit feedback.
3. Use refer-a-friend forms or scripts.
4. Provide discount coupon or logo imprinted giveaway rewards for telling a friend.
5. Utilize pre-existing social networks.
6. Participate in message boards or forums.
7. Add a signature line with a refer-a-friend tagline to all posts and emails.
8. Enable unrestricted access.
9. Facilitate website content sharing.
10. Write articles and e-books, and encourage free reprints with byline mention.
11. Submit articles with 'about the author' box to article directories, such as www.articlecity.com.
12. Develop attention-grabbing product line extensions to stay connected.
13. Do the unexpected by offering a surprise benefit.
14. Deliver a remarkable offering that exceeds client expectations.
15. Provoke a strong emotional response by getting involved with a cause that is important to your clients.
16. Provide referral incentives.
17. Get free samples into the hands of respected opinion leaders.
18. Educate clients, as to your product benefits and competitive advantages, to act as spokespersons for your company.

Explain Your Viral Marketing Program

_____
_____
_____
_____
_____

Marketing on Social Networking Websites

1. Place banner ads or Pay-Per-Click ads on social networking sites.
2. Create an account on the website and add your company logo.
3. Encourage word-of-mouth exchanges by posting comments on

friend's profiles.
4. Post surveys on your social networking pages to solicit feedback.
5. Create a profile that subtly and humbly tells everyone about you and your gift basket products and services.
6. Include links to your gift basket business website.
7. Make your profile keyword rich with keyword phases from your business specialty.
8. Use a soft sell approach, and focus on establishing your credibility and expertise as a gift basket marketing guru, to be trusted by prospective clients.
9. Name your social networking page exactly as your organization is named.
10. Have a strong presence in one channel rather than all of them.
11. Make sure you give visitors a strong call to action to supply their email address, so you can contact them later.
12. Include a signature line with your website contact info.
13. Blog often, but make certain that instead of selling, you are sharing your gift industry expertise.

Helpful Resources:
http://en.wikipedia.org/wiki/List_of_social_networking_websites
Examples: Facebook.com   Myspace.com
            LinkedIn.com   Ryse.com

Explain Your Online Social Networking Strategy
_____
_____
_____
_____
_____

Integrate Marketing into Daily Operations

Objective: To seamlessly integrate marketing processes into daily, routine operations.

Strategies:
1. Develop form to ask for referrals upon new client registration and annual renewal.

2. Present a sales presentation folder upon registration or contract sign-up with needs analysis worksheets, testimonials, new product introduction flyers, innovative application ideas, etc.
3. Develop a second sales presentation folder version for presentation upon job completion or sale, with referral program details, warranty service contract blank, and accessory suggestions.
4. Include business cards and coupons with all product deliverables.
5. Install company yard signs during job set-up.
6. Include a thank you note/comment card with all deliverables.
7. Include flyers and helpful articles in all client correspondence, especially mailed invoices and statements.
8. Attach logo and contact info to all finished products.
9. Conduct client satisfaction surveys while clients are waiting to be served.
10. Develop enclosed warranty card to build client database and feed drip marketing program.
11. Provide competitor product/service comparisons that highlight your strengths.
12. Incorporate feedback cards into merchandise displays.
13. Train all employees to also be sales and client service agents.
14. Print your Mission Statement or slogan on all forms and correspondence.
15. _____
16. _____

Indicate how you will incorporate marketing into daily operations.

Sales Stage	Business Processes	Opportunities to Incorporate Marketing Techniques
Pre-sale		
Transaction		
Post Sale		

Monthly Marketing Calendar

Instruction: Use to plan your monthly marketing events or activities and evaluate individual event results and marketing lessons learned for the month.

Month/Year: _____

| Event/ | Responsibility | Cost | Comments | Date | Results |

Activity   Evaluation

_____
_____
_____
_____
_____
_____
_____
_____
_____
_____
_____
_____
_____
_____
_____
_____
_____
_____
_____
_____
_____
_____

Monthly Evaluation of Lessons Learned:

_____
_____
_____

Form Strategic Marketing Alliances

Definition: A collaborative relationship between two or more non-competing firms with the intent of accomplishing mutually compatible and beneficial goals that would be difficult for each to accomplish alone. Also referred to as 'Collaboration Marketing'.

Note: Usually, potential alliance partners sell distinct or complementary products and/or services to the same target market audience.

Advantages: Improve marketing efficiency by achieving synergy in resource allocation with strategic partners.
Improve marketing effectiveness by creating a one-stop or wraparound shopping experience.
A way to inexpensively test the market for growth potential.

Types of Co-Ventures:
1. Informal Strategic Alliances
2. Contractual Relationships (Attorney review recommended)
3. New Business Entity (Set-up by attorney)

Informal Strategic Alliances
1. Most involve consultations regarding:
    a. Mutual Referrals
    b. Research for product improvements
    c. Promotion of products or services (affiliate programs).
    d. Creative product bundling arrangements.
2. May or may not require a written agreement.
3. May or may not require compensation.

Topics to be Covered:
1. The specific strategic goals and objectives of the alliance.
2. The performance expectations of the parties.
3. The scope of the alliance.
4. The period of performance.
5. Termination and renewal procedures.
6. Strategic marketing plan to promote the alliance.
7. Dispute resolution procedures.
8. Performance tracking methods.
9. Periodic evaluation of reciprocal benefits realized.
10. Website pages/links to promote alliance partners.

Example: The mutual referral relationship between a sports bar and a fitness club or physical fitness trainer.

Strategic Marketing Alliance Worksheet

Methodology:
1. Identify the assets and capabilities you can provide to the alliance.
2. Identify the assets and capabilities that the proposed partner will bring to the alliance.
3. Determine the benefits you are seeking from the alliance.
4. Determine the gaps in your offerings that the alliance partner can fill.
5. List any conflicting relationships with other businesses and benefits

received.
6. Research the potential alliance for strategic fit and other opportunities.
7. List the ways in which your clients will benefit from this alliance.
8. Assess any alliance risks.
9. Determine the ongoing actions needed to maintain the alliance.
10. Design a marketing plan to promote the alliance.
11. Develop a Mission Statement for the alliance.
12. Develop the Management Plan for the alliance.
13. Design the alliance appraisal and renewal procedures.

Potential Alliance Partner	Partner Strengths Offered	Your Offering Gaps Filled	Client Benefits	Alliance Risks

Referral Program Tips

Objective: To formalize your referral program so that it can be easily and consistently integrated into your operating processes.

1. Define the stages in the sales process when you will ask for a referral. Ex: Registration, Renewals, Annual Drive, etc.)

2. Document your referral asking script (include objection handling

responses).

3. Include a request for referrals in your client satisfaction survey and your registration forms.

4. Stress the dependence of your business on referrals in all your marketing communications.

5. Set-up a follow-up procedure and tracking form to convert referral leads into actual clients.

6. Publish your referral incentives, awards criteria and timetable for settlement.

7. Customize your referral program to the motivational needs of a select number of potential 'Bird Dogs' or 'Big Hitters'.

8. Educate potential referral agents as to the characteristics of your ideal prospect. (Develop Ideal Prospect Profile)

9. Set-up special, mutual referral arrangements with strategic business alliance partners and track the reciprocity of efforts.

10. Join or start a local lead group.

11. Set-up 'thank-you note' templates to facilitate your expression of gratitude.

12. Use logo imprinted giveaways, such as T-sheets, as referral thank you expressions.

Seminar Outline Worksheet

Objective: To establish your expertise on the subject matter, and produce future possible networking contacts by offering a newsletter sign-up and/or business card exchange.

Warning: Make seminar information rich and not a sales presentation.

1. Start with Attention-Grabbing Headline
   Ex: Hard-hitting Quotation, Thought Provoking Question, Startling Fact

2. Introduce Yourself and Establish Your Credentials

3. Present Seminar Overview

4. Discuss Attendee Participation Guidelines

5. Solicit a sampling of attendee interests, backgrounds and concerns.

6. Establish Learning Objectives

7. Preview the Bulleted Topics To be Covered

8. Share a Relevant Success Story (Case Study).

9. Use analogies and comparisons to create reference points.

10. Use statistics to support your position.

11. Conclusion: - Summarize Benefits for Attendees / Appeal to Action

12. Hold Question and Answer Session

13. Final Thoughts
    - Appreciation for Help Received
    - Indicate after-seminar availability

14. Handout A Remembrance
    - Business Cards
    - Seminar Outline
    - Glossary of Terms
    - Feedback Survey

Seminar Planning

Opening Discussion
Canvas participants' previous experience in relation to the topic.
Introduction
Provide a brief introduction to establish the context, perhaps one or two references to relevant literature and a mention of the departmental context. Link back to the participants contribution to the opening discussion.
Outline
    what it is you have been doing

what you learned
the conclusions you have reached.

Discuss
use the questions you developed in the planning phase to provide sequence and focus to the discussion

Learning Outcome:
what is that you want participants to learn?
how can you help them do that?

Time:
develop a time frame for the session.
mixture of input, activity and discussion.

Input:
Refer to the questions you developed in the planning

Input
Establish a series of sub topic headings that will enable you to quickly get back on track after a question or discussion and that will keep you moving through the material in a logical sequence

Learning reflection
Develop a key question that will enable people to discuss the relevance and possible application of your findings into their own practice or context

Evaluation
Develop two to three key questions that will enable the participants to tell you in what ways the seminar was useful to them.

Seminar Evaluation Process

The following is a simple checklist to help you focus on your own contribution to the seminar. Write a brief note beside each question.

Was the pre-seminar planning adequate?
Was the session plan appropriate?
Was there a balance between telling and discussing?
Did the entire group participate?
Were others able to contribute to the generation of new knowledge?
Did I introduce the topic sufficiently?
Did the first activity involve people in the topic?
What was the highlight of the session? Why?
What was the low point of the session? Why?
How could I present this seminar differently next time?

Video Marketing Tips

YouTube has become a big marketing operation for businesses and there are even marketing agencies to help businesses gain exposure from YouTube using proven viral video strategies. With so much exposure possible from a single video clip, YouTube should become a part of every business marketing plan.

1. Focus on something that is funny or humorous, so that people will feel compelled to share it with friends and family.
2. Make the video begin and end with a black screen and include the URL of your originating website to bring traffic to your site.

3. Put your URL at the bottom of the entire video.
4. Clearly demonstrate how your product works.
5. Create how-to videos to share your expertise and develop a following.
6. Build contests and events around special holidays and occasions.
7. Run a search on similar content by keyword, and use the info to choose the right category and tags for your video.
8. Make sure the video is real, with no gimmicks or tricks.
9. Add as many keywords as you can.
10. Make sure that your running time is five minutes or less.
11. Break longer videos into several clips, each with a clear title, so that they can be selectively viewed.
12. Encourage viewer participation and support.
13. Take advantage of YouTube tags, use adjectives to target people searching based on interests, and match your title and description to the tags.
14. Use the flexibility provided by the medium to experiment.
15. Use the 'Guru Account' sign-up designation to highlight info videos and how-to guides.
16. Create 'Playlists' to gather individual clips into niche-targeted context so viewers can easily find related content.
17. Use 'Bulletins' to broadcast short messages to the world via Your YouTube Channel.
18. Email 'The Robin Good YouTube Channel' to promote a new video release.
19. Join a 'YouTube Group' to post videos or comments to the group discussion area and build your network of contacts.
20. Use 'YouTube Streams' to join or create a room where videos are shared and discussed in real-time.
21. Use 'Active Sharing' to broadcast the videos that you are currently watching, and drive traffic to your profile.
22. Use the 'Share Video' link found under each video you submit and then check the box 'Friends' to send your video to all your friends.
23. Create your own YouTube Channel when you sign-up for a new YouTube account.
24. Create video responses to existing videos.
25. Accept and welcome video responses.
26. Comment on other videos to build relationships and tactfully promote your video.
27. Use tags and descriptions to help google searches.
28. Do wear thought provoking clothing items to provoke viewer comments.
29. Post your Youtube.com link to Twitter and Facebook, and forum discussions.
30. Use video sitemaps and include title, description, play page, thumbnail and player or content location.
31. Transcribe your video content into the description field.
32. Produce videos on a regular basis and announce your future production schedule.
33. Make sure your videos are easy to share by providing sharing features like embed codes, 'tweet this' button and 'email this' links.
34. Publish to more than one location, including niche video sites.
35. Make videos about a subject you are passionate about to broadcast your expertise.

36. Provide viewers with a rare behind-the-scenes look at your operations.
37. Encourage viewers to comment back via text, audio, photo and/or video.
38. Incorporate credited viewer feedback into your video content.
39. Tell your story with emotion to elicit an emotional response from viewers and stimulate the viral sharing of your video.
40. Link your Youtube video to your website or blog by copying and pasting the Youtube Embed Code into your website code.
41. Create a YouTube video title that arouses curiosity in viewers and prompts them towards watching the shocking evidence.
42. Use unique tags that relate to your niche market.
43. Do not spoil the viral potential of the video by making it entirely an ad.
44. Embed your website's URL into the video.
45. Create a video that is simple enough to be remixed by others.
46. Reach out to individuals who run relevant blogs and actually encourage/reward them to post your embedded videos.
47. Start new forum threads and embed your videos into the dialogue.
48. Get permission to embed your YouTube videos right in the comments section of MySpace pages of friends.
49. On Facebook share your videos with your entire friends list.
50. On Facebook create an event that announces the video launch and invite friends, writing a note and tagging friends, or posting the video on Facebook Video with a link back to the original YouTube video.
51. Send the Youtube video link to your email database list.
52. Change the title of the video several times, from something catchy to something more relevant to your brand and niche market.
53. Engage in thumbnail optimization by creating a thumbnail or middle frame that is clear, which suggests a high video quality, and it should have a face or at least a person in it.
54. Create controversy in the comments section below the video by getting a few people to log in throughout the day and post heated comments.
55. Start by using some unique tags that are common to all of your videos and, then after a few days, add some more generic tags that draw out the long tail of a video.
56. Get local non-competing businesses to sponsor your video with an opening ad and use the fees collected to help defray some of the video production costs.

Branding Strategies

Definition: What you do to shape what the consumer immediately thinks your business offers and stands for.
Objective: To reduce client perceived purchase risk and improve your profit margins.

Methodologies:
1. Develop processes, systems and quality assurance procedures to assure the consistent adherence to your quality standards.

2. Develop business processes to consistently deliver upon your value proposition.

3. Develop training programs to assure the consistent professionalism and responsiveness of your employees.

4. Develop marketing communications with consistent, reinforcing message content. (Testimonials should support your promises)

5. Develop marketing communications with a consistent presentation style. (Logo design, company colors, slogan, labels, packaging, stationery, etc.)

6. Exceed your brand promises to achieve consistent client loyalty.

7. Use surveys and interviews to consistently monitor what your brand means to your clients.

8. Consistently match your brand values or performance benchmarks to your client requirements.

9. Focus on the maintenance of a consistent number of key brand values that are tied to your company strengths.

10. Continuously research trends in your markets to stay consistently relevant to client needs and wants.

11. Attach a logo-imprinted product label and business card to all baskets.

Helpful Resources:
Logo Design Services: www.elance.com   /   www.logoworks.com

Document Your Branding Strategy

_____
_____
_____

Basic Monthly Marketing Plan Checklist

1. Send birthday greetings to existing clients. _____
2. Contact referral sources and express appreciation for their referrals. _____
3. Implement program to develop new referral sources. _____
4. Research new ways to solve more problems of your target clients. _____
5. Research possible new target audience needs. _____

6. Make your friends/family/associates/social contacts aware of your expanding capabilities. _____
7. Train all employees to assist in marketing efforts. _____
8. Conduct selected client interviews to assess performance, changing needs and suggestions. _____
9. Forward copies of articles of interest to contacts. _____
10. Take contact to breakfast, lunch or dinner. _____
11. Invite contact to sporting or cultural event. _____
12. Distribute articles that demonstrate your expertise. _____
13. Invite contacts to an informative seminar. _____
14. Send personal notes of congratulation. _____
15. Join organizations important to your contacts. _____
16. Update your mailing list. _____
17. Issue a press release on a firm accomplishment or planned marketing event. _____
18. Update your firm's list of competitive advantages. _____
19. Attend a networking event. _____
20. Update the helpful content on your website. _____
21. Arrange to speak on your area of expertise. _____
22. Become actively involved in the community. _____
23. Track your ad results to determine resource focus. _____
24. Develop alliances with complementary businesses. _____
25. Conduct client satisfaction surveys. _____
26. Implement client needs analysis checklist. _____
27. Distribute newsletter featuring clients. _____
28. _____ _____
29. _____ _____
30. _____ _____

Networking Insights

Definition: A reciprocal process in which you share ideas, leads, information, and advice to build mutually beneficial relationships.

Networking Tips:
1. Start your own local referral group with other business owners.
2. Understand your long-term networking goals.
3. Become a helpful resource to networking members.
4. Research people and companies to know their goals and interests.
5. Offer referrals, resources and recommendations to receive same in return.
6. Consistently try to meet new people and make new friends.
7. Develop good listening skills.

8. Frequently express your gratitude for assistance.
9. Know what interests, strengths and availability you bring to the table.
10. Stay in touch with a newsletter, blog, postcards or email messages.
11. Keep asking questions to get others to tell you more about themselves.
12. Show warmth, display confidence, smile and shake hands firmly.
13. Explore organizations that offer accreditation and directory listings.

Entrepreneur Networking Possibilities

1. Meet Up — www.meetup.com
2. FaceBook, Friendster, Myspace — www.facebook.com
3. LinkedIn — www.linkedIn.com
4. Ryze — www.ryze.com
5. Int'l Virtual Women's Chamber of Commerce — www.ivwcc.org
6. Business Network International — www.BNI.com
7. Club E Network — www.clubENetwork.com
8. Local Chamber of Commerce
9. Rotary Club — www.rotary.org
10. Lion's Club — www.lionsclubs.org
11. Jaycees
12. Toastmasters — www.toastmasters.com
13. Woman Owned Network — wwwwomanowned.com
14. Alumni Associations
15. Parent Teacher Associations (PTA)
16. Trade Shows — www.tsnn.com
17. Trade Associations — www.associationscentral.com
18. EONetwork — www.eonetwork.org
19. Prof. Organizations, Economic Clubs, Charities, Churches, Museums, etc.

Perfect Your Elevator Pitch

A brief, focused message aimed at a particular person or niche segment that summarizes why they should be interested in your products and/or services.

I am a/we are _____ (profession) **and we help** _____ (target market description) **to** _____ (primary problem solved).

Press Release Cover Letter Worksheet

Instructions: Use this form to build a ready-to-use cover letter.

Your Letterhead.

Date

Dear _____,

As a company located in your coverage area, we thought the attached Press Release

would be of special concern to your readers/viewers, as it touches upon something that we all have in common, an interest in
_____.

Brief overview purpose of the press release.
_____

I have also enclosed a media kit to give you background information on _____ Company and myself. I hope to follow-up with you shortly.

I also possess expertise in the following related areas:
- _____
- _____
- _____

Should you wish to speak to me or require additional information, I can be reached at _____ or via email at _____.
Additional assistance with company supplied photos can be requested at the same number. This Press Release can also be downloaded from my company website at www. _____.

Thank you for your time and attention,

Contact Name
Company Title
Phone Number
Email Address

New Release Template

News Release

For Immediate Release
(Or Hold for Release Until …(date)….)

Contact:
Contact Person   _____
Contact Title   _____

Company Name _____
Phone Number _____
Fax Number _____
Email Address _____
Website Address _____

Date: _____
Attention: _____ (Target Type of Editor)

Headline: Summarize Your Key Message: _____

Sub-Headline: Optional: _____

Location of the Firm and Date.
_____

Lead Paragraph: A summary of the newsworthy content.
_____

Answers the questions:
Who: _____
What: _____
Where: _____
When: _____

Second Paragraph:
Expand upon the first paragraph and elaborate on the purpose of the Press Release.
_____
_____

Third Paragraph:
Further details with additional quotes from staff, industry experts or satisfied clients.
_____
_____

For Additional Information Contact:
_____
_____

About Your Expertise:
Presentation of your expert credentials
_____
_____

About Your Business:
Background company history on the firm and central offerings.

_____
_____

Enclosures: Photographs, charts, brochures, etc.

Special Event Release Format   Notes

1. Type of Event
2. Sponsoring Organization
3. Contact Person Before the Event
4. Contact Person at the Event
5. Date and Time of the Event
6. Location of the Event
7. Length of Presentation Remarks
8. Presentation Topic
9. Question Session (Y/N)
10. Speaker or Panel
11. Event Background
12. Noteworthy Expected Attendees
13. Estimated Number of Attendees
14. Why readers s/b interested in event.
15. Specifics of the Event.
16. Biographies

Track Ad Return on Investment (ROI)

Objective: To invest in those marketing activities that generate the greatest return on invested funds.

Medium	Cost	Calls Received	Cost/Call	No. Act. New Clients	Cost/New Client
Formula:	A	B	A/B=C	D	A/D=E
Newspaper					

Classified Ads   _____
Yellow Pages   _____
Billboards   _____
Cable TV   _____
Magazine   _____
Flyers   _____
Posters   _____
Coupons   _____
Direct Mail   _____
Brochures   _____
Business Cards   _____
Seminars   _____
Demonstrations   _____
Sponsored Events   _____
Sign   _____
Radio   _____
Trade Shows   _____
Specialties   _____
Cold Calling   _____
Door Hangers   _____
T-shirts   _____
Coupon Books   _____
Transit Ads   _____
Press Releases   _____
Word-of-Mouth   _____
_____   _____
_____   _____
Totals: _____

Sample Sales Letter

Dear _____,

    Does Your Company have a Revenue Problem or a Cost Problem or Perhaps it has Both?

_____ (company name) has developed a comprehensive and highly effective analytical tool for evaluating the performance of companies like yours. The custom designed analysis tool very efficiently enables us to uncover and precisely define the nature of the problems facing your company.

Our "Business Performance Evaluation Analysis" is a well-conceived program that enables us to obtain relevant information, and therefore gain an understanding, of every major aspect of your company's operations. After we have completed the analytical work, we will then formulate a detailed strategic plan for your business that will enable you to move forward. This rigorous process cannot fail to benefit your company and improve its profitability.

Please contact us at your earliest convenience to explore how we can help you to optimize your company's performance. Indeed, you may want to take advantage of our "Free Consultation" offer, whereby we will discuss your needs and determine, at least initially, if and how we might be able to assist you in your business development plans.

Please contact the undersigned at _____ to schedule a free consultation or visit our website at _____ to arrange an appointment today.

Very truly yours,

How to Get Started Marketing on Twitter
1. **Import Your Contacts**
   Import contacts from Gmail, Hotmail and your own address book. Start with a solid base of people who you consider friends, following you on Twitter.
2. **Make Sure that Your Profile is Complete**
   Fill in all the fields (both required and optional) and include your website URL. Personalize your Twitter page to match your company's branding.
3. **Understand the Dynamics of Twitter**
   Use Twitter as a social tool, not a classifieds site and follow these tips:
   - Don't spam others about your specials.
   - Follow other users.
   - Don't promote your company directly.

           - Tweet about an informative blog posting.
4. **Build Your Followers Base**
    - Put a link to "Follow Me on Twitter" everywhere (your email signature, forums, website, and business cards)
    - Every time you post on your blog, invite people to follow you on Twitter
    - Follow people who are smart in your business and look for people who follow them for you to follow. Get a re-follow will build our follower list with the right profile of followers. Make sure that you look for people who might be interested in what you have to offer and don't send a Tweet that is overtly asking for a sale.
    - Start by actually reading what prospective clients say in their Tweets and give a smart "tweetback" before you follow him or her on Twitter.
5. **Balance Your Followers/Following Ratio**
    - Strike a balance between people you follow and people that follow you.
    - Grow slowly by adding 30 friends at a time, and then wait for them to follow you back.
6. **Make it Worthwhile to Follow You**
    - Tweet only interesting stuff about your industry, and relate your tweetbacks to it and even post in some links.
    - Clients develop real interest and attention when they realize that the people who are meticulously maintaining the Twitter profile really want to help them.
    - Make sure that at least an hour is spent in maintaining the Twitter account, so that the profile is active, and remains interesting to people.
7. **Learn from the Best**
    - Find users with several hundred followers and learn their best practices.
8. **Twitter Uses**
    - Use twitter to extend the reach of an existing blogging strategy and to deepen or further ties. Ex: Carnival Cruise Lines.
    - Use to announce sales and deals. Ex: Amazon.
    - Increase the ability for frequent updates to blogs or web sites or news.
    - Build consensus or a community of supporters.
    - Build buzz for a blog. /Update breaking news at conferences or events.

Internet Article Writing Template

1. Article Title

Maximum 100 characters (including spaces) - about 12 words.
Write it to catch the attention of readers and publishers. Start with your primary search engine keyword phrase. In printed media titles starting "How to…" or "10 top tips for…" are very popular, but they are not very helpful for search engines. The article title will go into the title of a web page.

2. Abstract

Maximum 500 characters - about 90 words but 50 or 60 is better.

Make it enticing to hook the publisher and make them want to read the full article. The abstract is primarily targeted at the publisher and will be displayed just below the title on the search pages in the directory, but is secondary to the title in getting attention. Some publishers may also use it.

3.   Description – Meta Tag

Maximum 200 characters but preferably 150 – two lines of text.
This should be a shorter version of the abstract, which must contain your primary keywords. The Mega Tag is needed if you publish on your own website.

4.   Keywords – Meta Tag

Maximum 100 characters - about 12 words comma separated
Start with your primary keyword of phrase then add the other relevant keywords that are used in the article.

5.   Article Text

Length depends on your topic, market and writing style. Research suggests about 500 to 800 words, but some publishers want more of an in-depth analysis. Research your specific market and be flexible, with a prepared mix of lengths, including long and short versions of the same article. Write the basic article with no formatting. If you are using word, disable all the auto-formatting like smart quotes, automatic hypertext links and paragraph spacing because they will all cause problems later.

Include the 'Primary Keyword Phrase' into the first sentence. Include the liberal usage of keywords throughout the article, but don't overdo it. The article still has to be a good read. Remember that even though you are writing for several audiences, content must still be king. Do not promote your own products and services or your article will not be published. Also, do not include self-serving links to your web site or affiliate sites in the body of the article, but rather save them for the 'Resource or Byline Box'. If you have links to resources show them as text, as many sites do not allow live html links in the body of the article.

Introduction
1.   Brief outline of what will be covered in the article.
2.   The motivating factor behind why this particular topic was selected and why you are qualified to address the subject.
3.   A brief statement on your credentials, experience and exposure.
4.   What you have achieved from your experience to convince readers that you know the subject very well.

Core Subject Matter
1.   Define the problem or address the subject areas that will define the gap between the uninformed and the knowledgeable.
2.   Provide the benefits the reader will realize from reading the article.
3.   Start with simple and general background knowledge, and gradually intensify the technicality of the subject matter.
4.   State the expected challenges to be faced in tackling the problem.

5. Discuss the pros and cons of your proposed solution to create the link between the norm and the desired state.

Expand Upon Subject Matter
1. Add technical information to convince readers of the merits of your solution.
2. State a range of requirements needed to implement your solution and their options.
3. Compare players in the market and promote good practice.
4. Place emphasis on desired actions, taking a chronological approach to each stage.
5. Attempt to indirectly answer any questions you think your readers may have.
6. Give supporting points to gain confidence in the approach you recommend.
7. Suggest other options based on price and availability.

Conclusion
1. Summarize problem solution recommendations.
2. Refer readers to other helpful resources.

6. Copyright

Copyright, date, name, country. Few directories ask for this but it makes sense to put it at the bottom of the article or in the field requested.

7. Resource Box

Maximum 500 characters, "including spaces and html code."
This is your opportunity to promote yourself but limit content to 1 or 2 self-serving links. Refer to the links in the "Third Person." The directory publisher has to function with this link on their site or ezine so make it acceptable to them. Offer an incentive or reward for people to visit your web site, but make sure that live links show the web address not just keywords. If the publisher doesn't use live links, you still want to present your website address for later referral.

Demonstrative Speech To-do Outline

1. Collect all the information for the speech.
    - Become a subject matter expert on all the topics related to the speech.
    - Do the research, and address all possible questions that could be brought up by the audience.

2. Determine a demonstrative manner for the speech.
    - Assemble any tools needed to complement the speech.
      Note: PowerPoint slides are an opportunity to use pictures, flow charts or parts of the actual speech to enforce what is being said.
    - Use role-play by the audience or persons brought in to enhance a

demonstrative speech.

3. Document all the steps in process of the demonstrative speech.
   - Cover all the areas that will educate the audience concerning the topic.
   - Include additional props that will be a part of the speech in the appropriate areas.

4. Rehearse the speech process or presentation in its entirety.

5. Create an outline descriptive enough to clearly lay out what is happening at every step in the process of the speech.

6. Ready any handouts and other props that will be used in the speech.

7. Distribute surveys at the end of the speech to solicit constructive feedback, testimonials, improvement suggestions and possible referrals.

Classified Ad Worksheet

Ad Budget: _____

Ad Objective:
___ Go to Website   ___ Request More Info   ___ Mail a Check
___ Introduce a new product/service   ___ Announce a Sale
___ Increase awareness of product
___ Other _____

Target Market: _____

Target Market:
Demographics:

- Age _____
- Gender _____
- Income _____
- Education _____
- Location _____

Reading Interests:
- Daily Newspapers _____
- Weekly Magazines _____
- Magazines _____
- Trade Journals _____

Product. Knowledge Level _____

Purchase Motivators _____

Best Category Heading _____

Select Type of Message
- Strong Offer with Best Value for Money _____
- Point of Difference from Competitors _____
- Listing the Benefits _____

Product Price: $_____

Ad Cost: $_____

Number of Responses: _____
Cost/Response: _____
Number of Sales: _____
Cost/Sales: _____

Marketing Plan   Month: _____

Planned Accomplishments for month:
_____
_____

Describe target audience:
_____
_____

Success Measures:
Number of New Prospects   _____
Number of New Contacts to Referral Network
Sales Revenues of _____ by _____

Other measure: _____

Referral Network Action Plan:
We will attend the following events:
    Event   Date   Objective

_____

_____

We will contact the following people in my network:
    Name   Date   Reason

_____

_____

We will meet the following people in person:
    Name   Date   Reason

_____

_____

We will keep in touch with the following people by sending them information, including articles and newspaper clippings:
    Name   Date   Information Type

_____

_____

Past Client Action Plan:
We will contact the following past clients:
Method Options: In-person, Mail, email, phone.
    Name   Date   Reason   Method

_____

_____

Prospecting Action Plan:
Distribution Methods: Publications, Website, Organizations, Email, etc.

Method   Date   Subject   Distribution Method

Article   _____

Speech   _____

Newsletter _____

Press Release _____

Other Activities:
    Activity Type   Date   Target

_____

Sample Thank-you and Referral Letter

Dear _____ (client name)

I wanted to take this opportunity to thank you for your business once again. If I can be of service to you in the future, I hope you will not hesitate to call.

In the meantime, I have enclosed a few business cards and referral cards. I would very much appreciate your passing them along to anyone in need of

Human Resources Consulting Services. As usual, I will mail you a referral fee for any business that comes my way from your efforts.

I have also enclosed a 'Client Satisfaction Survey' with a self-addressed and stamped return envelope. Your feedback is invaluable in helping us to improve the services that we offer, and we very much appreciate the time you will spend in completing the survey.

I hope you are enjoying your new surroundings and we look forward to serving you and your family in the future.

Please call me if I can be of any help. Thanks again.

Sincerely,

Top 20 Marketing Tips

The most important order you ever get from a client is the second order.

In direct mailing, spend 10% of your budget on testing.

Understanding and adapting to consumer motivation and behavior is not an option. It is an absolute necessity for competitive survival.

A well-designed catalog mailed to a qualified response list will probably bring a one percent response.

Processing and fulfillment costs incurred from the time an order arrives until it is shipped should be kept below $10 an order.

Know the power of repetition. Be sure your message is consistent.

The two most common mistakes companies make in using the phone is failing to track results and tracking the wrong thing.

Marketing activities should be designed to increase profits, not just sales.

It costs five times as much to sell a new client as an existing client.

Selling what your clients need, instead of what they want, can lead to failure.

Don't think that product superiority, technology, innovation or company size will sell itself.

Don't neglect or ignore your current clients while pursuing new ones.

People don't buy products, they buy the benefits and solutions they believe the products provide.

Any decent direct mail campaign will cost $1.25 per piece.

The average business never hears from 96% of its dissatisfied clients.

Fifty percent of those clients who complain would do business with the company again if their complaints were handled satisfactorily.

It is estimated that clients are twice as likely to talk about their bad experiences as their good ones.

Marketing is everyone's business, regardless of title or position in the organization.

Exaggerated claims can produce inflated expectations that the product or service cannot live up to, thereby resulting in dissatisfied clients.

Get to know your prime clients - the 20% of product users who account for 80% of the total consumption of that product class.

Made in the USA
Columbia, SC
21 February 2019